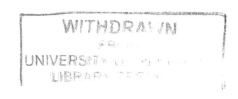

Language and Peace

War and Society

A series edited by S. P. Reyna and R. E. Downs

Volume 1
Feuding and Warfare: Selected Works of Keith F. Otterbein

Volume 2
Studying War: Anthropological Perspectives
Edited by S. P. Reyna and R. E. Downs

Volume 3
Troubled Times: Violence and Warfare in the Past
Edited by Debra L. Martin and David W. Frayer

Volume 4
Roots of Violence: A History of War in Chad
Mario J. Azevedo

Volume 5
Deadly Developments: Capitalism, States and War
Edited by S. P. Reyna and R. E. Downs

Volume 6
Language and Peace
Edited by Christina Schäffner and Anita L. Wenden

This book is part of a series. The publisher will accept continuation orders which may be cancelled at any time and which provide for automatic billing and shipping of each title in the series upon publication. Please write for details.

Language and Peace

Edited by

Christina Schäffner

and

Anita L. Wenden

harwood academic publishers
Australia • Canada • China • France • Germany • India • Japan • Luxembourg
Malaysia • The Netherlands • Russia • Singapore • Switzerland

First published 1995 by Dartmouth Publishing Company Limited, Aldershot
Second printing 1999 by Harwood Academic Publishers, Amsterdam

 Printed in Singapore.

Amsteldijk 166
1st Floor
1079 LH Amsterdam
The Netherlands

British Library Cataloguing in Publication Data

Language and peace. – (War and society ; v. 6)
1. Sociolinguistics 2. Language and languages – Political aspects
I. Schäffner, Christina II. Wenden, Anita L.
306.4′4

ISBN: 90-5702-480-2 (soft cover)
ISSN: 1069-8043

Contents

Part III: Language and Social Discrimination

Part IV: Language, Education and Peace

Foreword

This book will surprise adventurous readers. Though written by linguists, its potential interest goes far beyond that field. *Language and Peace* could easily be a text or supplementary reading for a broad spectrum of disciplines, including history, political science, psychology, sociology, communications, peace studies, foreign languages, and teacher or leadership training.

All of us can still remember the totalitarian anti-utopia of George Orwell's *1984*, wherein a 'Two Minute Hate Session' was set aside daily for the proletariat to scream hateful taunts at a video representation of the manufactured enemy. The startling result was that language, to a frightening degree, shaped politics and social behaviour.

This work starts at the same point. The central thesis, persuasively argued, is that language, as historically used, has been a significant factor in creating political oppression, and economic and social discrimination. As the editors see it, the challenge for the next century is to begin using language to inspire inclusion rather than exclusion, conciliation rather than conflict, and peace rather than war.

Unfortunately, such a challenge is more daunting than might at first appear. 'Inept' language, even if unintentional and even if used to express inherently noble ideas, can result in misunderstanding, resentment, even violence on the part of those whom we are seeking to pacify. The exhortation 'Watch your language!', often shouted by mothers at their exuberant teenagers, also applies in the most sobering degree to adult leaders of all varieties. As a young alderman in Philadelphia, Ben Franklin learned the hard way that language can be a tricky tool in seeking votes.

Because of this central theme, that language is the interface between thought and action, this book will prove to be a seminal work, inspiring a host of articles and other books on related themes in such areas as rhetoric, mass media, preventive diplomacy, and education. For example, to what extent did Serbian television's use of stereotypes provoke the Yugoslav war? Again, does the media's use of stereotypes, and of connotation rather than denotation, make its language almost part and parcel of its message? Why, as the contributors to Part II state, is metaphor such a highly powerful element of the media's language? Because it is 'imagistic'? — that is, because we can 'see' it in our minds?

As for preventive diplomacy, attempted for the purpose of avoiding conflict, anyone who has tried it knows that it requires first and foremost an open mind. Keeping, building, or making peace can only flow from a genuine tolerance of many different views. Such tolerance is the opposite of rigid ideology, with its self-defeating pre-judgements. Hence it follows, as the editors implicitly concede, that language cannot carry the whole burden of making peace. To achieve such an end, the diplomat must have mastered the techniques of conflict resolution. Even more important, his language must flow from a truly open mind, and that is where education comes or should come in.

The volume deals boldly with the relation of education to language and peace. In Part IV, there is a call for a change in the way teachers teach reading. It is advocated that lay persons be empowered to read critically rather than passively, so that they can evaluate the degree of fact and bias reflected in various media interpretations of public issues.

Some future article, building on that base, can explore other facets of an open mind, including awareness of human interdependence and the imagination to perceive issues through *other* people's frames of reference. Even on this point *Language and Peace* makes a powerful point, namely, that if medical doctors could experience their patients' roles, their attitude and language would change radically. The point applies to other professions as well.

Some scholars have argued that peace (or at least arms control, the prerequisite for peace) is an academic discipline. Such argument is delusory. Peace is not a discipline but a problem, in fact, the *ultimate* problem. And all academic fields, including art, poetry, and cinema, can help provide solutions to that problem. This book marks one of the first efforts by linguists to address the problem of peace. Let us hope it will not be the last.

Leland Miles, President Emeritus
International Association of University Presidents (IAUP)
and Chief, IAUP Mission to the United Nations

Contributors

Jan Blommaert is professor of African linguistics at the University of Gent, Belgium. His major interests include pragmatics, ideology research and political discourse in Africa and Europe.

Paul Chilton is presently professor of language and communication in the School of Languages and European Studies at Aston University, Birmingham, UK. Previously, he was at Warwick University and he was also a visiting fellow at the Center for International Security and Arms Control, Stanford (1988–90). His research includes the field of political discourse analysis and international relations.

Michael Clyne is professor and head of linguistics at Monash University, Australia. His major research interests are sociolinguistics, bilingualism/language contact, second language acquisition, and intercultural communication.

José Carlos Gonçalves is professor of discourse and conversation analysis in the graduate programme of languages and linguistics at the Federal University of Pernambuco (UFPE) in Recife, Brazil. His main research interests are in language and the professions and communication at work, mainly from the perspective of discourse and conversation analysis applied to the study of the relationship between language, social contexts and social actions in spontaneous and institutional settings.

Julieta Haidar is professor in the graduate programme in linguistics at the National School of Anthropology and History in Mexico City. Her earlier research focused on the study of native languages, especially Ecuatorian Quechuan. More recently she has concentrated on the analysis of discourse, power and ideology as well as the semiotics of culture.

George Lakoff is professor of linguistics at the University of California at Berkeley, USA. He previously taught at Harvard University and the University of Michigan and is a leading cognitive scientist and one of the founders of the field of Cognitive Linguistics.

Peter Lowenberg has been an associate professor in the Department of Linguistics and Language Development at California State University, San José since 1991. Previously, he was associate professor of linguistics at Georgetown University, Washington, D.C. He has published in the areas of language contact in Southeast Asia, language policy and planning, and the testing of English as a world language.

Luiz Paulo da Moita Lopes is associate professor at the Federal University of Rio de Janeiro in the Applied Linguistics Programme. He has lectured in England, Venezuela, Chile and around Brazil. His current research interests address issues related to discourse, power and identity in the language classroom.

Andreas Musolff is a senior lecturer in German in the Department of Modern Languages at the University of Durham, UK. His current research focuses on comparative studies of media language in Britain, France and Germany and on historical pragmatics.

Lidia Rodríguez is professor at the Autonomous University of Nuevo Leon in Monterrey, Mexico. She is interested in lexical semantic analysis as well as discourse analysis. Her recent research, based on a corpus of six hundred one-hour interviews, has been dedicated to a study of the argumentation of clearly differentiated social groups.

Christina Schäffner is a lecturer in German in the School of Languages and European Studies at Aston University, Birmingham, UK. Her research interests are political discourse analysis, metaphors, intercultural communication, and translation studies.

Teun A. van Dijk is professor of discourse studies at the University of Amsterdam, The Netherlands. His earlier research interests included literary studies, text grammar, the psychology of text comprehension, and the reproduction of racism through various types of discourse. He has published several books in each of these domains, many of which have been translated into a dozen languages. His present research in 'critical' discourse studies focuses on the relations between power, discourse and ideology.

Caroline Vaughan is Special Assistant to the Director of Specialist Services at the United Nations in New York, USA. She has also taught sociolinguistics at Columbia University, New York and English at the American University of Beirut, Lebanon. Her main research interests are in the fields of comparative discourse analysis and political text analysis.

Jef Verschueren is a research-director for the Fund for Scientific Research, Flanders. His main interests are theory formation in pragmatics, metapragmatics, and intercultural and international communication. He is founder and Secretary General of the International Pragmatics Association.

Anita L. Wenden is professor in the Department of Foreign Languages, ESL and Humanities, and former Coordinator of the Cultural Diversity Programme at York College, City University of New York, USA. Her research interests include the processes of adult learning and the role of language in the communication of ideology. She has published in the area of learner autonomy and peace education.

Acknowledgements

Acknowledgement is made to the Department of Educational and Psychological Research, School of Education, Lund University (Malmö, Sweden) for permission to reprint *Defining Peace: Spatial and Cross-Cultural Dimensions* from 'Making peace with people and planet: Some important lessons from the Gandhian tradition in educating for the 21st century' by Frank Hutchison in *Peace, Environment, and Education,* vol. 3, no. 3, 1992.

Support for some of the clerical work required in the production of the camera-ready copy was provided by the Aston Modern Languages Research Foundation.

Introduction

ANITA L. WENDEN AND CHRISTINA SCHÄFFNER

Social context

In his report to members of the United Nations on ways of strengthening and making more efficient the organization's capacity for preventive diplomacy, peacemaking, and peacekeeping in post-Cold War times, Boutros-Ghali (1992, pp. 7-8) recommends that UN endeavours be guided by the following aims:

(1) preventive diplomacy to prevent the eruption of conflict,

(2) where conflict erupts, to engage in peacemaking aimed at resolving the issues that have led to conflict,

(3) where conflict has been halted to engage in peacekeeping to preserve peace and to assist in implementing agreements achieved by peacemakers,

(4) to assist in peacebuilding through rebuilding institutions and infrastructures of nations torn by civil war and by developing bonds of peaceful mutual benefit among nations formerly at war,

(5) to address the deepest causes of conflict, i.e. economic despair, social injustice and political oppression.

These recommendations are a response to the following contradictory trends which, the Secretary General notes, characterize the post-Cold War era. On the one hand, there are attempts by associations of states to transcend nationalistic rivalries, to work cooperatively and to dismantle discriminatory social institutions that violate the political and social rights of their citizens. Yet, at the same time, groups within nation-states are aggressively pursuing their right to political autonomy, and racial, ethnic, religious, cultural and linguistic differences have become the causes of intergroup conflict within nation-states. Moreover, besides the wars that erupt in response to these differences, it has become clear that the unmonitored and unchecked advance of technology can have an equally destructive impact on the quality of human life and the integrity of Earth systems in the long term.

It is these contradictory trends characterizing social and political change in our global society which provide the context for *Language and Peace.*

Aims

As the title suggests, the book examines the relationship between language and peace. Specifically, it intends to demonstrate that language is a factor that must be considered, together with political and economic factors, in seeking to understand the structural causes of conflict, i.e. economic despair, social injustice, and political oppression, and the acceptance and use of war as a viable alternative for settling intergroup and international differences.[1]

To that end, *Language and Peace* seeks insight into the role that language plays in the interface between ideology and the social institutions and practices that hinder attempts (1) to prevent the outbreak of war, (2) to contain physical violence once it has erupted, and (3) to deal with the structural violence that violates human rights whether or not wars are being waged. It hopes to make explicit what remains implicit in the *Agenda for Peace*: the relationship between ideology and peace. The volume also points to the need for language and peace education to raise awareness about and critically evaluate the ideology embedded in and communicated by language.

Language, politics and social change

Social change, politics, and language (i.e. discourse) are inextricably intertwined. While there is no direct, immediate relation between them, political and social upheavals caused by the socio-economic factors referred to in the *Agenda*, for example, and the regional wars that come in their wake, go hand in hand with discursive transformations. Social and economic changes are usually reflected in discourse, and the interpretation and subsequent influence of such changes are decisively determined by language. Language provides access to our experience of the world. It is an indicator of ways of thinking and acting, even if only indirectly mediated and refracted. Language can also disguise the world. It can channel access to it in a specific way or structure it according to particular and not always honourable aims and purposes. As Halliday says, "our 'reality' is not something ready made waiting to be meant - it has to be actively construed; and ... language evolved in the process of and as the agency of, its construal ... hence language has the power to shape our consciousness; ..." (Halliday, 1990, p.11).

It is the above view of language which underlies the aims of *Language and Peace* and which is implicit in the theoretical discussions, the research, and the educational recommendations found in the various chapters.

Definition of peace

Lexical semantics, the linguistic subdiscipline that is concerned with word meanings, has traditionally defined 'peace' in opposition to 'war'. From a textlinguistic and discourse analytic perspective, however, it has become obvious that not every instance of non-war can be called peace and that those instances which are called peace do not necessarily share identical features. Moreover, word meanings are not fixed or stable entities. They have to be explained relative to specific historical, social and cultural circumstances. The notion of 'peace' implicit in *Language and Peace* is based on this broader perspective. It reflects the understanding of the term proposed by peace researchers.

According to Galtung (1964), 'peace' refers to a reality that extends beyond the absence of war to include the absence of discriminatory and inegalitarian social structures and institutions, in other words, the absence of structural violence. If viewed in these terms, it follows that the achievement of peace entails not only the containment of war but also the development of just and equitable social structures that respect and enhance the human rights of all. The former condition is referred to as 'negative peace' and the latter as 'positive peace'. The term 'comprehensive peace' has been used to indicate the need to include both of these dimensions in a definition of peace.

Critical discourse analysis

The term 'discourse' has varied meanings in linguistics. Sometimes it is synonymous to 'text'; sometimes it is viewed as a label for a sequence of (mutually related) texts. The term can be linked to situations (e.g. the discourse of advertising), to individuals (e.g. the discourse of Gandhi, Martin Luther King), or to topics (e.g. the Cold War discourse, the discourse of racism). In this volume, 'discourse' is used predominantly in an actional and functional manner, i.e. discourse and discursive elements are regarded as manifestations of actions used to perform specific functions.

Originating in the late 1960s, text and discourse analysis are fairly 'modern' (sub)disciplines of linguistics. The main aim of discourse analysis has been to analyse language and the functioning of language in its social context. In this volume, therefore, linguistic or textual forms and structures are analysed, interpreted, and explained in terms of the social, political and cultural context in which they are embedded. Such an analysis goes beyond the 'mere' linguistic structures of the text and takes the social and institutional conditions of the text production and text reception into account. The underlying assumptions are that the study of language is not distinct from the study of society (social structures, processes, agencies) and that structure is not independent of function, process and use (see Kress and Hodge, 1993, p. 202) Thus, language is "irreducibly a social practice" (Kress and Hodge, 1993, p. 202).

Recently, it has become more and more obvious that by relating text/discourse and (contemporary) history, discourse analysis is the link between linguistics and other social sciences and the humanities. Thus, the social function of discourse analysis is stressed. As van Dijk says, "we needed to go beyond mere description and explanation, and pay more explicit attention to the sociopolitical and cultural presuppositions and implications of discourse analyses" (van Dijk, 1993c, p. 131). This means that social, institutional and situational determinants and effects of discourse have to be identified. The terms 'critical linguistics' or 'critical discourse analysis' refer to such an approach.

Fairclough (1993, p. 135) defines 'critical' discourse analysis as "discourse analysis which aims to systematically explore often opaque relationships of causality and determination between (a) discursive practices, events and texts and (b) wider social and cultural structures, relations and processes; to investigate how such practices, events and texts arise out of and are ideologically shaped by relations of power and struggles over power; and to explore how the opacity of these relationships between discourse and society is itself a factor securing power and hegemony."

Critical discourse analysis (or critical linguistics), thus, deals with power, dominance, hegemony, inequality and the discursive processes of their enactment, concealment, legitimation and reproduction (see van Dijk, 1993c, p 132). Wodak and Matouschek (1993, p. 227) list the following among the most important characteristics and goals of critical discourse analysis:

(a) Research interest: uncovering inequality, power relationships, injustices, etc.

(b) Object under investigation: language behaviour in natural speech situations of social relevance is to be investigated (institutions, media, etc.). ...

(f) Social and political practice is aimed at: results of the research should not only imply success in the academic field, but they should also include proposals for practical implementation (school materials, training seminars for teachers, doctors, lawyers, etc.).

For the greater part, the chapters in this volume are instances of critical discourse analysis. They illustrate the approach, characteristics, and goals of this emerging specialization within the (sub)discipline of discourse analysis. The link between the linguistic methodology and the social/political context is self-evident.

Content and organization

Language and Peace is divided into four sections: Language, Ideology and Peace (Part I), Language and War (Part II), Language and Social Discrimination (Part III), Language, Education and Peace (Part IV).

Language, Ideology and Peace

Part I of *Language and Peace* provides the conceptual foundation for the chapters that follow. The various dimensions of the concept 'peace' as it is understood in peace research are explained. A rationale is presented for exploring the relationship between language and ideology together with a framework of discourse structures that can provide the focus of such research.

Based on insights from peace research, Wenden's analysis (Chapter 1) of how the concept 'peace' is understood by various peace organizations reveals an expanded meaning of the term that acknowledges the following distinctions:

negative peace	versus	positive peace
absence of war	versus	absence of discriminatory social structures
physical violence	versus	structural violence or absence of conditions that reduce length of life span *or* quality of life

It is one or other dimension of the expanded view of peace represented by these distinctions that underlies the critical analysis of discourse in Parts II and III.

In the presentation of his theory of ideology van Dijk (Chapter 2) includes the following functions of ideology, which suggest the relationship between ideology and peace. That is, ideologies organize, maintain and control specific group attitudes; they influence personal cognition, including the planning and understanding of discourse and other forms of social interaction. In other words, ideologies shape group and individual attitudes which, communicated in discourse and determining other social practices, can either facilitate or hinder the achievement of peace.

The chapter argues that discourse analysis can be seen as ideological analysis, thus suggesting the relationship between language, ideology and peace. That is, language provides the interface between ideology and social practices that impede or facilitate the achievement of peace. Viewing discourse analysis in this way, van Dijk maintains, allows for a critical examination of discourse as the medium through which ideologies (such as those that justify social discrimination and war) are formulated and communicated. His chapter also provides a framework of discourse structures that can guide the critical analysis he advocates. The value of the approach is illustrated in the reports that follow (Parts II and III), each of which utilizes one or more of these discourse structures as a research focus.

Language and War

The social context for the analysis provided by each of the chapters in Part II is war: the making of foreign policy in matters relating to war and national security during the Cold War and in post-Cold War times (Chilton and Lakoff); the 1982 war between Israel and Lebanon (Vaughan); the Cold War (Schäffner); the Gulf War (Musolff). Implied in this focus on war as a means of settling intergroup differences is an understanding of peace as the absence of war. Recognizing the important role played by the media in shaping and transforming political reality and in influencing readers' attitudes about politics, the four chapters in this section have analysed media discourse (e.g. editorials of four national newspapers on the Israeli/Lebanese crisis; leading articles in a British weekly on East-West relations; Western TV media reports on the Gulf War). The analysis of these data reveals language as implicitly representing an ideological stance that accepts and promotes war, i.e. organized and legally sanctioned physical violence, as a viable alternative for the settling of intergroup conflict and/or regulating international relations.

All four chapters focus on the use of metaphor in war discourse. According to van Dijk (Chapter 2) metaphors are rhetorical devices that can be drawn upon in the communication and consolidation of group ideologies. However, metaphors are more than rhetorical devices. As noted by Chilton and Lakoff (Chapter 3), they are ways of conceptualizing (i.e. thinking about) the world. Through metaphorical thinking, familiar concepts are applied to unfamiliar realities, and in matters relating to national security and relations between nations, the outcome of this conceptualization, i.e. the metaphor, provides the basis and justification for the formulation of government policy and its potential execution.

The chapters in Part II, therefore, illustrate the indirect role metaphors and metaphorical thinking play in the maintenance and promotion of social beliefs regarding the acceptability of war. Three of the chapters focus on specific metaphors, i.e. the state-as-person and the state-as-container metaphor (Chilton and Lakoff), the balance metaphor (Schäffner), the Rescue Scenario (Musolff). One chapter (Vaughan) describes four categories of metaphor used in war discourse, i.e. military metaphors, images of primitivity, images of bipolar divisions, familial images. Together, the four chapters illustrate how metaphors are used to:

(1) shape, represent and justify foreign policy regarding war and/or matters of national security (Schäffner; Musolff),

(2) indirectly convey that war is an acceptable means of settling international disagreements (Schäffner; Musolff),

(3) unquestioningly promote values, sustain attitudes, and encourage actions that create conditions that can lead to war (Chilton and Lakoff; Schäffner),

(4) serve to create the enemy image essential to provoking and maintaining the hostility that leads to war (Vaughan).

Two of the chapters in Part II further illustrate how a macro or global analysis of a text can reveal the ideology that guides the making of policy in matters relating to war and national security. Through her analysis of keywords and recurring themes, Vaughan (Chapter 4) identifies general principles that justified the use of war as a means of settling the Palestinian problem. Schäffner (Chapter 5) outlines a set of macropropositions which defined the policy of deterrence that led to nuclear proliferation during the Cold War. Thus, Part II reveals the indirect but key role language plays in promoting values, beliefs, and social practices that justify the use of war as a means of settling intergroup differences and/or regulating international relations.

Language and Social Discrimination

While the focus of the analysis in Part II is peace between nations (or the absence of it), in Part III peace is viewed from a national perspective as it may or may not exist between and among social groups. The individual chapters focus on the relationship between language and discriminatory social structures and practices based on race (Chapter 7), social class (Chapter 8), ethnicity (Chapters 9 and 10). Implied in these chapters is the fact that when basic human rights are violated through discriminatory and inegalitarian institutions and practices, structural violence exists, reducing the length of life and diminishing its quality. In such cases, while a society may not be at war, it is not at peace. Thus, underlying the research in Part III is a view of peace as the absence of structural violence.

Again, as in Part II, media discourse is the focus of the analysis, e.g. American racist newspapers, German far-right pamphlets, suburban Melbourne newspapers and a Sydney talkback radio show (Clyne); a televised public debate between the students and administration of the National Autonomous University of Mexico (Haidar and Rodríguez); articles on ethnic conflict from the mainstream daily press in eastern and western Europe (Blommaert and Verschueren); leading English language newspapers in Malaysia (Lowenberg). Discussions regarding collective agreements between Mexican textile industries and the trade union and interviews concerning the crisis experienced in Mexico in 1985 are also analysed (Haidar and Rodríguez). Just as the research in Part II leads to the conclusion that language supports and justifies the use of war, in Part III, the research illustrates two ways by which language contributes to the maintenance of structural violence, i.e. discriminatory and inegalitarian social structures.

Two of the chapters in Part III provide insight on how language is used to communicate and consolidate ideologies that sustain social discrimination. Clyne examines linguistic devices that sustain the *us* versus *them* antithesis that is one component of a racist ideology. He lists examples of (1) lexical choices (e.g. dysphemisms, euphemisms, complex symbols, labels of ethnic groups, ...) used in overt racist discourse and (2) semantic strategies (e.g. concession, tolerant talk, playing down, ...) utilized in covert racist discourse. Haidar and Rodríguez address the question of how meaning is managed in discourse so as to communicate and consolidate social beliefs which maintain and justify inegalitarian social structures. Their analysis illustrates how this is done through (1) conditions which govern the production and reception of discourse (e.g. rules that determine what is permitted or selected as a form of argument/evidence in particular discourses) and (2) discursive devices (e.g. ideological stereotypes, the choice of personal pronouns, modal verbs, and imagery).

While Clyne, Haidar and Rodríguez demonstrate the indirect role language plays in maintaining structural violence, Blommaert, Verschueren and Lowenberg focus on language as a direct instrument of discrimination and oppression. From their examination of the assumptions underlying reports of interethnic conflicts in mainstream newspapers, Blommaert and Verschueren identify the ideology that shapes nationalist movements in Eastern and Western Europe, i.e. the doctrine of homogeneity. Excerpts from their corpus illustrate how, according to this doctrine, culturally diverse societies are viewed as dangerous, i.e. unstable, and the ideal or preferred society is constituted of a 'natural group' defined in terms of a common language, descent, history, culture, and religion. Among these identity markers, language is key. It is a unifying force necessary for social coherence and the predictor of a natural group. Their data show how this doctrine is manifested in immigrant policies and interethnic strife. In the case of the latter, language is used as an instrument of oppression, with the dominant group using the denial of language rights as a means of controlling or suppressing the subordinate group.

Lowenberg's analysis of lexical shifts (the borrowing of words that are denotatively but not connotatively equivalent) further illustrates how language is used to discriminate and institutionalize inequalities among competing groups. When used to replace English, the official (and supposedly neutral) language of Malaysia, lexical shifts, such as banner words (words or expressions that trigger complex schemata or values and associations), legitimize the exclusion of non-Malays from opportunities enjoyed by Malays. Furthermore, Lowenberg demonstrates, they define non-dominant ethnicities in terms of the nationally dominant Malays, thus neutralizing their ethnic identity.

Language, Education and Peace

While Parts II and III have, in fact, demonstrated that language contributes either indirectly or directly to war and to discriminatory and inegalitarian social institutions and practices (i.e. structural violence), Part IV assumes that it need not play such a role. Demonstrating how discursive practices are the result of educational practices and beliefs (Gonçalves, Lopes), the chapters in this last section argue for an educational strategy that can enable participants in written and spoken discourse to acquire the knowledge and skills to critically assess both text and talk. The purpose of such a strategy would be to make them aware of what they assent to and to empower them to dissent and seek alternative views and/or change discursive practices (Wenden). The implementation of such a strategy would require further research into the linguistic practices that take place in those contexts where professionals provide services (e.g. the medical consultation and the language classroom), and the re-training of professional trainers who apprentice novices (e.g. the trainers of teachers and doctors) - recommendations emerging from both Gonçalves' and Lopes' research.

According to Gonçalves, institutionalized discourse reflects, creates, disseminates and perpetuates asymmetry in social relations, and in his critical conversational analysis of a medical consultation, he illustrates how such asymmetry is manifested in the different topic management styles and conversational strategies utilized by both doctor and patient. These differences, he argues, reflect the conflicting frames of reference and expectations that each one brings to the medical interview and, in the case of the doctor, the beliefs and practices acquired as a result of his professional training. Noting that such differences can obstruct the restoration of the patient's health, Gonçalves argues for programmes to provide for the re-education of physicians. Such programmes, he recommends, should include opportunities for doctors to (1) study medical discourse, (2) experience the patient's role in the doctor-patient relationship and, then, (3) consider the implications for their practice of the insights derived.

From his ethnographic analysis of teacher-student interaction in secondary schools in Brazil, Lopes concludes that a logocentric view of language underlies the teaching and learning of reading both in first and second language classrooms. Rather than learning to interact with a writer through the application of their own schematic knowledge when faced with written text, novice readers acquire the belief that, somehow, meaning is inherent in the text. Lopes further illustrates how teaching strategies induce the acquisition of such a logocentric view of language. He argues that acquired simultaneously with this view is the belief that language users play a passive rather than an active and critical role in social discourse. To change these teaching strategies, he maintains, it will be necessary to design teacher education programmes that will enable teachers to review and revise their own understanding of language and of reading in particular. Language teaching syllabi that translate these new understandings into classroom practice will also be required.

In the last chapter of Part IV, Wenden outlines a content schema for a language curriculum in critical language education - an educational strategy appropriate both for training teachers (and other professional trainers), and for teaching students. Consisting of the discourse structures that were the focus of the research reported in this volume, the schema is intended to be a guide to language educators who wish to help readers and listeners develop the knowledge and skills necessary to assess critically both text and talk. Moreover, while it is not the intention of this last chapter to argue for language change, implied in such a critical approach to language education is the empowerment of discourse participants to raise for critical discussion and change long-held assumptions and practices, including discursive practices, which hinder the achievement of a comprehensive peace.

Conclusion

In the declaration issued at the outcome of a 1988 meeting of 45 university presidents from nearly two dozen countries held at Tufts University's European Centre (Talloires, France), the participants state:

> In a world that is plagued by war, hunger, injustice and suffering, we ... join in supporting research and teaching programs that will increase our common understanding of the causes of conflict and their resolution, the relationship between peace and development and the sources of injustice and hunger ... (Bedarida, 1988, p. 37)

Dimitru Chitoran, Chief of UNESCO's Higher Education Section, has outlined a similar role for higher education. He advocates the design of curricula and the promotion of research on global problems so as to provide students, particularly future researchers and those destined for positions of responsibility, with the necessary knowledge of problems related to peace, democracy and respect for human rights (Chitoran and Symonides, 1992).

Language and Peace is a response on the part of one group of linguistic scholars to these challenges to higher education. At the same time, illustrating as it does how critical discourse analysis can be applied to investigating the relationship between language and peace, the book reflects the characteristics and goals of critical linguistics cited earlier in this introduction.

However, the book is not intended exclusively for those linguists who do critical discourse analysis. It is hoped that it will provide insight into the crucial role of language in social life and suggest directions for future research that scholars in the wider field of sociolinguistics and peace research will find relevant. It is also intended for language educators and peace educators, aiming to provide them with an understanding of discourse that they can incorporate into their language curricula. Finally, it is hoped that laypersons, who must make sense of the varying interpretations of social issues provided by media reports, will be empowered with an awareness of how discourse subtly and imperceptibly shapes their understanding of these issues, especially those that relate to social and ecological violence, its causes and consequences upon the quality of life on our interdependent but fragile planet.

Notes

1 Earlier versions of most of the papers in this volume were presented as part of a special symposium on *Language and Peace* organized for the 10th Congress of the International Association of Applied Linguistics (Amsterdam 1993).

Part I

Language, Ideology and Peace

1 Defining Peace: Perspectives from Peace Research

ANITA L. WENDEN

Introduction

In *Agenda for Peace* (Boutros-Ghali, 1992), a report commissioned by the United Nations Security Council to recommend ways of strengthening the work of the United Nations, the Secretary General states that peace is an easy concept to grasp. Its definition, however, has proven somewhat problematic for peace researchers who have found it easier to define peace in terms of what it is not rather than what it is. Thus, earlier definitions referred to peace as the absence of war (Wright, 1942). Expanding the concept, Galtung (1964, 1969) introduced the notion of *negative peace* to refer to the absence of war and contrasted it with *positive peace* to refer to the absence of structural violence. This latter term refers to inegalitarian and discriminatory social structures which also indirectly inflict violence upon individuals or groups in a systematic and organized way because of the institutions and practices they condone. Slavery was an example of structural violence in the past, and discrimination on the basis of race, ethnicity, or gender is an example of structural violence in our age. According to peace researchers, such as Galtung, a society in which such social structures exist is not at peace even though it may not be at war.

Writing from a feminist perspective, Brock-Utne (1989) expands Galtung's definition. She acknowledges the existence of negative peace (the absence of war) and positive peace (the absence of structural violence). However, she introduces a distinction that separates structural violence that *shortens* the life span from structural violence that reduces *quality of life*. Finally, she points out that there is a distinction between organized violence manifested in a systematic way on an intergroup level and unorganized physical and structural violence manifested on an interpersonal level, within the home, for example.[1] In other words, even if there are no wars going on (*organized physical violence*), peace cannot be said to exist when children or women are abused within the home (*unorganized physical violence*). There is no peace if life span is lessened because of the effect of inequitable economic structures or damage on natûre by pollution, radiation, etc. (*organized structural violence*) or if a girl child's needs for food, health, clothing are not provided for adequately because of gender (*unorganized structural violence*). Finally, there is no positive peace if quality of life is reduced as when, for example, free speech or the right to organize are denied (*organized structural violence*) or when educational opportunities in a home are determined according to gender (*unorganized structural violence*).

The purpose of this chapter is to determine whether or not the above view of peace, based on Galtung - one of the seminal thinkers in the field of peace research - and expanded by Brock-Utne - who uses the tools of feminist analysis to review concepts from peace research - represents an emerging consensus by examining how peace is understood by:

(1) the major cultural traditions
(2) peace educators
(3) Nobel Peace Prize Committees (from 1901-1993)
(4) the editors of the Peace Encyclopedia (1986)
(5) peace organizations (i.e. peace research institutes and the peace movement).

Cross-cultural definitions

According to Chernus (1993), the meaning of peace must be considered in the context of past and present cultural *political* realities. In other words, he maintains it is probably impossible to have a culturally neutral definition of peace. On the other hand, earlier research considered cultural views from a linguistic perspective. Ishida (1969) described the various meanings of the word 'peace' in some of the world's major languages, i.e. Greek, Latin, Arabic, Hindi and Japanese. The Greek word 'eirene' and the Roman word 'pax', he noted, are closely related to the state and to its form of government, the Greek concept referring to a country that is orderly, untroubled by civil disturbances. In contrast, the Hebrew word for peace, 'shalom', implies a unity with God and the people of God. Islam has a similar concept - the Arabic word 'al-Islam', which means 'to be at peace'. In India, there are three words for peace. 'Santi' means a well-ordered state of mind - it refers to inner peace. 'Samdhi' indicates the absence of national war, and 'Sama' means a well-governed social order. 'Heiwa', the Japanese word for peace, implies harmony within the culture and adaptation to the social order. 'Ahimsa', nonviolence against any form of life, eloquently expressed by Gandhi, acknowledges that the concept peace must also be defined in terms of human relationships with nature - a view found in African and Native American cultures and among members of some Asian religious groups (Stanford, 1976).

Looking at cultural differences more broadly, Hutchison (1992) introduces some distinctions which expand and refine Ishida's linguistic perspective. His schema (Table 1.1), representing the cultural views of European, West Asian, East Asian, Indigenous, and African traditions distinguishes four levels of peace - peace with our planetary ecosystem, international, interpersonal, and inner peace.

In this schema, 'peace with our planetary ecosystem' is seen as the first and one of the main categories of peace, emphasizing the need for humans to live in harmony with nature rather than conquer it. Hutchison's description of 'Pax Romana' adds to Ishida's - he refers to an absence of open hostilities, perhaps imposed through the use of arms. The Hebrew and the Buddhist traditions introduce a view of peace as justice, equity, and compassion among and between nations. Finally, according to Hutchison, to achieve interpersonal peace, relationships are to be characterized by non-possessive love (early Christian), harmony (Confucian), non-aggression and concern for the welfare of others (Inuit), and skills in interpersonal conflict resolution (Africa).

Views from the cultural traditions include the main categories peace researchers use to discuss peace while, at the same time, refining them. The notion of a stable social order, as represented by Pax Romana, is a form of negative peace. The Hebrew and Buddhist concern for justice and equity reflects the notion of a positive peace though the structural implications are not recognized. The notion of ecological peace, a subcategory of positive peace, receives more prominence in the cultural views derived from Asian and Native American traditions. In including the notion of peace with nature, these traditions implicitly recognize that earth, too, is an object of violence, as does Brock-Utne in her analysis. Finally, in some cultural traditions, peace is viewed in personal terms, as a tranquil inner state of mind or unity with God, or interpersonal terms, as harmonious social relationships, a perspective not found in peace research.

Table 1.1
Defining peace: Spatial and cross-cultural dimensions

Macro Level				
PEACE WITH OUR PLANETARY ECOSYSTEM (ENVIRONMENTAL SECURITY) ↑			*Ahimsa (India)* Non-violence at all levels: Hindu-Jainist-Buddhist traditions. Taoist concept of living in harmony with nature (Chinese).	Cherokee Indian (North American). Koorie (Australian Aborigine). Peace with nature/the land rather than conquering and taming the natural environment. INGOs (internationalist/globalist values).
INTERNATIONAL PEACE	*Pax* (Roman) Peace seen as absence of open hostilities. Armed or imposed peace. 'Negative peace'. Still dominant view of peace in the modern world (eg Pax Britannica, Pax Russica, Pax Americana), although there are important currents of social change for broader rather than narrower definitions of peace/security.	*Shalom* (Hebrew) *Salaam* (Arabic) A durable peace seen as dependent on justice & equity. 'Positive peace'. Peace as more than an interval between wars.	*Metta* (Buddhist) Loving-kindness and compassion to humanity and other life-forms.	*Ho'oponopono* (Hawaiian) Traditional ways of resolving interpersonal conflict peacefully.
INTERPERSONAL PEACE		*Agape* (Early Christian) Non-possessive rather than possessive love as important to building peaceful relationships.	*Hoping-p'ingho* (Chinese) Confucian notion of peace as harmony and order in the world and in social & personal organisation. *Satyagraha* (Indian) Non-violence as social action Mahatma Gandhi.	*Ekimi* (Mbuti, Zaire, Africa) Skills in interpersonal conflict resolution from early childhood. *Ihuma & Naklik* (Inuit, Canada) Non-agression in interpersonal relations - humanity, maturity, concern for the welfare of others.
INNER PEACE ↓			*Shanti* (Indian) Peace of the inner self. Personal peace.	
Micro Level	EUROPEAN	WEST ASIAN	EAST ASIAN	OTHER

← **Cultural Traditions** →

Peace education

With curricular antecedents dating back to the beginning of the century, peace education began to emerge as a specialized discipline in education in the 1940s and 1950s. In *Comprehensive Peace Education,* Reardon (1988) presents an overview of the educational goals that characterized the field as it evolved - each one implying a particular understanding of the notion of peace. (See Aspelagh, 1986, and Pradhan, 1986 for similar overviews.)

Nuclear education, disarmament education, and conflict studies, earlier forms of peace education, view peace as the absence of war. Assuming that the nuclear arms race would lead to war between the superpowers, the key concern of *nuclear education* was the prevention of nuclear war. Peace educators, therefore, concentrated on informing the public about the possibility and catastrophic effects of nuclear war. *Disarmament education* took a comprehensive view of the arms race and extended its educational efforts to both nuclear weapons and conventional weapons. In advocating the notion of general and complete disarmament, it basically questioned the viability of war as a social institution. *Conflict studies,* in its earlier and contemporary forms, sees the central problem as the way conflict is handled. Therefore, its efforts have focused on conflict management and/or conflict resolution skills. Unlike nuclear education and disarmament education, which define peace narrowly as the prevention of war, the field of conflict studies perceives peace as the absence of all physical violence.

Development education, environmental education and human rights education are three more recent curricular approaches based on the notion of a positive peace. In other words, they recognize that life-diminishing damage can be inflicted by forces other than weaponry or armed struggle on both humans and nature. *Development education* uses the term 'structural violence' to refer to the life-diminishing effects of inequitable economic structures. In *environmental education*, the term 'ecocide', i.e. the total destruction of the ecosphere, means that violence can be done to earth systems - a notion also recognized in Indian and Native American cultures. In *human rights education,* the term 'violation' is used to describe the denial or abuse of rights, especially civil and political rights, thus indicating that structural violence also diminishes the quality of life. Moreover, all three approaches are value based. Development education emphasizes the importance of increasing material well-being, environmental education of preserving the eco-system, and human rights education of recognizing the dignity and worth of all human beings. By thus suggesting that alternative values be taken into account in the making of public policy and the shaping of social institutions, these three forms of peace education highlight the value foundation of social structures and the role values play either in inhibiting or facilitating the achievement of a positive peace.

In sum, peace education also recognizes the two main dimensions of peace outlined by Galtung and Brock-Utne. Its focus on the prevention of war reflects the notion of a negative peace and its concern for equitable social structures, for preserving the eco-system, and for human rights reflects the notion of a positive peace. Moreover, Reardon (1988) introduces the notion of a *comprehensive peace* thus recognizing that both negative and positive peace are essential conceptual components of the term.

Nobel Peace Prize

The Nobel Peace Prize is considered the most prestigious recognition of work for peace and humanitarian causes (Abrams, 1986). In his will, Alfred Nobel (1833-96), whose estate provides the finances for the prize, specified that the peace award be given to the person "who shall have done the most or the best for fraternity among nations, for the abolition or reduction of standing armies and for the holding and promotion of peace congresses in the preceding year" (Abrams, 1986, p.52). According to Abrams, while remaining faithful to Nobel's larger purpose as they have understood it, the Nobel Committees have given an ever-broader interpretation to the phrase 'fraternity between nations', eventually coming to consider any distinguished achievement for human solidarity as qualifying for an award. Thus, their reasons for awarding the prize to a particular individual or organization provide another data source on the emerging notion of peace.[2]

Of the 90 prizes awarded from 1901-93, 63, or 70 per cent, recognized work done to achieve a 'negative peace'. Taking into account Nobel's explicit request, Nobel laureates were recognized for the work they had done to prevent war. The other 27, or 30 per cent, which represented work done to promote fraternity or solidarity among nations, implicitly acknowledged the notion of positive peace or the absence of structural violence. The recipients were selected primarily because of their humanitarian contributions in the area of social and economic justice and human rights.

Those Nobel laureates who received awards for their efforts towards achieving a negative peace were commended for contributions towards settling conflict either through arbitration, negotiation, or through work to promote citizen movements that advocated nonviolence. Others were selected because of their work to prevent war by:

(1) promoting education for peace and international understanding,
(2) helping the peace movement,
(3) extending law into international relations, and

(4) establishing and strengthening the League of Nations or the United Nations.

Others, yet, were selected because of their work as pacifists and because of their efforts to abolish war or achieve disarmament. Finally, prizes recognized contributions of individuals and groups towards mitigating the effects of war (e.g. the plight of refugees, postwar hostilities).

It was not until 1977, with the awarding of the Nobel Prize to Amnesty International, that the Nobel Committee expressed its conviction that peace is more than merely the absence of war. That is, until then the concept of positive peace was never *explicitly* referred to as a dimension of peace in the Committee's award statements. However, the notion did emerge *indirectly and implicitly* with the recognition of contributions that shed insight on conditions that lead to war.

Thus, the first Nobel prize (in 1901) was awarded to Frederick Passy for the years spent tracking the causes of war and just over a decade later, the twelfth prize went to Elihu Root for pinpointing the causes of race and local prejudice. Then, in 1919, when the prize was awarded to Woodrow Wilson for introducing the basic concept of justice into international politics and arbitration, the relationship between peace and justice was firmly and explicitly established and, therefore, the notion of positive peace implicitly introduced. Subsequent contributions that prompted the award of the peace prizes, listed in Table 1.2, suggest how the notion of positive peace emerged in the thinking of the Nobel Peace Prize Committee.[3]

Acknowledgement was made of factors which contribute to shortening the life span in prizes awarded to Brantung, who struggled against the inequalities between the powerful and less powerful nations; to Hull, who strove for fair economic interchange, and to Orr and Borlaug for their crusade against famine; to Jouhaux and later to the International Labour Organization (ILO), who attempted to reduce social and economic inequalities through the labour movement and UNICEF for similar attempts through their work with the world's children; to Marshall whose plan for European rehabilitation after World War II was based on the view that political stability (i.e. absence of physical violence) is based on economic health and freedom from poverty.

Intolerance based on differences in race, nation, ethnicity, gender can also inhibit the achievement of a positive peace. This happens when the institutionalization of intolerance leads to lack of economic opportunity and the consequent shortening of the life span *or* to the limiting of freedom of choice and fulfilment, thus diminishing the quality of life. This notion emerged in the thinking of the Nobel Committee members when prizes were awarded to Jane Adams, John Mott, and the Quakers.

Table 1.2
References to positive peace in the Nobel Peace Prize

Year	*Nobel Laureate*	*References to positive peace*
1920	Leon Bourgeois	worked for peace through arbitration and international justice
1921	Karl Brantung	worked for justice
1931	Jane Adams	worked for justice through understanding of different classes, races, and points of view
1934	Arthur Henderson	worked to make the League of Nations bring peace through justice
1935	Carl von Ossietzky	struggled against the suppression of free opinion
1936	Carlos S. Lamos	emphasis on social justice in the field of labour relations
1945	Cordell Hull	peace through fair economic interchange among nations
1946	Emily Balch	contributed to peace and justice
1946	John Mott	brought young people together to work for peace and tolerance among nations
1947	Quakers	relief work which transcended differences based on race and nationality
1949	John Boyd Orr	worked to reduce hunger
1951	Leon Jouhaux	worked in the labour movement to remove social and economic inequalities
1952	Albert Schweitzer	discovery of the ultimate social value 'reverence for life'
1953	George Marshall	worked to remove the causes of war, economic depression, fear, poverty
1965	UNICEF	strove toward an equitable sharing of the earth's resources among the world's children
1968	René Cassin	authored the Declaration of the Rights of Man
1969	ILO	promoted work based on social justice
1970	Norman Borlaug	crusade against famine
1974	Sean McBride	introduced human rights legislation globally
1975	Andrei Sakharov	defended human rights
1977	Amnesty International	fought for human rights
1979	Mother Theresa	emphasis on respect for the individual and the individual's worth and dignity
1980	Adolfo Esquivel	worked for human rights and justice in Latin America
1981	Lech Walesa	struggled for human rights
1991	Aung San Suu Kyi	non-violent struggle for human rights, democracy, and ethnic conciliation
1992	Rigoberta Menchú	promoted rights of indigenous people
1993	Nelson Mandela and F. W. de Klerk	helped to end apartheid and promoted nonracial democracy

The key role that human values play in shaping social institutions and, therefore, in inhibiting or facilitating the achievement of positive peace was recognized when prizes were awarded to Albert Schweitzer and Mother Theresa. Underlying any kind of violence is a violation of human rights. Tolerance and justice, key components of a positive peace, refer to conditions that ensure that human rights will not be violated. Thus the awarding of nine prizes for work done to forward the cause of human rights (1935, 1968, 1974, 1975, 1977, 1981, 1991, 1992, 1993) also marked, albeit implicitly, a broadening notion of peace to include the absence of structural violence.

Peace Encyclopedia

According to its executive editors, the most recent *World Encyclopedia of Peace* (Laszlo and Yoo, 1986) is an attempt to present an integrated body of information on peace in all its aspects. It has two predominant themes: peace research and peace activism seeking to demonstrate the interrelationship between them and the ways in which they have fostered each other. Consequently, according to the editors,

> "... peace is discussed ... from a very broad spectrum of perspectives: from the idealist to the realist; from the global to the subnational; from the cultural to the economic; from the religious to the feminist; from the historical to the contemporary." (Laszlo and Yoo, 1986, p. xiii)

The subject classification (Table 1.3, based on Laszlo and Yoo, 1986), used to commission the articles that constitute the main body of the *Encyclopedia* (volumes 1 and 2), reflects this broad spectrum of perspectives. Representing the views of the executive editors and their advisors, the classification is yet another data source for examining evolving perceptions on the notion of peace.

Eight of the eighteen topics reflect the view of peace as the absence of war. These refer to ways of better understanding war and aggression from a theoretical point of view (a) or by looking at actual conflicts (e). Or they consider ways to replace war as a means of resolving disputes through dispute resolution (b), the use of international law (d), nonviolence (n) or to abolish it (i, k, and j). Five of the eighteen topics suggest a view of peace as the absence of structural violence. Items (m) and (l), terms that point to belief systems that present alternative values (i.e. feminism and religion), implicitly acknowledge that peace is more than an absence of war - that it is values embedded in social structures that influence instability (c). Human rights, social justice (o), and issues related to the world economic order (f), point to specific values and institutions that are necessary to ensure a non-violent social structure or a positive peace. (Items h, p, q, r were not sufficiently specific to be classified.)

Table 1.3
Subject classification for commissioning articles for Peace Encyclopedia

(a)	theories of aggression, conflict, and war
(b)	theories of, and approaches to, conflict and dispute resolution
(c)	the modern states system - ideologies, structures, and individuals which have shaped it; how shaped it; how these have influenced the current instability of the world
(d)	attempts to regulate the states system - through international law and through institutional frameworks
(e)	East-West conflict and related issues of nuclear war and militarization
(f)	North-South conflict and related issues of development, nonalignment, and world economic order
(g)	world order and internationalism
(h)	integration: theory and practice
(i)	disarmament and arms control
(j)	peace movement: history and contemporary
(k)	pacificism
(l)	religion and peace
(m)	feminism and peace
(n)	nonviolence: theory, practice and pioneers
(o)	human rights and social justice
(p)	peace research: pioneers and theories
(q)	peace education
(r)	peace - history, advocates, plans, psychology, sociology

Peace organizations

Peace research institutes

The descriptions of the forty-eight peace research institutes included in the *World Encyclopedia for Peace* were also reviewed to determine the view of peace underlying their stated goals and objectives.

The majority reflected a view of peace as the absence of war citing research topics which included:

(1) a better understanding of violence: its origins, existing evidence of war in contemporary international systems, and regions where peace was at risk

(2) conflict resolution: at all social levels, the theory of conflict, the manifestations of conflict, its management, the application of Gandhian thought and the analysis of conflict processes
(3) disarmament
(4) issues related to defence and national security.

Other peace research institutes listed research topics related to the notion of positive peace. These topics included:

(1) conditions that would establish and maintain peace
(2) alternative societies
(3) the role of religious values in nurturing peace
(4) the effects of structural violence
(5) how to build an equitable and sustainable economy
(6) how to protect human rights and global ecology
(7) the study of peaceful societies
(8) evidences of peace in contemporary international systems.

Peace movements

Peace movements consist of citizen groups that organize to alter foreign and/or military policies of governments. Their strategies vary from ending an existing war, preventing an impending war, or educating contemporaries to a different view of world order. The earliest examples of peace movements were groups calling themselves 'friends of peace', established in the United Kingdom and the north-eastern United States in 1815-16 (Cooper, 1986). First efforts towards bringing these national groups together on an international scale began in 1890 (Abrams, 1986). The action goals of the twenty-five organizations in the peace movement included in the *World Encyclopedia for Peace* indicated an appreciation of both negative and positive peace.

Perceptions of peace as the absence of war are evidenced in those organizational goals which sought to abolish war or to avoid it by working:

(1) to deal with confrontation
(2) to develop confidence building structures
(3) to influence the formation of nuclear policy
(4) to promote the use of negotiation or international law
(5) to achieve total disarmament
(6) to introduce nonviolence as an approach to solving group differences.

Perceptions of peace as the absence of structural violence are reflected in organizational goals which sought structural changes (referred to as peacebuilding by one group) that would:

(1) end poverty
(2) support the recognition of human rights
(3) achieve a secure peace with freedom and justice
(4) eliminate colonialism and racial discrimination
(5) provide for beneficial trade relations
(6) eliminate the destruction and deterioration of the life systems of the planet.

Conclusion

Certainly, one may conclude that the notion of peace as absence of war (often taken to mean the ending of a particular war) is easy to grasp. The sources examined all recognize this more traditional and narrower notion of peace, i.e. negative peace. In fact, it was the dominating view in the selection of Nobel Peace Prize laureates and in the selection of research topics by peace research institutes. The subject classification that determined the focus of articles commissioned for the *Peace Encyclopedia* was similarly biased in favour of the narrower view of peace.

However, the complexities represented by the notion of a positive peace are more elusive. There is a growing recognition of the impact of structural violence on the life span and on quality of life, but the sources vary in the emphasis and explicitness with which they refer to social justice and the recognition of human rights as manifestations of positive peace. Moreover, as yet to achieve a prominent place within this emerging concept of a positive peace is the notion of peace with nature or ecological justice. Only peace educators and the Indian and Native American cultures have explicitly recognized the absence of ecological violence as key to a peaceful society. Similarly, the distinction between organized and unorganized violence, which acknowledges, for example, that the perpetration of direct physical violence on an interpersonal level reduces the quality of peace enjoyed by a society, is a notion recognized only by Brock-Utne, one of the two peace researchers, and, implicitly, by the cultural traditions that include the concept of interpersonal peace in their definition of the term.

In sum, as regards the notion of peace put forth at the outset of this paper (i.e. by Galtung and Brock-Utne), there is consensus on the notion of a negative peace, and the notion of a positive peace has come to be recognized as a necessary complement to the more traditional view. However, the distinction between organized and unorganized violence is not generally recognized. Nor is there, as yet, a clear agreement on all of those conditions that constitute a positive peace. Consensus on what that term represents is still emerging. Still the relevance of clarifying these emerging meanings of 'peace' and of extending recognition of these clarifications beyond the world of peace research is underlined by the constructivist view of language underlying this volume. For such a view, which recognizes language as a dynamic force that shapes the world of meaning guiding human endeavour, suggests that, ultimately, it is the meaning represented by the word 'peace' that will inform the goals and determine the efforts of those who strive to achieve it.

Notes

1 While the notion of organized violence focuses on intergroup relations (national groups, ethnic groups, racial groups), in the last analysis it is the *individual* who is its recipient. In that sense all violence may be viewed as personal.

2 Information on reasons for awarding the Nobel Peace Prize to particular groups or individuals was drawn from articles in the *World Encyclopedia for Peace* (1986) written to reflect the thinking of the Nobel Committee, from *The World Almanac and Book of Facts* (1987-94), and from *Facts on File Yearbook* (1987-92).

3 Of course, several of the laureates listed in Table 1.2 were also selected for work they did to prevent war. Here, only those criteria referring to positive peace are listed.

2 Discourse Analysis a Ideology Analysis

TEUN A. VAN DIJK

Introduction

This chapter focuses on the 'expression' of ideologies in various structures of text and talk. It is situated within the broader framework of a research project on discourse and ideology which has been conducted at the University of Amsterdam since 1993. The theoretical premise of this study is that ideologies are typically, though not exclusively, expressed and reproduced in discourse and communication, including non-verbal semiotic messages, such as pictures, photographs and movies. Obviously, ideologies are also 'enacted' in other forms of action and interaction, and their reproduction is often embedded in organizational and institutional contexts. Thus, racist ideologies may be expressed and reproduced in racist talk, comics or movies in the context of the mass media, but they may also be enacted in many forms of discrimination and institutionalized by racist parties within the context of the mass media or of Western parliamentary democracies. However, among the many forms of reproduction and interaction, discourse plays a prominent role as the preferential site for the explicit, verbal formulation and the persuasive communication of ideological propositions.

Theory of ideology

The theory of ideology that informs the discourse analytic approach of this paper is multidisciplinary. It is articulated within a conceptual triangle that connects society, discourse and social cognition in the framework of a critical discourse analysis (van Dijk, 1993b). In this approach, ideologies are the basic frameworks for organizing the social cognitions shared by members of social groups, organizations or institutions. In this respect, ideologies are *both* cognitive *and* social. They essentially function as the 'interface' between the cognitive representations and processes underlying discourse and action, on the one hand, and the societal position and interests of social groups, on the other hand. This conception of ideology also allows us to establish the crucial link between macrolevel analyses of groups, social formations and social structure, and microlevel studies of situated, individual interaction and discourse.

Social cognition is, here, defined as the system of mental representations and processes of group members (for details, see, e.g., Fiske and Taylor, 1991; Resnick, Levine and Teasley, 1991). Part of the system is the sociocultural knowledge shared by the members of a specific group, society or culture. Members of groups may also share evaluative beliefs, viz., opinions, organized into social attitudes. Thus, feminists may share attitudes about abortion, affirmative action or corporate 'glass ceilings' blocking promotion, or other forms of discrimination by men. Ideologies, then, are the overall, abstract mental systems that organize such socially shared attitudes. The feminist attitudes just mentioned, for instance, may be internally structured and mutually related by general principles or propositions that together define a 'feminist' ideology. Similar examples may be given for racist, anti-racist, corporate or ecological attitudes and their underlying ideological systems.

Through complex and usually long-term processes of socialization and other forms of 'social information processing', ideologies are gradually acquired by members of a group or culture. As systems of principles that organize social cognitions, ideologies are assumed to control, through the minds of the members, the social reproduction of the group. Ideologies mentally represent the basic social characteristics of a group, such as their identity, tasks, goals, norms, values, position and resources. Since ideologies are usually self-serving, it would seem that they are organized by these group-schemata. White racists, for example, represent society basically in terms of a conflict between whites and non-whites, in which the identity, goals, values, positions and resources of whites are seen to be 'threatened' by the Others. They do so by representing the relations between themselves and the Others essentially in terms of *us* versus *them*, in which *we* are associated with positive properties and *they* are associated with bad properties.

Such ideologies of groups and group relations are constructed by a group-based selection of relevant social values. Feminists, on the one hand, select and attach special importance to such values as *independence*, *autonomy* and *equality*. Racists, on the other hand, focus on *self-identity*, *superiority* of the own group, and hence on *inequality*, while at the same time advocating the *primacy* of their own group and the *privilege* of preferential access to valued social resources.

The contents and schematic organization of group ideologies in the social mind shared by its members are a function of the properties of the group within the societal structure. The *identity* category of a group ideology organizes the information as well as the social and institutional actions that define membership: who belongs to the group, and who does not; who is admitted and who is not. For groups who share a racist ideology, this may mean, among other things, resentment, actions and policies against immigration and integration in 'our' culture, country, city, neighbourhood, family or company. Similarly, the *goal* category of groups who share a racist ideology organizes the information and actions that define the overall aims of the group, e.g., 'To keep our country white'. The *position* category defines the relations of the group with reference groups, such as, 'foreigners', 'immigrants', 'refugees' or 'blacks'. In sum, the social functions of ideologies are, among others, to allow members of a group to organize (admission to) their group, coordinate their social actions and goals, to protect their (privileged) resources, or, conversely, to gain access to such resources in the case of dissident or oppositional groups.

As basic forms of social cognitions, however, ideologies also have cognitive functions. We have already suggested that they organize, monitor and control specific group attitudes. Possibly, ideologies also control the development, structure and application of sociocultural knowledge. To wit, feminists have special interest in acquiring and using knowledge about the dominance of women by men. Generally though, we shall assume that ideologies more specifically control *evaluative* beliefs, that is, social opinions shared by the members of a group.

At this mental interface of the social and the individual, however, ideologies and the attitudes and knowledge they control, also - indirectly - influence the personal cognitions of group members, e.g., the planning and understanding of their discourses and other forms of (inter)action. These personal mental representations of people's 'experiences' of such social practices are called *models* (Johnson-Laird, 1983; van Dijk, 1987b; van Dijk and Kintsch, 1983). Models are mental representations of events, actions, or situations people are engaged in, or which they read about. The set of these models represents the beliefs (knowledge and opinions) people have about their everyday lives and defines what we usually call people's 'experiences'. These models are unique and personal and controlled by the biographical experiences of social actors. On the other hand, they are also socially controlled, that is, influenced by the general social cognitions members share with other members of their group. This combined presence of personal and (instantiated, particularized, 'applied') social information in mental models allows us not only to explain the well-known missing link between the individual and the social, between the micro and the macro analysis of society, but also to make explicit the relations between general group ideologies and actual text and talk. That is, models control how people act, speak or write, or how they understand the social practices of others. We, thus, have the following, highly simplified elements in the relations between ideologies and discourse at various levels of analysis (outlined in Table 2.1):

Table 2.1
Ideologies and discourse: Levels of analysis

1 Social Analysis

- Overall societal structures, e.g., parliamentary democracy, capitalism
- Institutional/Organizational structures, e.g., racist political parties
- Group relations, e.g., discrimination, racism, sexism
- Group structures: identity, tasks, goals, norms, position, resources

2 Cognitive Analysis

2.1 Social cognition

- Sociocultural values, e.g., intelligence, honesty, solidarity, equality
- Ideologies, e.g., racist, sexist, anti-racist, feminist, ecological ...
- Systems of attitudes, e.g., about affirmative action, multiculturalism ...
- Sociocultural knowledge, e.g., about society, groups, language, ...

2.2 Personal cognition

2.2.1 General (context-free)

- Personal values: personal selections from social values
- Personal ideologies: personal interpretations of group ideologies
- Personal attitudes: systems of personal opinions
- Personal knowledge: biographical information, past experiences

2.2.2 Particular (context-bound)

- Models: ad hoc representations of specific current actions, events
- Context models: ad hoc representations of the speech context
- Mental plans and representation of (speech) acts, discourse
- Mental construction of text meaning from models: the 'text base'
- Mental (strategic) selection of discourse structures (style, etc.)

3 Discourse Analysis

- The various structures of text and talk (see below)

In other words, ideologies are localized between societal structures and the structures of the minds of social members. They allow social actors to 'translate' their social properties (identity, goal, position, etc.) into the knowledge and beliefs that make up the concrete models of their everyday life experiences, that is, the mental representations of their actions and discourse. Indirectly (viz., through attitudes and knowledge), therefore, ideologies control how people plan and understand their social practices, and hence also the structures of text and talk.

Ideologies define and explain the similarities of the social practices of social members, but our theoretical framework at the same time accounts for individual variation. Each social actor is a member of many social groups, each with their own, sometimes conflicting ideologies. At the same time, each social actor has her/his own, sometimes unique, biographical experiences ('old models'), attitudes, ideologies and values, and these will also interfere in the construction of models, which, in turn, will influence the production (and the comprehension) of discourse. Hence, the schema given above may be read top down, or bottom up. The relations involved are dynamic and 'dialectic': ideologies partly control what people do and say (via attitudes and models), but concrete social practices or discourses are themselves needed to acquire social knowledge, attitudes and ideologies in the first place, viz., via the models people construct of other's social practices (including others' discourses) (van Dijk, 1990).

At many points, our theoretical approach to ideology is at variance with classical and other contemporary approaches to ideology (see Eagleton, 1991; Larrain, 1979; Thompson, 1984, 1990). Ideologies in our perspective are not merely 'systems of ideas', let alone properties of the individual minds of persons. Neither are they vaguely defined as forms of consciousness, let alone as 'false consciousness'. Rather, they are very specific basic frameworks of social cognition, with specific internal structures, and specific cognitive and social functions. As such, they (also) need to be analysed in terms of explicit social psychological theories (see also Rosenberg, 1988), which obviously has nothing to do with mentalist reductionism. At the same time they are social, for they are essentially shared by groups and acquired, used, and changed by people *as* group members in social situations and institutions, often in situations of conflicting interests between social formations (Eagleton, 1991). However, ideologies are not restricted to dominant groups. Oppositional or dominated groups also share ideologies. The main problem of most critical approaches to ideology is that they are exclusively inspired by social sciences and rather confused philosophical approaches. They ignore detailed and explicit cognitive analysis, and so they are unable to explicitly link social structures with social practices and discourses of individuals as social members. Ideologies or other social cognitions in our approach are not reduced to or uniquely defined in terms of the social 'practices' they control (Coulter, 1989), nor to the discourses that express, convey or help reproduce them (Billig et al., 1988; Billig, 1991), or to the institutions in which they are reproduced. (For different but related approaches, see, e.g., Fairclough, 1989, 1992a; Kress and Hodge, 1993.)

Discourse analysis as ideological analysis

The sketch of the theory of ideology presented above provides us with a conceptual framework that also allows us to engage in 'ideological analyses', and, hence, a critique of discursive practices. After all, we have seen that ideologies, though variably and indirectly, may be expressed in text and talk, and that discourses similarly function to persuasively help construct new and confirm already present ideologies. In both cases, this means that there may be discourse structures that are particularly relevant for an efficient expression or persuasive communication of ideological meanings. For instance, headlines in newspapers, taken as prominent expressions of the overall meaning or gist (semantic macrostructure) of a news report in the press, form a special discourse category that is probably more likely to express or convey ideological 'content' than, for instance, the number of commas in a text.

On the other hand, we have no a priori theoretical grounds to exclude any textual structures from expressing underlying ideological principles. Indeed, virtually all discourse structures are involved in the functional expression of mental models of events or communicative contexts, and, therefore, of the opinions that are part of such mental models. To wit, a racist opinion of a speaker about his black interlocutor, may be subtly expressed (involuntarily or not) by minimal intonation variations, interpreted by the black interlocutor as a racist way of addressing her, while sounding unwarrantably 'insolent' or 'impolite' (for many such examples of everyday racism, see Essed, 1991). Let us now examine these levels and properties of discourse and the ways ideologies may be expressed and conveyed more systematically.

However, before we present a summary of 'preferential' discourse structures for the expression and communication of ideological meanings, we should be clearly aware of what we are looking for. Given the theory of ideology presented above, we need to attend primarily to those properties of discourse that express or signal the opinions, perspective, position, interests or other properties of groups. This is specifically the case when there is a conflict of interest, that is, when events may be seen, interpreted or evaluated in different, possibly opposed ways. The structures of ideologies also suggest that such representations are often articulated along an *us* versus *them* dimension, in which speakers of one group will generally tend to present themselves or their own group in positive terms, and other groups in negative terms. Thus, any property of discourse that expresses, establishes, confirms or emphasizes a self-interested group opinion, perspective or position, especially in a broader socio-political context of social struggle, is a candidate for special attention in such an 'ideological' analysis. Such discourse structures usually have the social function of legitimating dominance or justifying concrete actions of power abuse by the elites.

Surface structures

The 'surface' structures of discourse refer to the variable forms of expression at the level of phonological and graphical 'realization' of underlying syntactic, semantic, pragmatic or other abstract discourse structures. With a few exceptions, such surface structures of text and talk do not have explicit 'meanings' of their own. They are only the conventional manifestations of underlying 'meanings'. Yet, such surface structures may express and convey special operations or strategies. For instance, special stress or volume or large printed type may strategically be used to *emphasize* or attract attention to specific meanings, as is the case when shouting at people or in 'screaming' newspaper headlines. In the same way, special intonational contours may help express irony, (lack of) politeness or other semantic or interactional meanings and functions.

These examples already suggest that surface structures may express or control the ways in which events are interpreted by speech participants. A large banner headline may emphasize the biased summary of a news event, about a 'race riot', for instance, and 'insulting' volume or intonation may similarly signal social inequality between speaker and hearer. Theoretically, this means that ideologically controlled models of events or of communicative contexts may represent women or minorities in a negative way, and such opinions will not only influence the meanings of the text but also, indirectly, the sometimes subtle variations of the graphical or phonological surface structures. Indeed, whereas the meanings of the text may not explicitly express or encode prejudice or social inequality, surface structures may let 'transpire' such 'hidden' meanings anyway.

In general this means that such surface structures must be 'marked'. They must be out of the ordinary and violate communicative rules or principles, i.e., those of 'normal' size headlines, 'normal' volume or intonation in polite speech, and so on. Depending on meaning and context, then, such 'deviant' surface structures may signal, express, or convey similarly 'deviant' properties of models, such as a specially negative opinion about the competence of a woman or a black man. In other words, ideological surface structures primarily function as signals of 'special' meanings or model structures, and may, thus, also contribute to special processing of such interpretations of text and talk.

Special graphical or phonological emphasis may also manage the importance of information or beliefs, and, hence, the hierarchical organization of models in which important information is located at the top. Conversely, meanings and beliefs may be de-emphasized or concealed by non-prominent graphical or phonological structures when they express meanings that are inconsistent with the goals or interests of the speaker. Intonation, such as the tone of racist insults, may also conventionally signal specific social relations, and hence also ideologically based inequality. That is, they also influence the context models of the communicative context. The same is true for other forms of non-verbal communication, such as gestures, facial expression, proximity, and so on, which also may signal interpersonal and social relations, and, therefore, ideological meanings.

Finally, it is well known that 'accented' speech of sociolects or dialects express or convey social class, ethnicity, gender, or social relations of familiarity or intimacy, as has been shown in much sociolinguistic and social psychological research (Giles and Coupland, 1991; Montgomery, 1986). Again, it is obvious that such social relations may also be structured in conflict and inequality, and so presuppose ideological differences. Accents may thus signal or express prestige, accommodation, dominance, resistance or other ideologically controlled social relations.

Syntax

The ideological implications of syntactic sentence structures referred to in the literature are familiar. For example, it has often been shown that word order as well as transactional structures of sentences may code for underlying semantic (or indeed, cognitive) agency (Fowler et al., 1979; Kress and Hodge, 1993). In general, at least in English, responsible agency is associated with grammatical subject, and initial position. This means that ideologically monitored opinions about responsibility for socially positive or negative acts may be differentially expressed in different syntactic forms. Negative properties attributed to outgroups (e.g. black youths) may be enhanced by focusing on their responsible agency (Hamilton and Trolier, 1986). In that case minorities will tend to be subject and topic of the sentence. The same is true for the *positive* actions of *us*. Conversely, the agency of ingroup members who engage in negative actions will be syntactically played down by the use of passive sentences, and their role may be wholly dissimulated by agentless passives or nominalizations. A typical discourse location for this kind of syntactic management of opinions are news headlines (van Dijk, 1991a).

Again, the theoretical explanation of such ideologically based syntactic variation should be given in terms of model structures. Syntactic prominence expresses or suggests semantic prominence, which, in turn, may be related to prominence of actors and their properties in mental models. If negative properties of outgroups are prominent in the model, this may affect syntactic word order and clause structure in such a way that agency and responsibility of outgroup actors is syntactically highlighted (for details of these relations between discourse structures and models, see van Dijk and Kintsch, 1983).

Another link between syntactic structures and ideology, well-known from sociolinguistic research, is the one between sentence complexity, on the one hand, and education or social position of speakers, on the other hand. Elite speakers and institutions may restrict comprehensibility of their discourses in this way and, thereby, control access to public discourse, e.g., to political and media text and talk. The public may, for example, be excluded from elite debate and decision making (Ghadessy, 1988; Renkema, 1981; Sandig, 1986; Wodak, 1987; Wodak, Menz and Lalouschek, 1989). Medical and legal discourse also restricts access to 'outsiders' through sentence complexity (Halliday, 1988; Edelman, 1977; Fisher and Todd, 1986; Di Pietro, 1982). Alternatively, ideologically based condescension, e.g., with respect to immigrants who do not speak the language well, may be expressed by various forms of simplified 'foreigner talk' (Dittmar and von Stutterheim, 1985). Thus, social power may translate quite directly into language variables that are instrumental in getting symbolic access to the resources of public discourse.

Lexicon

Lexicalization is a major and well-known domain of ideological expression and persuasion as the well-known 'terrorist' versus 'freedom-fighter' pair suggests. To refer to the *same* persons, groups, social relations or social issues, language users generally have a choice of several words, depending on discourse genre, personal context (mood, opinion, perspective), social context (formality, familiarity, group membership, dominance relations) and sociocultural context (language variants, sociolect, norms and values). Many of these contexts are ideologically based, as is the case for the representation of speech participants, and their mutual relations in context models, and the representation of participants and actions in event models.

Examples abound and need not be discussed in detail. Racist or sexist slurs directed at or used about minorities and women, directly express and enact relationships of power abuse grounded in inegalitarian ideologies (Essed, 1993; Greenberg, Kirkland and Pyszczynski, 1987; Hurtado and Arce, 1987; Schultz, 1975). Political ideologies are variously expressed in differential, if not polarized lexicalization of political actors (as in the 'terrorist' example) (Edelman, 1985; Wodak and Menz, 1990). Other social ideologies, about abortion, for example, may make use of words and slogans such as 'Pro Choice' or 'Pro Life' that emphasize the positive implications of ingroup opinions and values and the negative ones of those of the Others. The lexicon of military and political discourse may also distinguish between the 'peaceful' nature of our weapons or military operations and the catastrophic and cruel nature of theirs (Chilton, 1985; Geis, 1987a). Euphemisms, such as 'surgical strikes' or 'smart bombs' are well-known here, as was evident in the military propaganda and news reports about the Gulf War (Chomsky, 1992; Media Development, 1991). During the Cold War, the Soviet Union was characterized as the 'Evil Empire'. Similarly, in the Middle East conflict, our opponents are often 'terrorists', whereas especially Muslims and not Christians, are called 'fundamentalists', 'zealots' or 'fanatics'. A similar use of euphemisms is made in elite discourse on ethnic or race relations, in which 'racism' is typically denied, and replaced by less harsh words such as 'xenophobia', 'prejudice', 'discrimination' or 'resentment' (van Dijk, 1993a). On the other hand, the credibility of refugees may be undermined in political and media discourse by calling them 'economic' refugees, or 'illegal aliens' instead of 'undocumented' immigrants. In all these examples, we find the general pattern of ideological control of discourse, viz., a positive self-presentation of the ingroup and a negative other-presentation of the outgroup.

Local semantics

What has been shown for lexicalization is more generally true for the management of meaning. Local coherence depends on models, that is, on ideologically controlled representations of the situation. Biased reasons and causes that define relations in the model may, therefore, appear in partisan local semantics. The attribution by employers of high minority unemployment in the Netherlands to cultural differences, the lack of motivation or knowledge of the language by minorities is an example (van Dijk, 1993a). Well-known socio-cognitive processes underlying positive self-presentation of ingroups and negative presentation of outgroups, such as the fundamental attribution error (Pettigrew, 1979) and blaming the victim (Ryan, 1976), may also translate as 'biased' local coherence in the semantics of text and talk. Conversely, such ideologically shaped discourse semantics may, in turn, affect the biased construction of models by recipients if these have no alternative information sources. In both cases, ideologies and attitudes used in the self-serving 'explanation' of social inequality are assumed to control (or result from) self-serving representations of social events in mental models (Schuman, Steeh and Bobo, 1985).

Another important property of discourse semantics and its relations to underlying mental models (and hence to social cognitions) is implicitness. Since parts of models may be known to recipients, speakers are allowed to presuppose such information. Such normal processes of mutual knowledge may also be ideologically managed when it is suggested that knowledge is shared even when it is not as when newspapers speak about 'rising crime', or about 'the linguistic deficit of immigrants' (Fowler 1991; van Dijk, 1988a, 1991a). More generally, we find that, in principle, all information that is detrimental to the ingroup will tend to remain implicit, and information that is unfavourable to the outgroup will be made explicit, and vice versa (our negative points and their positive points will remain implicit).

The same holds for the variation in levels of generality and the degrees of specificity in describing events. Not only are 'our' blunders or crimes described in euphemistic terms and attributed to circumstances beyond our control or blamed on our victims, but they are also described in more general, abstract terms. On the other hand, when describing 'their' mistakes, 'we' use specific, low level, 'gory detail'. In both cases, the ideologically controlled goal of such discourse is the management of self-serving and preferred models of social situations.

Underlying ideologies also control communicative contexts, and hence the self-definition and impression management of speakers, who will generally try to make a good impression or avoid a bad impression (Goffman, 1967; Tedeschi, 1981). This is particularly clear in the strategic use of disclaimers. Examples of such semantic strategies in our own research on the reproduction of racism in discourse of such semantic strategies are well-known and comprise such classical moves as the disclaimers of the *apparent denial* ('I have nothing against Blacks, but ...', 'Refugees will always be able to count on our hospitality, but ...'), the *apparent concession* ('There are of course a few small racist groups in the Netherlands, but on the whole ...'), or *blame transfer* ('I have no problem with minorities in the shop, but my customers ...') (van Dijk, 1987a). These moves essentially do two things. They contribute to the overall strategy of positive self-description (viz., 'we are tolerant citizens'), or the avoidance of a negative impression, on the one hand, and of negative other-presentation, on the other hand, because the second term of these moves, introduced by 'but', is always negative about the Others.

More generally, elite ideologies are known to de-emphasize social inequality by semantic strategies that aim to legitimate, justify, naturalize, rationalize, authorize, universalize, or deny injustice, to transfer it to other groups (as when elites attribute racism to 'popular resentment') or to blame the victim (Eagleton, 1991).

Global semantics: Topics

Topics or semantic macropropositions of discourse subjectively define the information in a discourse that speakers find the most relevant or important. This means that topicalization may also be subject to ideological management. Ingroup speakers may be expected to de-topicalize information that is inconsistent with their interests or positive self-image and conversely they will topicalize information that emphasizes negative outgroup properties. This happened, for instance, in the British media accounts of urban disturbances sparked by the shooting of a black woman during a police raid in Brixton in 1985. The aggression of the police was de-topicalized in favour of an explanation of the 'race riots' in terms of the deviance of young black and crime (drugs, aggression, etc.) (van Dijk, 1991a). Similarly, immigration fraud and minority crimes are prominent topics in the press, but not the (equally documented and accessible) everyday discrimination by 'our' politicians, employers, journalists, police or professors. This difference cannot simply be attributed to preference for 'negative' information or crime in the press. Both topics are negative and represent social crimes. In the same way, the civil war in Bosnia will be readily topicalized (by male journalists) as an 'ethnic conflict' or as a 'tribal war' rather than as a prominent form of male aggression or nationalistic macho-chauvinism or as a likely consequence of the presence of arms and armies and the freedom of the international arms trade. In sum, undesirable interpretations (models) of social and political events will, generally, not be topicalized in ingroup discourse.

Schematic structures

Overall meanings, i.e. topics or macrostructures, may be organized by conventional schemata (superstructures), such as those that define an argument, a conversation or a news report. As is the case for all formal structures, schematic structures are not directly controlled by ideological variation. A reactionary and a progressive story are both stories and should both feature specific narrative categories to be a story in the first place. Similarly, a 'Pro Choice' or a 'Pro Life' editorial or other argumentative discourses are both, formally speaking, editorials and argumentations. So the question is: How do such overall schematic structures of text and talk signal underlying ideologies?

Since schematic categories also define the (canonical) order of discourse, they may signal importance or relevance. Initial summaries, such as *headlines* in the news, for instance, have the crucial function of expressing the topic highest in the macrostructure hierarchy, and, therefore, the (subjectively) most important information of a news report (van Dijk, 1988b). This means that this link between macrostructures and superstructures may be ideologically manipulated. Semantically subordinate topics (that is, topics that organize little local information in the text) may be 'upgraded' and put in the headline, thus assigning more prominence to them, and vice versa. A main topic may be 'downgraded' to a lower level of the schema and realized as a subordinate topic in a *background* category of the news. In one story the same events may be presented as the *circumstances* category of the *setting*, whereas in another story they may constitute the crucial *complication* of the story. Such possible variations of relevance and importance are, of course, open to ideological control. Information that is inconsistent with the interests of powerful groups may be downgraded, and information about outgroups be given more prominence by assigning it to a more prominent category. Political discourse may also feature specific text schema categories (such as *problem* and *solution*) that highlight ideologically based opinions (Schäffner and Porsch, 1993).

Argumentation is another major domain in which ideological points of view may be expressed. The study of numerous argumentative fallacies has shown that powerful arguers may manipulate their audiences by making self-serving arguments more explicit and prominent, whereas other arguments may be left implicit. Strategic argumentation is a major means of manipulating the minds of the recipients. This may involve many of the features we have studied above: the use of specific lexical items, rhetorical devices, and so on (Kahane, 1971; Windisch, 1990; van Eemeren and Grootendorst, 1992). One analysis of the argumentation of British press editorials on the 'riots' of 1985 is an example. It noted how the racist ideologies of right-wing tabloid editors were revealed by their attribution of the violence to the criminal nature of young male Caribbeans (van Dijk, 1992).

Rhetoric

Specific 'rhetorical' structures of discourse, such as surface structure repetition (rhyme, alliterations), or semantic 'figures' such as metaphors, may be a function of ideological control when information that is unfavourable to *us* is made less prominent whereas negative information about *them* is emphasized. Many of the figures we know from classical rhetoric have this specific effect as their main function (e.g. over- and understatements, hyperbole (exaggeration), euphemism and mitigation, litotes and repetitions).

The semantic operations of rhetoric, such as hyperbole, understatement, irony and metaphor, among others, have a closer relation to underlying models and social beliefs. Racist, sexist and other inegalitarian ideologies, for instance, may typically be expressed, not only by derogating lexical items referring to minorities or women, but also by demeaning metaphors that belittle, marginalize or dehumanize the 'others'. Thus, Nazi propaganda associated Jews, communists and other ethnic and social minorities with dirty animals (rats, cockroaches) (Ehlich, 1989). Similar tendencies may be observed in the contemporary rhetoric of the right-wing press when it writes about immigrants, minorities, refugees or white anti-racists. The following are some typical examples from the British conservative press in 1985 (for further analysis, see van Dijk, 1991a):

(1) Snoopers (*Daily Telegraph*, 1 August, Editorial)
(2) Unscrupulous or feather-brained observers (*Daily Telegraph*, 30 September)
(3) Race conflict 'high priests' (*Daily Telegraph*, 11 October)
(4) The multi-nonsense brigade (*Daily Telegraph*, 11 January)
(5) He and his henchmen ... this obnoxious man, left-wing inquisitor (*Mail*, 18 October)
(5) Left-wing crackpots (*Sun*, 7 September)
(6) Unleashing packs of Government snoopers (*Sun*, 16 October)

Similarly, political discourse is replete with variously demeaning metaphors that derogate the 'enemy', as when Bush referred to Saddam Hussein as 'Hitler'. However, political metaphors may also have other ideological functions, as when Gorbachev referred to Europe as our 'common European House' (Chilton and Ilyin, 1993) or when the Western press writes about the unification of Europe by using architectural metaphors (Schäffner, 1993). That such variations may be ideologically constrained is also shown by the fact that different groups, cultures or countries may use different metaphors to denote the 'same thing'. France and Great Britain, for example, use different metaphors to refer to 'security' (Thornborrow, 1993). Similarly, press reporting about refugees systematically uses 'flow' metaphors ('stream', 'flood', 'deluge', 'swamp', 'tide', etc.) to emphasize the catastrophic and threatening nature of the immigration of refugees (van Dijk, 1988c). In the Netherlands, the 'natural' response to such metaphors is to 'protect' the country against such floods by building dikes.

Pragmatics

According to our theory of ideological discourse production, the social control of speech acts should operate through context models that represent the communicative situation and its participants, goals, and other relevant appropriateness conditions. For instance, if speakers share sexist or racist attitudes and ideologies featuring propositions that imply the inferiority of women or minorities, such general opinions may also be applied to women and minorities as speech participants. Such negative evaluations, and, generally, relations of inequality between speech participants, also control speech act production. Commands and threats, for instance, presuppose relations of dominance and power, and may be issued to women or minority participants only because of group membership. Prejudices about the intellectual inferiority of Others, similarly, may occasion speech acts such as giving advice or even plain assertions (in situations were none is asked or otherwise appropriate), since both presuppose ignorance of the recipient.

Similar remarks hold for other interactional strategies, e.g. those of politeness, self-presentation, impression management, and so on, as we have already seen above. Obviously, ideologically based inferiorization of Others may lead to inferiorization of speech partners in such a way that normal rules of respect and politeness are not respected (Brown and Levinson, 1987). Evidence from minorities confronted with racist events shows that lack of respect, rudeness, and other forms of impoliteness are routine forms of everyday verbal discrimination (Essed, 1991). Again, the same is true for the ways many men treat women in conversation (Kramarae, 1981; Kuhn, 1992; Trömel-Plötz, 1984).

Dialogical interaction

These examples finally bring us to the ideological structures of discursive interaction. What has been said above for speech acts and politeness more generally holds for interaction and, hence, also for conversation. We have already seen that sexist and racist ideologies generally tend to favour overall strategies of positive self-presentation and negative other-presentation implemented by local semantic strategies, such as disclaimers. This will also be apparent in dialogues with and about women and minorities.

Similarly, ideologies define relationships of power, which in turn also may control interaction, i.e., who has more or less access to the use of specific dialogical features, such as setting agendas for meetings, making appointments, opening and closing dialogues, turn management (e.g. interruption), the initiation, change and closure of topics, style selection and variation, and the more general properties of discourse also dealt with above (van Dijk, in print). Recent research on the relations between conversation, institutions and social power has familiarized us with these strategies (see, e.g., Boden and Zimmerman, 1991; Drew and Heritage, 1992; R. Lakoff, 1990; West, 1984) .

The more specific interactional nature of dialogue may reflect the ideologically based power of interaction strategies more generally, by which speakers who share egalitarian ideologies may feel entitled to verbally treat their speech partners as inferior. This usually happens when the 'normal' rules of conversation are broken: by irregular interruptions, not yielding the floor or taking very long turns, avoiding or changing 'undesirable' topics, negative meta-comments about the other's style (choice of words) or other attributed 'breaches' of etiquette, using inegalitarian speech acts, as discussed above, and so on.

Virtually all work that has been done on power abuse in talk presupposes tacit assumptions of speakers about their own and the Others' social position and relations. Obviously, underlying ideologically based attitudes about others may not always be conscious, and so the subtle details of dialogical interaction are not always fully controlled and controllable. Non-verbal as well as subtle interactional, pragmatic and stylistic means of controlling the other speech partner may, therefore, yield valid diagnostics for inferences about underlying inegalitarian ideologies.

Conclusion

Ideologies need to be analysed as the socio-cognitive interface between societal structures, of groups, group relations and institutions, on the one hand, and individual thought, action and discourse, on the other hand. In such a combined cognitive and social approach to ideology, we assume that ideologies are constructed by a biased selection of basic social values and organized by group self-schemata in which categories, such as *identity, task, goal, norms, position* and *resources* play an important role. Such ideologies have social functions. They influence social interaction and coordination, group cohesion, and the organized or institutionalized activities of social members aimed towards reaching common goals.

Similarly, ideologies were found to have important cognitive functions. They organize clusters of social (group) attitudes and monitor their acquisition and change, viz., as a function of group interests. These attitudes, in turn, provide the socially shared opinions that may be 'applied' by social members in the construction of mental models of concrete events and communicative contexts. These interactions of personal and social knowledge and opinions, as represented in mental models, control the production or the comprehension of text and talk. That is, discourse structures express ideologies only indirectly, that is, through their 'instantiation' in concrete models, which are the mental basis of the unique and situated nature of each occasion of text and talk.

Our brief review of ideologically controlled discourse structures at various levels of text and talk first of all shows that both in graphical and phonological surface structures, as well as in syntactic and semantic structures, we encounter similar patterns and strategies of expression and management of biased mental models. Overall, we find that preferred, consistent or otherwise self-serving information will be emphasized, highlighted, focused upon, and made explicit and prominent, whereas the converse is true for dispreferred information. In persuasive communication, this means that such discourse structures have obvious functions in the management of the minds of the recipients. There will be a higher chance that recipients will activate preferred old models or construct new models in agreement with the goals or interests of the speaker, if no alternative information is present.

Surface structures essentially serve to underline important or prominent beliefs, whereas syntactic organization may express and convey the role organization of social actors represented in biased mental models.

As is the case for virtually all strategic choices at the semantic level, such 'forms' will signal and emphasize *our* good actions, and *their* negative actions. What is preferred information in mental models results not only from personal goals and interests, but also from group-based attitudes and ideologies. Such social cognitions will in turn be acquired and reproduced precisely by the discursive structures that allow speakers to manage the minds (models) of recipients, viz., by emphasizing important, relevant or otherwise preferred information, and doing the opposite for dispreferred information. The ideological conflict between *us* and *them* may similarly be signalled in many ways in discourse, e.g., by stress and intonation, syntactic word order, and especially semantic disclaimers such as *apparent denials* ('We have nothing against them, but ...').

In sum, ideologies seldom express themselves directly in text and talk, and do so only by general ideological propositions, which, however, may be less efficient in persuasion. More subtle and indirect ideological control and reproduction is effected through general attitudes and specific personal models, which form the basis of discourse production and are the result of discourse comprehension. Thus, ideological control of discourse takes place through the control of mental models, and the same is true for the acquisition, change and reproduction of ideologies themselves. They involve general opinions and values that are represented in the models of the speakers and indirectly inferred from the opinions expressed or signalled in discourse. Adequate ideological analysis should always take into account these various steps or interfaces between discourse structures and ideological structures, as is more generally the case for the relations between discourse and society.

Part II
Language and War

3 Foreign Policy by Metaphor

PAUL CHILTON AND GEORGE LAKOFF

The metaphorical nature of foreign policy concepts

Government policy makers and academic experts not infrequently speak of a foreign policy 'concept'. This refers to a principle in some way summarizing or guiding the particular policies that a government, often a new incoming government, will adopt on taking office. The concept may be 'containment', 'bridging the missile gap', 'de-escalation', or 'spreading democracy', but all are metaphorical, and inevitably so. Metaphors are not mere words or fanciful notions; they embody modes of thought, and they structure the 'discourse' of foreign policy in the deepest sense - not just the words used but also the mode of thinking.

The conceptual processes used in foreign policy discourse are, of course, complex. By focusing on metaphor, we are picking out just one element, but it is a vital element, as we shall see. However, even if we limit our focus to metaphor, there is an important difference to be noted between everyday ('folk') concepts and discourse on the one hand, and those of foreign policy theorists, policy makers and politicians, on the other. Yet the two are not entirely separate, if only because the specialists themselves participate in both. Moreover, in the existing democracies, the specialists, and especially the politicians, ultimately have to justify their foreign policy discourses in public terms, communicating with legislators, business leaders, and journalists. It is possible, of course, that specialists and politicians secretly say and think one thing while using different concepts and language in addressing their voters. In what follows, however, we assume some degree of continuity between the specialist and the everyday discourse of foreign policy, without seeking to specify different degrees of secrecy or deception.

Metaphor, concepts and action

In our education systems and scholarly traditions, metaphor has, over centuries, been relegated to the domain of the poetic, the persuasive, or the purely deceptive. However, metaphors are one of our primary means of conceptualizing the world. What has been learned over the past decade in cognitive science and in linguistics is that a vast proportion of our conceptual life is metaphorical. We think automatically, effortlessly, and without being aware of the fact that we are using metaphors with which we have grown up, metaphors we have accepted unquestioningly. Here are two examples.

Dante began the *Inferno* with the line, 'In the middle of life's journey, I found myself in a dark wood.' In the Western tradition, we conceptualize purposes as destinations and purposeful lives as journeys toward goals. This metaphor of life as a journey is so seemingly natural that its presence in the language seems inevitable. To Americans, for example, it is important to 'have direction, to know where one is going', and it is desirable to have 'a head start'. What is more frustrating to an American than a sense of 'not getting anywhere with your life'? Such expressions are not merely arbitrary 'signs' that might mean anything at all. They represent an idea that is of vital importance in the West but that would be meaningless in many cultures, present and past, although it is possible that the march of modernism has spread it further.

Movement through space, as in journeys, involves time. The dimension of time itself is conceptualized metaphorically in a way especially appropriate to the modern era. Time, in much of the industrialized world, is understood as a money-like resource. We can 'save time', 'waste time', 'spend time', 'budget time', and 'use time wisely or foolishly'. When we understand our experience through metaphorical concepts, create institutions based on those metaphors, and live our lives according to those metaphors, our metaphors appear real to us. If you live by a time-as-resource metaphor, someone really can 'waste' an hour of your time. If you understand life as goal-oriented, you may really feel 'lost' and 'without direction' and worry about whether you are 'getting anywhere with your life'. Metaphor is a means of understanding one domain of one's experience in terms of another - time in terms of money, life in terms of travel. Such metaphors are so automatic, conventional, and widespread as to seem natural. It takes an acquaintance with cultures where lives are not journeys with goals and time is not a money-like resource to realize the metaphorical character of our own cultural concepts.[1]

Such metaphors are not dispensable. We cannot comprehend such abstract and overwhelming concepts as life and time unless we can make sense of them in terms of something more familiar. We know how to reason about travel and resources. Metaphor allows us to transfer those modes of reasoning to more problematic arenas, and the conclusions we reach on the basis of metaphoric reasoning can form the basis for action. If we are to understand ourselves, to see why we act as we do and to see new possibilities for action, we must be aware of the metaphors we are using.

The study of foreign policy discourse has lagged far behind research in the cognitive sciences on the nature of metaphorical understanding. Despite the enormous effort that has been spent, on both theoretical and practical fronts, in conceptualizing and reconceptualizing foreign policy, virtually no effort has gone into understanding the metaphorical concepts on which our current policies are based. This is hardly an accident. In the main, foreign policy theorists in the universities, the think-tanks, the government departments and the media pride themselves on what is referred to as 'realism'. Metaphor, in the traditional view adopted in such circles, is taken to be anything but 'realistic'. Yet the current understanding of foreign policy, in the popular mind, in the theories of international relations experts, and in the practices of policy makers themselves is metaphorical through and through. Indeed, the expert theories typically use versions of the popular metaphors; it is this that makes those theories seem intuitive, a manifestation of 'common sense'. The point is not that it is wrong to use metaphor - it is in fact inevitable - but that the traditional view that metaphors are mere words places the use of metaphor beyond serious consideration, comment, and criticism.

States as persons

The major metaphor that dominates thought about foreign policy is that the state is a person. It is understandable that this should be the case. Organizations of all kinds tend to be personified. Legal discourse speaks of corporations as 'legal persons'. Since states have become the most powerful form of political organization over the last four hundred years, and have their origins in the power of individual princes, it is not surprising to find this metaphor.

As persons, states enter into social relationships with other states, which are seen typically as either friends, enemies, neighbours, neutral parties, clients, or even pariahs. States are also seen as having personalities: they can be trustworthy or deceitful, aggressive or peace-loving, strong- or weak-willed, stable or paranoid, cooperative or intransigent, enterprising or not. Given our folk understandings of what animals are like, we will often use animal metaphors to characterize the personalities of states: thus, Russia is seen as a bear and England as a bulldog.

Our policies are designed to be consistent with such metaphorical estimations of 'national personalities'. Thus, for example, if Russia is seen as aggressive, deceitful, incompetent, paranoid, and intransigent, we will treat it very differently than we would a country seen as trustworthy, peace-loving, competent, and cooperative. Such metaphorical preconceptions about national personality lie behind policy.

Person, society, state

The effect of employing the state-as-person metaphor depends on one's view of what a person is like, and this, of course, may vary. A person can be seen, in essence, as being

(1) an isolated individual, pitted against all others;

(2) a socially cooperative and responsible autonomous individual; or

(3) a member of a collective in which individual identity is secondary, or entirely submerged.

These are crude distinctions, but they correspond approximately to the views of the person in various social and political philosophies. The first suggests theories, such as Hobbes's, social darwinism, sociobiology, or certain aspects of rational choice theory. The second suggests liberal political theorists. The third suggests two perspectives: totalitarian philosophies, such as fascism and Stalinist communism on the one hand, and on the other, utopian communitarianism.

These three different ways of conceptualizing what a person is are carried over metaphorically into theories of the international world, which are generally presented to students of international relations (IR) (Booth and Wheeler, 1992). Thus, the IR paradigm known as 'realism' (and its successor 'neorealism') treats nations as persons motivated by the pursuit of power, and is often linked with Hobbes. A second paradigm, associated with Grotius and sometimes termed 'rationalist', treats states as autonomous agents but also as interdependent and cooperative actors in a community. The third perspective is suggestive and disturbing in its implications. It could lead to concepts of world empire, world order and world government which may or may not be benign, as well as to pluralist concepts of global ecology, economic interconnectedness and the like.

Each of these three perspectives yields somewhat different versions of the state-as-person metaphor, different because the assumptions of the source domain (the beliefs about individuals and society) are different. The differences in the source domains give rise to different entailments, or different selections, or differently emphasized entailments. Thus, in a

Grotian perspective that emphasizes international law, person-states are seen as members of a 'world community', a community of nations. Treaties are promises, and keeping one's word and working together are important.

In government and academia, the most influential of these paradigms since World War II has been the realist and neorealist, based on the view of a person as a self-interest maximizer. The state-is-a-person metaphor is fundamental among academic theorists of international relations as well as in the state department. What is important is the fact that the metaphor inevitably carries theories and beliefs of human personality with it. Thus, in the 'realist' and 'neorealist' paradigms of international politics, person-states are viewed as logically consistent individuals with judgements untainted by emotion, i.e. rational decision-makers who know their self-interest and act to maximize it. What counts as 'rational' is defined as maximizing the economic and military self-interest of the state as a whole.

'Realist' and 'neorealist' theorists (the best known representatives are Hans J. Morgenthau and Kenneth Waltz, respectively), make it a fundamental assumption that states have basic 'instincts' and 'desires', namely, an overarching desire to survive and a desire to dominate. This further view of a state as a predatory animal leads to a kind of social darwinism for person-states. Waltz (1979), for example, used this metaphor of the 'instinct for survival' to argue that nations will attack if they feel threatened, and so great powers need to feel that they will survive and that they are not threatened.

It is also common for 'realists' to psychologize the person-state, postulating natural desires, such as the desire to make others like oneself. The metaphor is also prevalent among those who are less theory-oriented, but who write nonetheless explanation-oriented narrative. Michael Mandelbaum argues that the 'impulse' for 'strong states' to 'expand' is in part explained by the desire 'to extend the collective self', "to spread its domestic characteristics throughout the international system ... to make the world like itself" (Mandelbaum, 1988, p. 137). Robert Osgood and Robert Tucker, twenty years earlier, had seen extension of self as the person-state's 'purpose' or 'mission' and had linked it to a 'survival instinct'. This has led to the foreign policy view that it is the mission of the Western democracies to spread democracy throughout the world. As they say, attributing to the person-state more than a mere body, "a nation may preserve its body and yet perish through the loss of its soul or the abandonment of its purpose" (Osgood and Tucker, 1967, p. 272).

Law and order

Specific cultural experiences can contribute to the source domain of the state-as-person metaphor. In the United States, the world community is often conceptualized as a kind of frontier town, with law-abiding states (the United States itself plus currently favoured allies) and outlaw states (perhaps 'wild', 'crazy', 'irrational', or 'sociopathic' states). Specific entailments follow. Because there are outlaws (and 'Indians'), a sheriff is needed, and the United States has been playing sheriff for the past four decades. Without the sheriff, there would be anarchy. President Roosevelt and his advisors imagined that after World War II international society would be patrolled by 'four policemen', the United States, Britain, Russia and China (the 'Big Four'). In this type of model, the frontier is an important concept. The civilized community is conceptualized additionally in terms of the important basic image of a container - a protective boundary keeping the uncivilized from the civilized. When Truman succeeded Roosevelt, his advisors (notably George Kennan) emphasized a dividing line between East and West which would 'contain' the Soviet hordes. Winston Churchill expressed a similar concept in his 'iron curtain' speech. As the Cold War neared its end and the USSR was replaced by a Russia accepted by the West into the 'family', other states effectively took the place of principal enemy. They were referred to as 'rogue' states - states such as Libya and Iran.

The end of the bipolar structure of the Cold War also left questions as to the future roles of its former protagonists. With the Soviet bloc fragmenting and reforming, what was to be the role of the United States, of NATO, and of the United Nations? The United States appeared to be the world hegemon. President Bush spoke of a 'New World Order'. The concept remained vague but was to a large degree structured by the law-and-order metaphor. The debate frequently raised the question whether the United States should adopt the role of 'world policeman', and the notion of 'policing' the world came to the fore once again. This metaphorical way of looking at the problem had several implications. First, it suggested that one power alone not only had the might but also the right. Second, it took for granted that the legitimacy of the policeman in relation to lawful authority within states could be translated to the inter-state domain, and that the United States (and its allies) as law-enforcer was legitimized by some superior authority, the United Nations.

This was the position at the time of the Gulf War. Doubts were expressed that the concept would turn out to be a cloak for unilateral American interests under the authority of the United Nations, and extend NATO's role 'out of area'. The disorder in the former Yugoslavia did not arouse the serious attention of any new world policeman, American or European, unlike the war in the Gulf where American and British assets were directly threatened. Nonetheless, the scope for American use of NATO and the United Nations increased in 1993-94 when NATO's strategic concepts were extended in a way that envisaged operations outside the European theatre under UN or CSCE mandate.[2]

Body-politic

Any particular international relations perspective that sees states as persons is liable to make use of a wide variety of entailments. Such widespread, natural-seeming metaphors help to structure and legitimize policies and programmes. For hundreds of years we have used the metaphor of the 'body-politic'. If the state is a person, it has a body, and bodies can grow, mature, decline, be healthy, be developed, underdeveloped, weak, strong, diseased, and so on. Of course, what metaphorical 'strength', 'development', etc. corresponds to is understood in concrete terms, though often tacitly.

Metaphorical foreign policy views the health of a person-state, or body-politic, in terms of national wealth and the strength of a person-state as military force - instead of, say, the health or well-being of its individual citizens. Maturity for a person-state is industrialization. From this it follows that an 'underdeveloped country' is one which is less industrialized than Western countries. Therefore, an unindustrialized country is not considered mature even though its ecology is still largely intact. 'Growth' and 'development' are assessed in terms of industrial economics. States that are not 'fully developed' are, therefore, seen as metaphorical children, who need the help of their elders if they are to grow up to be mature adults. They are natural dependents requiring both paternalistic help and a strong hand to keep them in line if they get naughty. Given this metaphor, it is impossible for a third world country to know more about the kind of economic system that will best suit its culture and geography than the grown up industrialized nations. Metaphor is, thus, far from inconsequential.

The state-as-person metaphor also permits a body-politic to be seen as 'diseased', and, therefore, as a patient requiring treatment. George Kennan, in his famous 1946 *Long Telegram* that set the tone of US foreign policy for decades thereafter, urged that we must 'study' the Soviet Union with the same "objectivity ... with which the doctor studies the unruly and unreasonable individual" (Kennan, 1946, p. 708). If the Soviet Union is mentally deranged, the United States must take on the role of doctor. One way of treating mental patients is to strap them in a strait-jacket. In some respects this is what the policy of 'containment' was: it not only held back Soviet expansion and penetration, but also excluded the Soviet Union from the normal society of nations, as the Soviet Union itself sometimes complained. This is certainly not to say that the Soviet Union did not have its own metaphors (not considered here) which exacerbated the situation.

The metaphors that fed American foreign policy at the beginning of the Cold War can help us understand not only that formative period but some of the features of the post-Cold War period too. If a body-politic is sick, its 'disease' can 'spread', and 'infect' other bodies. In 1946, Kennan telegraphically told the State Department that "World communism is like the malignant parasite which feeds only on diseased tissue" (Kennan, 1946, p. 708). It followed from this metaphor that American society must be kept in a condition of 'health and vigour', which meant military 'strength'. In 1947, Dean Acheson, Truman's Secretary of State, appealed to Congressmen to continue and extend American involvement in Europe: "... the corruption of Greece would infect Iran and all to the east. It would also carry infection to Africa through Asia Minor and Egypt, and to Europe through Italy and France" (Acheson, 1987, p. 219). The disease was communism, and this was not the last time that the metaphor would be used. Senator McCarthy's 'purge' of the American body-politic involved the same metaphor. It has two parts: internal disease and external contagion. Both, together with other metaphors, were inherent in the American concept of 'security' after World War II.

In the 1990s, American involvement in the Balkan region could not easily be accepted by the American people: threats to American health and strength had for forty-five years been associated with communism, and communism was now presumed dead and no threat to American economic or military interests (health or strength) could be perceived. Indeed, the opposite was the case: involvement in the Balkans could be costly, both economically and militarily. It was involvement, not non-involvement, that was seen as sapping American health and strength.

The end of the Cold War has led to a metaphor crisis in European and American foreign policy. No new metaphorical concepts have been formed to handle what are very potent dangers in the new Europe. New security threats, though they are often linked to the old communist guard in new garb, are not metaphorized as contagious disease (they are not effectively conceptualized at all). Ironically and tragically, the body and disease metaphors constitute a major part of the new authoritarian, nation-state based mode of thinking and talking that characterizes many parts of Europe. The most shaming example is the Serbian (and Croatian) concept of 'ethnic cleansing' - the purging of territorial containers by murder or removal of 'foreign bodies' defined by 'ethnic group'. This is another form of 'containment', justified by the concept of territorially self-contained, 'sovereign', nation states. 'Cantonization', a proposal promoted by peace negotiators at Geneva, rested in essence on similar principles. The West has not seriously challenged these metaphorical structures, and cleansing metaphors are not, indeed, limited to the Balkans. From Russia to Germany and France, extreme nationalist parties exploit discourses that use the same metaphors of the bodily purity of the nation-state. Racist and nationalist discourse depends crucially on disseminating the metaphor of the nation-state as body, together with its entailments. These entailments include: maintaining the wholeness or integrity of the body, avoiding penetration, contamination and impurity; and these in turn entail: protection, exclusion, purging and cleansing (see Chilton, 1994).

Interestingly, such metaphors had by no means been absent from documents creating the original Cold War, the Cold War settlement, or from the subsequent Cold War culture. When they reappeared in the wake of the Cold War in the form of racism and nationalism, there was no effective challenge and there were no effective counter-concepts.

Fist fights

Seeing the state metaphorically as a power-hungry person seeking domination leads naturally to a metaphorical conception of foreign relations as competition above all else. Competition between persons takes numerous forms, all of which can serve as source domains for metaphors. One of these metaphors is war is a fist fight. Such fights typically take place between two and only two opponents. During the Cold War, the Soviet Union was the other fighter from the western point of view - a bully, rational enough not to fight someone equally strong, but bully enough to attack anyone weaker, with or without provocation. Here strength is measured by the number of troops in some cases and total nuclear capability in others. The United States, in this metaphor, is seen as having to be strong enough to stand up to this bully, not only to protect itself, but also the weaker kids in the schoolyard. The theory of nuclear deterrence is defined in this metaphor: the United States must be strong enough to deter the Soviet bully from starting a fight. This, of course, depends crucially upon the bully's rationality and accurate judgement. It also depends upon the bully's assumption that the hero is willing to fight.

This metaphor was not confined to conceptualizing Cold War deterrence. It can be replicated in other situations. In the Vietnam War, one of the many ways in which military violence was masked involved the use of the fight (specifically, boxing) metaphor. For example, right-wing critics of the war operations said the armed forces were 'fighting with one hand tied behind their back'. The metaphor appeared again in the Gulf War of 1991. Thus, the United States sought to 'push Iraq back out of Kuwait', to 'deal the enemy a heavy blow', 'to deliver a knockout punch'. Implicitly, the western alliance took on the role of the champion of a weaker victim, 'standing up to' an aggressive, domineering bully.

Rational choice and games

In contrast to fist fights, competition may take the form of organized games. Viewed theoretically, games are presumed to depend on strategic choices dependent on logical decisions. If there is a claim to 'science' in the IR community, it comes with the use of game theory - often called the theory of rational choice. The mathematics of game theory in itself is just mathematics: it happens to be a variety of abstract formal language theory with a certain set of constraints, including 'tree axioms'. The question to be asked is what does this rather abstract mathematics have to do, if anything at all, with either rational action or foreign policy. The answer is that there are three levels of metaphor mediating between pure mathematics and foreign policy.

The first level of metaphor maps the abstract mathematics into a 'tree' - it spatializes the mathematics so that it can be conceptualized in terms of locations (or nodes) and paths from one location to another (or lines). The players, or actors, are conceptualized as travellers that move from one location to another, choosing a path to continue along at each location (or node). The second level of metaphor maps this spatialization in terms of motion from location to location onto the concept of rational action. There are two common metaphors that accomplish this. The first is called the *event structure metaphor*. According to this metaphor, States are Locations and Causes are Forces that result in a motion from one location to another, Actors are Travellers, Actions are Self-propelled Motions, and Resulting States are Final Locations. A path through this 'tree' is conceptualized as a course of action, and the choice of which path to take is conceptualized as a choice of which action to take. A second common metaphor, called *well-being is wealth*, conceptualizes increases in well-being as 'gains' and decreases in well-being as 'losses' or 'costs'. This metaphor maps the vector of numbers at the terminal nodes of the game theory tree onto 'payoffs' - increases of well-being (gains) and decreases of well-being (losses). Rationality is then defined as maximization of profit. A maximally rational course of action is a route through the tree that maximizes gain. The third level of metaphor maps rational action, so conceived, onto international relations. The principal metaphor that accomplishes this is the state-as-person metaphor.

Thus, at the level of pure mathematics, a letter in an alphabet of symbols gets mapped onto a traveller at the level of spatialization of the mathematics. This traveller then gets mapped by the event structure metaphor onto an actor, and the actor is mapped by the state-as-person metaphor onto a state. Thus, the relationship between the letter in the alphabet of the formal language and the state in the foreign policy is mediated by three common metaphors and two intermediate levels. The commonness of these metaphors makes it seem 'natural' that such a mathematics should be applied to foreign policy.

The use of game theory allows any form of competition, including international relations, to be conceptualized as a game, typically with two players. It is important, here, to distinguish between 'play' and 'games'. The first is not goal-oriented. The second, however, is oriented typically towards winning. It is true that cooperative games can be imagined, but the prototypical game in our culture is oppositional. People, in fact, live in particular cultures and are socialized into the concept of what a game is and what its practices are. These include such things as having (usually) two 'sides', team spirit, loyalty, opposition, desire to win. Wars and games are used as metaphors for one another: games have their victors and vanquished; wars have their 'sides', 'oppositions', 'players', etc.

The game metaphor, taken seriously, makes it seem natural to use the mathematical theory of games in theorizing about international relations. Although it is true that there are theoretical games like the iterated prisoner's dilemma, where the optimizing strategy for both sides is cooperation, the use of game theory in international relations typically focuses on opposition, duality, and winning. However, the mathematics does not model real, culturally embedded games, played with the interaction of calculation and passion. All it models are abstract, idealized models of completely rational actors. Failure to appreciate this difference can lead to unrealistic expectations of what game theory can tell us about conflicts between groups of people, where passion does exist and cool rationality may not.

Game theory has been extensively used in economic theory as a way of conceptualizing an idealized model of the behaviour of economically rational individuals in a pure market. International relations theorists (notably Kenneth Waltz) have applied this in a fashion that is metaphorical. The international system is a market and states are rational economic actors. Defenders of such an approach may say this is merely an 'analogy', but it is, in fact, linked to a wider nexus of metaphors in the IR discourse, the key metaphor being, once again, 'the state is a person'. This is an element of the argumentation in IR discourse that is usually taken to be common-sensical, with a minimum of discussion or none at all (see Buzan, 1991). The use of economic metaphors should be carefully distinguished from the study of international political economy, which seeks to understand economic processes in international integration and conflict. The consequence of the combination of game theory and economic theory in the metaphorical representation of international relations is that international actions are thought about and talked about in terms of commercial cost-benefit analysis.

Closely linked to the metaphors involved in game theory is the uncertain-action-is-gambling metaphor. This metaphor had important entailments for the Gulf War, enabling President Bush to limit the media debate on the Gulf War in the United States by referring to strategic moves as a 'poker game' in which he could not be expected to 'show his cards'.[3] The well-being-is-wealth metaphor also had important implications for public discourse during the Gulf War. It defined the principal issue discussed by the US Congress in the debate over the war and the issue accepted by the press as the right one for debate, namely, what were the 'costs' and 'gains' to the United States of various courses of action. Thus, during the war, the press constantly sought to assess gains and costs. When General Powell was asked if there would be any cost if Saddam Hussein released oil into the Gulf, he replied that, since the American amphibious vehicles could land perfectly well on oil-slicked water, there would be no cost. The possible destruction of the Gulf's ecology was not a 'cost' to the United States, because it was not an American asset. Similarly, the 'cost' for civilians of the bombing of Iraq was discussed only in terms of propaganda value, not in terms of human suffering. Again, since Iraqi civilians were not US assets, their suffering could not count as 'costs' or 'losses' to the United States.

The notion of 'rationality' implicit in this set of metaphors, that of maximizing 'gains' and minimizing 'losses', derives its prestige from the Western conception of a person as a self-interest maximizer. Though such a view of person is not universal by any means, this notion of rationality is treated as a universal value by advocates of rational actor models in international relations.

Two points follow. First, when an international crisis requires open deliberation (as in western democracies), the public and the media, as well as the experts, assume that they are rational. Second, they may proclaim the irrationality of political or military opponents, and with it metaphors for madness. When the Cold War mentality was first established in the 1940s, texts (memos, reports and other documents) assumed and argued that the West was rational, had gone to the limits in the search for a rational 'solution', while the Soviets were irrationally suspicious, secretive, paranoid and megalomaniac. After the end of the Cold War, in 1990-91, it similarly had to be shown that the current enemy, Saddam Hussein, would not 'listen to reason', that he was not only irrational but refused to keep communication open. By any standards Saddam Hussein was and is cruel and tyrannical, but it does not follow he was not following his own rationality, maximizing his own benefits and the perceived interests of the Arab world.

The arms race and beyond

Another form of competition is a race, and during the Cold War decades, foreign policy placed us in an arms race with the Soviets. In such a metaphorical race, having enough weapons to blow up the world many times over was beside the point, and so was having enough invulnerable submarine-based missiles to assure the destruction of the enemy. There are many reasons why parity was never accepted by the West in the forty-odd years of the arms race after World War II, but the prevalent conceptualizations of East-West relations had something to do with it, either because it moulded perceptions that favoured the desire to 'stay ahead' in the 'nuclear contest', or because it provided a way of justifying and explaining the American 'lead'. It is natural to want to win a race, so if the East-West relationship was a race, then of course 'we' should strive to stay 'out in front'. An entailment of the race metaphor is 'winning' the race, but because of the nature of weapons involved, 'winning' the arms race was not commonly spoken of. Similarly, only a few specialists spoke of winning a nuclear war, though the fact that anyone at all could speak in these terms and be understood is testimony to the cognitive influence of race metaphors.

Race metaphors appear to be a constant of modern foreign policy thinking, and they are used to conceptualize historically different and changing situations. In 1994 President Clinton attended a major NATO summit in Brussels, the aim of which was to establish the role of this essentially Cold War organization in the rapidly changing continent of Europe. In his speech, he spoke of a new kind of race, a 'race between rejuvenation and despair':

> Today the race is being played out from the Balkans to Central Asia. In one lane are the heirs of the enlightenment, who seek to consolidate freedom's gains by building free economies, open democracies and tolerant civic cultures. Pitted against them are the grim pretenders to tyranny's dark throne - the militant nationalists and demagogues who fan suspicions that are ancient, and parade the pain of renewal to obscure the promise of reform.[4]

Since, like all metaphors, this race metaphor necessarily imposes cognitive and discursive limitations, one needs to question its usefulness. First, this race metaphor vastly oversimplifies the complexities and insecurities of Europe after the Cold War. The idea that there are two 'contenders', each one acting in a unified way to outstrip the other (as Communism and Capitalism were depicted in earlier years) is certainly false, and ignores the many local and historical differences in the transformation of Europe. There may be similarities between the Russian extremist leader Zhirinovsky and the Serbian President Milosevic, and they may not be totally accidental, but they are different and the differences matter.

Second, like all metaphors, Clinton's new race metaphor has to specify who the racers are, who is running in one 'lane' and who is running in the other. The most significant point here is that American policy has decided (as many speeches and documents testify) that the Russian President Boris Yeltsin is running in the lane not just for free economies, but also for open democracies and tolerant civic cultures. This seems a strange claim in the light of Yeltsin's own authoritarian style, his reneging on promises of elections, his readiness to act outside a constitution, and his silencing of media opposition.

Third, and perhaps most frightening, President Clinton may actually be taking this metaphor seriously, using it to structure a philosophy of history, and perhaps with it, a foreign policy. Let us hope not, since what he says is highly questionable. For instance, the metaphor of the race, interpreted as a binary competition, takes for granted only one particular interpretation of the Enlightenment and subsequent political philosophies. But some historians would argue that Marx and socialist political philosophies were also heirs of the Enlightenment, just as much as the capitalist democracies the president claims as its descendants. Further, applied to history in this fashion, the metaphor induces the idea of a grand all-or-none struggle between good and evil, reminiscent of Cold War thinking.

States as containers

Territoriality is important in human social experience. Space is experienced as bounded in various ways - by the surface of the body, by clothes, by protective armour, by buildings, by fences, walls, by natural barriers such as rivers, mountains and forests, and, last but not least, by boundaries and frontiers. The last two do not necessarily coincide with unambiguous natural features, and their definition has often been the motivator of conflict. Because frontiers are not always naturally self-evident in the geophysical sense, they attract all sorts of conceptualization in discourse, including the use of metaphor.

The state-as-container is an image that is deeply rooted in political discourse, and it provides the conceptual basis for much of the argumentation in international relations also. This is evident when one considers the Greek city-states, and perhaps the medieval towns and principalities. The container image came to be applied to the state when this particular form of political organization emerged in the sixteenth and seventeenth centuries; it was extended naturally to the nineteenth century notions of nation-states. In the medieval period the political entities of Europe were mostly such that they could not naturally be conceptualized as having an inclusive inside, an excluded outside, and a separating line around them. Medieval Europe was a collage of multiple and overlapping political and religious jurisdictions. It is with the emergence of a new form of political organization, the modern nation-state, that the container concept became crucial to political discourse with its characteristic notions of sovereignty, centralized control, fixed boundaries and diplomatic recognition. It is now so well rooted in the mind that it is difficult to think of the present state-as-container system as anything other than a natural and immutable fact.[5]

States as objects in a force field

From the sixteenth century onwards, the west European tradition of international relations used physical metaphors to conceptualize the relations between states. In the twentieth century, physical metaphors were adopted by the realist and neorealist schools.[6] Central to the discourse that emerged was the balance of power metaphor. It is linked to the state-as-person nexus via the view of war as a fist fight that can be avoided only if the two strongest people are about equally strong. The balance of power metaphor generalizes this, reifying the two participants as physical objects exerting force in a force field. The objects are stable as long as the two forces remain equal; if one comes to exert more force, the balance is upset, just as one fighter who becomes stronger can knock down the other.

The balance of power metaphor overlaps with the war-as-fist fight metaphor, but it is different in two important ways. First, the use of physics as a metaphorical source gives the metaphor a scientific air. Second, it removes any notion of human will: the bully may choose not to start the fist fight, but an object exerting a more powerful physical force will always knock over an object exerting a weaker force. The effect is to make conflict seem inevitable unless an arms increase on one side is countered by one on the other side.

Just as the typical fist fight involves two participants, so a balance of physical forces is much more achievable with two major forces than with more, since the two-body problem is solvable but the three-body problem is not. In the Cold War, the physics-based metaphor was commonly used to justify a world order with exactly two superpowers on the grounds that 'stability' is more achievable with two bodies exerting force than with more (see Schäffner, this volume).

A special case of force is magnetic force, which happens to be bipolar; there are magnetic dipoles, but no tripoles. Merely thinking about force in international relations as magnetic force with 'poles' imposes a conception of world politics with a binary superpower structure. Consider the following example in which a historian of the international system argues that a bipolar world is the best of all possible worlds:

> Strong states are like powerful magnetic poles; weaker ones can seldom evade their fields of force. Independence, therefore, must be redefined as equidistance among - or between - the most powerful states in the international system. Even this position is not always feasible. If the pull of one pole is stronger than that of the other, if one of the great powers is more threatening than the other, then independence requires not equidistance but closer association with the orbit of the other to offset the threat from the first. (Mandelbaum, 1988, p. 201).

The magnet metaphor does at least two things. It makes international power politics seem as inevitable as the laws of physics, and therefore divorced from questions of freedom and rights; and it makes it seem both natural and necessary that international power politics should result in two and only two antagonistic coalitions, alliances, or blocs.

Balance of power and bipolarity did not disappear with the end of the Cold War. These metaphors shaped foreign policy in the Gulf War as well. Why, one might ask, was Saddam Hussein left in power? Why were his elite guards not eliminated? The Bush administration's rationale was balance of power and bipolarity. It was reasoned that Iraq had to remain a viable counterforce to Iran - the balance of power had to be maintained in the region. If Saddam Hussein were weakened further, the Shiites in the south and the Kurds in the north of Iraq might split off, with the Shiites possibly joining forces with fellow Shiites in Iran and the Kurds fomenting revolution of fellow Kurds in Turkey. The remainder of Iraq, without the elite guards, and without the Shiite south and Kurdish north, would, it was reasoned, be weakened enough so as to throw the balance of power to Iran, which would 'destabilize' the region. Thus, US policy ceded the Shiite south and the Kurdish north to Saddam Hussein, who has since carried out massacres in those regions in order to maintain them as part of the country. Those massacres are the legacy of bipolarity and the balance of power metaphors.

Not all of our foreign policy metaphors have the same status. The state-as-person metaphor is part of our everyday conceptual system; it is part of a folk conceptualization of governments that is widespread. It has been adopted and expanded upon by expert theorists. But we should notice where the metaphorical folk portrait of the state ends and the hand of the theorist enters the picture.

The folk view has a state-person replete with a personality, a community, a susceptibility to disease, a home, a tendency to get into fist fights, and a body that can topple under force. It is the theorist who elaborates the metaphor, portraying the person-state as a rational actor trying to maximize his personal gains, who sees states as being like children going through inevitable stages of development, who defines security in military terms and health and maturity in economic terms, who sees competition as a game with a mathematical structure, who defines strength by counting warheads. It is the theorist who reifies states as physical objects exerting force within a political space, subject to natural expansionary pressures, knocking over other objects as they expand unless the force they exert is countered by an equal and opposite force. And it is the theorist who claims that only a bipolar force is stable.

Containment

The key terms of American foreign policy after World War II were 'security' and 'containment'. They were defined relative to the state-as-a-container metaphor. Security for a state is conceptualized in terms of being inside an overwhelmingly strong container that stops things from getting in or out. We have 'security leaks' on the one hand, and 'security penetration' on the other, 'internal' and 'external' security threats. This metaphor sees the boundary as all-important - the 'security perimeter' of American postwar policy. It is surprising now to recall that the very term 'national security' was not current until 1945-46, when it began to emerge in Washington as a unifying 'concept'. But it is not so surprising, given the naturalness of container metaphors, that it should be appealing and get developed in the way it did. Nor should it be at all surprising that the most central foreign policy concept of all - the concept of 'containment' - should have been so quickly adopted. It works like this: States are containers and their contents have a tendency to get out, say, by leakage, spillage, boiling over or even explosion, and get into or 'penetrate' the secure containers of other states.

Another possibility (as we have seen in our account of force field metaphors) is that the container itself may expand. If the metaphor that states are objects projecting an outward force is combined with the states-as-containers metaphor, what one gets is the idea of 'state expansion', in which there is natural 'lateral pressure' and possible 'penetration' of the boundaries of other states. Essentially, this is how the Soviet Union was conceptualized in foreign policy immediately after World War II. It followed from the perspective of the United States, that it needed to be 'contained'. That is, the Soviet container had to be prevented from expanding, and its communist contents from oozing out and filtering or flooding into capitalist containers.

The state-as-house metaphor

The state-as-house metaphor is a special case of the container metaphor. However, it is related not to physics metaphors but to the state-as-person metaphor. If a state is a person, its land-mass and sovereign territory is its 'home', for a home too is a bounded territory. The concept 'home' is closely bound to the concept 'house', which is a kind of container very special to humans, and intimately linked to concepts of safety and security. Therefore, it is not surprising to find that states-as-persons live, as it were, in houses. Bismarck, the great 19th century unifier of Germany, used the house metaphor to conceptualize his project of national unification. As the organization of states developed, one came to speak of 'domestic' affairs and foreign affairs. It is not difficult to find important house metaphors in American foreign policy discourse. One's home must be 'secure' against 'outside' intruders. Americans have a 'backyard' (Cuba, Mexico, and Central America, in general), where they do not want other people's missiles. In the Cold War period, it was not accepted that the Soviet Union might have a 'backyard' (Turkey), from where it could be threatened by NATO missiles. The home metaphor surfaced even in such expressions as 'window of vulnerability', a phrase powerfully deployed by those who lobbied to increase American strategic missile capability in the 1970s and 1980s. An even more powerful special case of this metaphor, conceptually speaking if not technologically, was President Reagan's vision of the protective 'roof' of the Star Wars space shield. It would keep from our heads what Truman (threatening, in August 1945, further atomic bombing of Japan) called a 'rain of ruin'.

Like all metaphors, particular historical meanings of the state-as-house metaphor depend on how speakers use it in discourse. The metaphor also depends on the particular cultural properties of the source domain, that is, on what kind of structure and social environment a 'house' is imagined to be. Further, there is nothing inevitable about the link between the house image and the concept of state, the same metaphor can be used to structure concepts of various forms of political organization. As the Cold War closed, the house metaphor played an interesting role in international discourse between the East and West.

The new foreign policy of the Soviet Union ('New Thinking'), initiated largely by Mikhail S. Gorbachev, was a conceptual challenge to the West as well as to traditional Soviet ways of thinking. It was in large part a metaphorical challenge. One of the key concepts of this new approach to the West was the 'common European house' metaphor. It was a metaphor that provoked debate in several national discourses and may in the end have backfired on its originator. A brief history indicates the importance of understanding the workings of metaphor in transnational discourse.

The first point to make is a cognitive and linguistic one. The metaphorical entailments or the house metaphor are affected by the culturally bound nature of the source image. In late Soviet society the word *dom* was typically associated with a communal tenement block containing separate individual apartments. In the United States, Britain and perhaps in other parts of western Europe, the conventional (prototypical, or, better, stereotypical) image of the home, is the one-family owner-occupied house: a free-standing box-like structure on its own, fenced land. When the metaphor was translated out of Russian into the language and cultural setting of other European states, the entailments were different. In the Russian context the entailments included (stereotypically, at least): collective responsibility, a plurality of separate independent units but common structure (roof, entrance, etc.). However, in the American, German, French settings, for example, the entailments included: a single unit, a family structure, no internal separations, no common structure, boundary walls or fences. Translated into political terms, this meant the West would perceive Gorbachev proposing a unitary structure in a circumscribed space. Would that include or exclude America? What would happen to independent states? This cognitive difference probably contributed to the suspicion with which Gorbachev's metaphor was greeted (Chilton and Ilyin, 1993; Schäffner and Trommer, 1990).

Gorbachev himself first used the metaphor in the context of the deployment of medium-range missiles in the European theatre. The house metaphor enabled him to say, or imply: the occupants of a communal house are concerned with the security of the whole tenement block; Europeans are in the same block, therefore, they should not threaten to destroy the whole structure with nuclear weapons. This argument was of course perceived as a threat to the NATO deployment policy. In addition, in the western cognitive perspective it looked as if Gorbachev was assuming a single container-like space in which the USSR and the rest of Europe were all united, perhaps without North America.

Gorbachev persisted with the metaphor, even making what he called 'philosophy' out of it. He used it to speak of the official Soviet abandonment of the 'Brezhnev doctrine' - which had sanctioned Soviet intervention in the countries of eastern Europe. He used it to speak of the right of separate countries and social systems (the socialist and the capitalist systems) to continue not just in 'peaceful coexistence' but in some form of 'neighbourly' cooperation, which had its institutional expression in the Conference for Security and Cooperation in Europe (CSCE).

The metaphor of the European house was much debated in western Germany, where different political groupings sought to specify the metaphor in different ways, and to emphasize different entailments. The house metaphor was a natural metaphor for the nation state and had also historically been used for a united Germany. Consequently, the various transformations of Gorbachev's metaphor in the German domestic debate were influenced by the anomaly of the Berlin wall and the post-war division into two states. Initially, there was talk of unification 'under a European roof', which was perhaps consonant with an apartment-house model. But eventually, as unification approached, the public discourse turned to a unitary family-dwelling model with talk of 'das deutsche Haus' ['the German house'].

It is possible that Gorbachev's metaphor implied a valuable conceptual model of security for the emergent new Europe, one that would have had the CSCE as a major institutional framework. In the transatlantic discourse that developed around 1990, however, this possibility was opposed. Germany was united on the American insistence that NATO provide the dominant security framework, and the 'house' metaphor was replaced by the conceptually related, but significantly distinct, 'architecture' metaphor. One conceptual and discursive effect of this was to set the limits of the reconceptualization of European security by focusing on organizations (NATO, CSCE, the West European Union, the European Union) and the structural relations between them. The political effect, it might be argued, was that the old patterns of NATO thinking persisted, with the result that there was no way of handling the new type of insecurity and conflict that appeared among the post-communist states. For example, there were no concepts or institutions capable of handling the horrendous conflicts of post-communist Yugoslavia.

Why metaphors matter

The political 'realist' who uses the metaphor systems described above might claim that they are mere words, convenient labels that accurately describe the nature of world politics. But metaphors are not just words. They are concepts that can be and often are acted upon. As such, they define in significant part, what one takes as 'reality', and thus form the basis and the justification for the formulation of policy and its potential execution. Because metaphors are rooted in everyday discourse, they tend to be taken for granted. Specialist discourse that may be ultimately based on them may, thus, be difficult to change at this fundamental level. At the end of the Cold War almost half a century of conceptual - and largely metaphorical - habits remained, and their perseverance led to serious failures to reformulate ideas and policies in the post-communist aftermath.

Metaphor and interests

A natural question to ask is whether the theorist's metaphors characterize an 'objective' political reality as is commonly claimed or whether they are self-serving means for legitimizing the policies of governments. Take, for example, the metaphor of the bipolar world. When the United States was one of two superpowers, it served American interests for there to be no third superpower. Since it is a rich nation, it serves American interests to view poorer nations as childlike, to be both helped and kept in line and told that they, too, will all inevitably develop by natural stages into wealthy adults if they accept the American guidance. Another possibility for the self-serving use of metaphors is in their application to particular situations. Why was Cuban intervention in Angola seen as expansionism while American intervention in El Salvador was not? As is often the case, foreign policy experts apply their metaphors to serve their government's interests. Such cases are anything but a characterization of an 'objective' reality - at least in the sense of a reality existing prior to its designation by concepts and words. Such interest-based projections can, however, end up being the 'objective' reality in which states do, in fact, operate although it is not the only possible reality.

What metaphors hide

Metaphors also hide important aspects of what is real, and it is vital that we know what realities our foreign policy metaphors are hiding. The state-as-person metaphor hides the most basic realities of the lives of individual citizens. The state may be secure in its home while many of its citizens are not. The state may be 'healthy' in that it is rich, while its citizens may not be able to afford real health care. Security for individual people is very different from 'national security'. Individual people need food, shelter, employment, health care, and education in order to be secure. The metaphorical notion of 'national security' in IR discourse has little to do with this. Spending more money on 'national security' means spending less on what makes individual people secure. Not only does the welfare of individual citizens stand outside the state-as-person metaphor, but so does the possibility of the contributions of individual citizens to international cooperation and communication: scientists, artists, scholars, and businessmen play no role in foreign policy as conceived of in terms of the nexus of metaphors we have described. In short, civil society is hidden and effectively excluded from international relations discourse.

The container concept of the state used by IR discourse hides the contents. Governments deal with other governments perceived as being in some sense legitimate, even if non-democratic. Wars, such as the Gulf War, are then seen as waged against governments, and the effects on inhabitants are marginalized in official discourse. Focus on the 'external affairs' of container-states, typical of Cold War discourse, also hides potential ethnic and other forms of conflict that are the most serious forms of threat in the post-Cold War period as events in the Balkans, the Caucasus and other border regions of the former Soviet empire tragically testify. In such cases, massacres can remain out of focus, because they can be categorized as 'internal conflict' and 'civil war'.

The state-as-person metaphor also hides most environmental issues. A few cases like the ozone hole, rain forests, and certain forms of pollution have recently been seen as threats to the world community and have begun to be taken seriously as appropriate foreign policy matters. But the full range of environmental issues does not arise in the state-as-person metaphor; this leaves them outside the domain of standard foreign policy concerns.

Imagine

It is probably impossible to formulate a concept of what a state or any other organization is without metaphor. Moreover, the folk version of the state-as-person metaphor may not be entirely eliminable since it is an automatic, largely unconscious, and long-standing conventional means for conceptualizing states. The possibilities for change are limited by our everyday metaphors. What can be changed, however, are the theorist's elaborations of the folk metaphors. Among the things that policy makers can do is to find new metaphorical elaborations that highlight realities that their current metaphors hide.

One way to reveal what has been hidden is to conceptualize the properties of the state-as-person in terms of the corresponding properties of the least fortunate quarter of its citizenry:

> Imagine conceptualizing the health of a state in terms of the health of the least healthy 25 per cent of its citizens.
>
> Imagine defining the educational level of a state in terms of the education of the least educated 25 per cent of its citizens.
>
> Imagine defining the fairness of a state by comparing the wealth of the least wealthy 25 per cent of its citizens to that of its wealthiest 25 per cent.
>
> Imagine defining the security of a state in terms of the personal security of the least secure 25 per cent of its citizens.
>
> Imagine defining the rationality of a state in terms of the degree to which it devoted its resources to satisfying the fundamental human needs of its entire citizenry.

The United States would not fare well by such definitions - it would be seen as sick, ignorant, unfair, insecure, and irrational for having overspent so much on Cold War weaponry to the detriment of the well-being of its citizens.

Such new elaborations of the state-as-person metaphor would highlight realities that our present metaphors for the state hide. They would refocus the attention of policy makers on the needs of citizens, which provide the ultimate rationale for external policy. In short, they would link external policy to internal policy as it affects the full range of citizens.

It is important, however, to realize that new metaphoric elaborations cannot be prescribed at will by experts or leaders. The fate of Gorbachev's European house metaphor, for all its merits, is testimony to that. Re-metaphorizing is anything but easy. For example, imagine a modified metaphor: 'common world house'. There would seem to be advantages: it would focus on the fact that weapons of mass destruction destroy not somebody else's house, but rather everybody's; it would stress the necessity for cooperation in the management of common living quarters; and it would bring global ecological issues into centre stage.

However, this prejudges the question as to whether there is some universal concept included in the English word 'house'. The category 'house' is structured differently in different cultures. Different languages, discourses, and cultural contexts will produce variant entailments. What this indicates is that the role of metaphor in discourse requires theoretical scrutiny and practical vigilance. Metaphors are among our most important tools for comprehending the world. They are necessary tools for understanding the nature of world politics and for formulating policy. They need to be better understood.

Metaphors need to be discussed out in the open - both in academic and in public discourse. What metaphors hide is a vital topic for discussion in the media. What metaphors entail is a crucial topic for theoretical discussion. Alternative metaphors need to be formulated and thoroughly aired. For all the public political discourse in the West, the main intellectual tool we have for conceptualizing international politics goes virtually undiscussed.

Notes

1 On journey metaphors, see Lakoff and Johnson (1980), pp. 90 ff.; on 'time is a resource', see Lakoff and Johnson (1980), pp. 66 ff., also Lakoff (1987), pp. 210, 439.

2 This envisaged use of United Nations authority was presented as 'support' for the UN ('peace support').

3 See Lakoff (1992) on metaphors in the Gulf war, also Chilton (1991a).

4 Speech in Brussels, 9 January 1994 ('Official Text', United States Information Service, p. 3).

5 But for a critique of this conception, see Camilleri and Falk (1992) and R.B.J. Walker (1993).

6 The classic account is in Morgenthau's *Politics among Nations*.

4 A Comparative Discourse Analysis of Editorials on the Lebanon 1982 Crisis

CAROLINE VAUGHAN

Introduction

ubi solitudinem faciunt pacem appellant[1]

The distrust and hatred that begets violence and war between peoples does not spring suddenly and wholly formed from a culture. It is nurtured and rationalized in the everyday discussion and interpretation of political and social events deemed newsworthy by that culture. In modern society, the interpretations expressed in the elite newspapers carry great weight in influencing opinion about every aspect of society that is reported on, especially during times of conflict and war.

This chapter presents findings of an analysis of approximately sixty editorials from four newspapers looking at an ongoing crisis from very different points of view. The newspapers are major, respected organs within four societies involved in the crisis, the initial phase of which took place over four months, from June to September 1982, when Israel invaded Lebanon to get rid of the Palestine Liberation Organization. The four involved nationalities and their newspapers are:

(1) Americans, *New York Times* (*NYT*)
(2) Israelis, *Jerusalem Post* (*JP*)
(3) Lebanese, *An-Nahar* (*AN*)[2]
(4) Palestinians, *Al-Fajr* (*AF*)

I would like to suggest that selected texts, editorials in this case, produced at times of crisis may be analysed and compared for the following:

(1) clues about underlying ideologies

(2) actual arguments and attendant justifications put forth to convince the populace of whatever actions (or non-actions) are being proposed

(3) ways in which the keywords are characterized

(4) how imagery and metaphor are used to support and illuminate points.

Texts produced during a crisis may reveal more about the way other nations see themselves and other nations than the carefully thought-out pronouncements of a more stable period.

Why choose editorials to illuminate these issues? Editorials perform important roles in our literate, but hectic societies. In the editorial, the editor has the opportunity to organize seemingly disparate events in such a way that the reader can interpret them in a coherent framework. As well as being internally consistent, this framework needs to fit into other frameworks familiar to the reader so that the editorial point of view "makes sense" (Garfinkel, 1967) and builds on previous knowledge and understanding of the world (McQuail, 1972).

Usually the editorial offers advice (indirectly or explicitly) to those in power, based on the argument presented. That advice can range from a directive for explicit action to a mere nudge towards a reformulation in attitude. Sometimes, on the other hand, the editorial focuses on explaining why certain choices have been made and whether or not these choices have turned out to be good ones in light of what has happened since. In either case, the function of the editorial is to highlight and contextualize, to say that certain events (events can be defined as statements as well as actions) are of key importance and so require a good citizen's moral attention. This is what Garfinkel (1967) might have termed the 'common sense' understanding of the function of editorials.

Unfortunately, editorials in important, trusted newspapers may be letting us down. They may, in fact, (even inadvertently) be leading us to accept violent solutions to international conflict rather than reasoned discourse. The problem is that we as nations are not co-existing well. At times of crisis, we may resort to using language to promote violence and to make war a favourable option.

I do not wish to imply that communication is wholly one-sided from the leaders to the people. The media provide a forum for discussion of weighty issues from which a consensus emerges, socially and politically constructed by all interested parties in a society. Nevertheless, those in a position of greater power have the resources to promote their point of view. It is important for ordinary citizens to empower themselves through education to analyse language used to explain war, to realize when they are being manipulated, to see the entwining of language choices and political/social issues, in order to make better choices.

The aim of this study has been to seek out how some nations involved in war with each other (directly or indirectly) use language to argue and to characterize each other and the events in the war in the process of constructing a coherent viewpoint. Another aim has been to uncover implicit ideologies (or what van Dijk, 1993d, has recently called "ideologically grounded meanings or beliefs"), concepts and propositions about war and peace and the role of nations.

Research drawn upon[3]

In this study I have drawn upon previous work in the following research traditions (some of which overlap):

(1) the analysis of media (e.g., Geis, 1987b; Glasgow University Media Group, 1982; Said, 1981; Tuchman, 1978)

(2) discourse analysis - including critical linguistics (Brown and Yule, 1983; van Dijk, 1985, 1988b; Fairclough, 1989, 1992a; Lee, 1992; Wodak, 1991)

(3) metaphor (Lakoff and Johnson, 1980; Rosch, 1977)

(4) linguistics and ideology (Billig, 1991; van Dijk, 1993d; Kress and Hodge, 1979; Trew, 1979)

(5) linguistics and peace (Bok, 1990; Bruck and Roach, 1993; Cohn, 1988; G. Lakoff, 1990).

Two other works have been provocative, but do not seem to fit any of these categories: Goffman's *Frame Analysis* (1974) and Garfinkel's *Ethnomethodology* (1967).

This list is meant only to provide a broad categorization of influences and to cue other researchers to useful and thought-provoking studies.

Research questions

The original guiding research questions were as follows:

(1) How is language used in important 'texts of public opinion' to deal with (explain, criticize, justify, ...) a society's involvement in war (in what is generally accepted to be a rational manner)? and

(2) What is revealed by the comparison of texts from different 'sides' involved in an international conflict that shows similarities and differences about the role of the nation in war and peace?

These very broad questions were then operationalized for this corpus into four specific questions:

(1) What are the main arguments[4] presented in the editorials?

(2) What are the keywords? How are they characterized, and how do these characterizations work to support the main arguments?

(3) How does the use of imagery, metaphor in particular, work to support the main arguments and the characterizations of the key terms?

(4) What underlying concepts and propositions concerning war, peace, the control of territory and the justification of nationality are revealed in the use of language, and how do these figure in an overall ideological stance?

Method

An editorial, by definition, argues a point or points. If one were analysing some other kind of text, advertisements, for example, one would be in search of how the language is used to 'sell' something: sales language would be the basic unit of the analysis. In this case, it is the argument.

Because one of the issues in discourse analysis and critical linguistics revolves around how to make the unwritten context part of the analysis without lapsing into unmitigated subjectivity, the corpus was built from sets of editorials that were expected to present different arguments. The intersection of all the sets, then, whatever all agree on, constitutes a core 'text' (even though it does not exist on its own). The arguments that lie outside that intersection constitute the context that is allowable in the overall analysis. In other words, Set A did not argue a, b and c, but Set B did, so they are part of the context of possible arguments; on the other hand, none of the sets argued x, y or z (even though an individual researcher might have thought these were important), so these are not allowable. As mechanistic as this may seem, it is a way of reducing the researcher bias possible when contextual material is entirely up to the individual or individuals carrying out the study.

In this study, between three and ten separate arguments were found in each editorial. These were then distilled into a set of five themes per set of editorials. The themes do not necessarily appear in every editorial, but all run through the set, providing an underlying argumentation that was found to cohere with the characterizations of the key players (the nations or nationalities) and events.

Grouping the themes as they relate to each of the key players involves bringing in the second research question, "What are the keywords? How are they characterized, and how do these characterizations work to support the main arguments?" I am extending Halliday's term 'keywords' (1985, p. 289) to fit the genre of editorials and the topic at hand, the discussion of how nations should proceed during an international crisis.

In any text or set of texts, keywords include both the primary referents of the topic(s) discussed and underlying concepts that may be gleaned from a careful reading of the texts. The content and genre of the texts chosen dictate the keywords; in this case, they include the names of the four major participants (Israel, the United States, the Palestinians, and Lebanon), four key events or stages during the summer, and one key concept per set of editorials found to underlie the arguments and themes of that set. The four key concepts will be discussed under **Findings**.

The key events are:

(1) The invasion of Lebanon by Israel (7-28 June 1982)

(2) The siege of Beirut (1 July - 19 August 1982)

(3) PLO and Syrian troop departures / Election of the president of Lebanon (20 August - 13 September 1982)

(4) Assassination of president-elect / Massacre of Palestinian civilians in a camp near Beirut (14 September - 1 October 1982).

A brief synopsis of the events is this:

(1) On 7 June 1982, the Israeli Defence Force (IDF) invades Southern Lebanon, moving quickly up the coast past Tyre and Sidon and capturing Beaufort Castle, a stronghold of the PLO.

(2) By early July, the IDF has surrounded Beirut and laid a siege, complete with regular bombing raids on the city. The United States becomes involved in trying to negotiate between the PLO and Israel during this period.

(3) Eventually, on 21 August, the PLO begins to depart. The election for president, won by Bashir Gemayel, is held on 23 August, having been postponed until after the PLO had formally begun leaving. On 30 August, Syrian troops from the Arab Deterrent Force begin departing Beirut.

(4) Bashir Gemayel is assassinated in a massive explosion at Phalange (his party) headquarters on 14 September. Two days

later the massacre of hundreds of Palestinian civilians (by Phalangists) in camps south of Beirut begins.

Findings

The findings are grouped under the four specific research questions that frame the study.

Themes and arguments / keywords

What are the main arguments presented in the editorials? What are the keywords? How are they characterized, and how do these characterizations work to support the main arguments?

As was hypothesized, it was found that the four sets of editorials view the situation very differently, both in theme choice and in characterizations of the four nations/nationalities (keywords) involved. The themes are grouped here according to their stance taken vis-à-vis each nation/nationality.

Lebanon

(1) The Lebanese must unify among themselves to rebuild their country. (*AN*)

(2) Lebanon is in such chaos that it may not be worth trying to save it as a nation. (*NYT*)

(3) Israel must help Lebanon set up a strong government that is friendly to Israel. (*JP*)

(4) The world must witness what Israel is doing to the Palestinians: it is a moral outrage, and a historical continuation of its policy towards them. As the siege progresses, Israel is criticized for extending an expansionist policy by oppressing Lebanese militias and by trying to form a puppet government in Lebanon. (*AF*)[5]

In light of what has just been said about the other arguments providing allowable context, the core that is left above is that Lebanon was foundering as a country at this point in history. The attitudes about what to do about that differ along a continuum from caring deeply (*AN*) to wanting to distance itself if the country goes under (*NYT*). The *JP*, as a neighbour, sees the need to shore up a friendly government. *AF* is suspicious of just such an attempt. The effect of the invasion and the siege seem to worsen the situation for Lebanon according to all but the *JP*, which sees it as an opportunity the Lebanese were hoping for.

Israel

(1) Israel is trying to harm Lebanon through its invasion. (*AN*)

(2) Because power entails responsibility, both the United States and Israel must accept their responsibility in this crisis and act accordingly. (*NYT*)

(3) Israel's actions now are the outcome of its having been attacked so often verbally and physically. (*NYT*)

(4) The present government of Israel does not always act in the best interests of the Israeli nation. (*JP*)

(5) The world must witness what Israel is doing to the Palestinians: it is a moral outrage, and a historical continuation of its policy towards them. (*AF*)

All these themes have in common a criticism of the way that Israel was acting during the crisis. It was carrying the military campaign in Lebanon too far, acting too aggressively; on that, all agree at least to some extent, even the *JP*. Again, the attitudes toward the situation branch off in different directions, the *NYT* being ambivalent in that at some times it supports Israel while at others it censures this ally. *AF* and *AN* are the most critical of Israel. The *JP* goes through a process of self-examination, concluding that its government is leading the country astray.

Palestinians

(1) The Palestinians are fellow sufferers. (*AN*)

(2) A solution granting Palestinians in Israel autonomy must be found. (*NYT*)

(3) The PLO and the Palestinians in the Occupied Territories who are ready to negotiate are two different groups and should be treated as such. (*NYT*)

(4) The PLO must be driven away from Lebanon. (*JP*)

(5) The problem of Palestinian nationalism must be solved. (*JP*)

(6) The Palestinians demand their own state. (*AF*)

(7) The PLO is the sole legitimate representative of the Palestinians, so it must be allowed to represent them. (*AF*)

(8) The Palestinians in the occupied territories and those in Beirut struggle together for their rights. (*AF*)

Taking up the majority of the themes, the characterizations of the Palestinians, the PLO, the Palestinian resistance, however differently they are named, create the most diversity among the newspapers. Yet a core can still be uncovered. All do agree that some answer to the problem of Palestinian nationalism needs to be found, and that finding it is likely to lead to solving many other problems in the Middle East. *AF* is the most fervent proponent of the position, with the *NYT* a relatively close second. The *JP* is the most reluctant to suggest moving in this direction. *AN* primarily looks to the past and commiserates with how the Palestinians have been treated until now, wishing that this would not continue, but not being especially optimistic.

United States

(1) Lebanon needs to stay with and rely on the United States. (*AN*)

(2) This crisis is part of a larger Middle East one in which many nations are involved. (*AN*)

(3) Israeli-US relations are vitally important. (*JP*)

(4) The United States - and to some extent the world - may be found guilty of neglecting the Palestinians and permitting Israel to harm them and the Lebanese. (*AF*)

(5) Because power entails responsibility, both the United States and Israel must accept their responsibility in this crisis and act accordingly. (*NYT*)

In all, the United States is recognized as being a major power with great influence in the Middle East, and in this crisis, particularly in its ability to influence Israel. Whether this influence is positively or negatively viewed depends on the newspaper. In fact, such a reduction is too simplistic. *AN*, for instance, seems to admire the power that the United States has in the region, and wants to make use of it to help Lebanon. *AF* tries to reason with the United States using their terms of reference: 'human rights issues', 'democratic elections', etc. The *JP* is concerned that it may be harming its strong relations with this powerful ally through its actions this summer. The *NYT* itself is positive in its assessment that its power entails concomitant responsibility to act out its principles and to get its allies to do the same.

The core then is this: Lebanon is foundering, Israel is reacting too violently, the Palestinian problem must be solved, and the United States is probably the most powerful nation involved in the crisis. On these, at least, there is agreement across editorials. The list of themes found to be running through each set of editorials reveals a Rashomon-like story, as each newspaper focuses on different arguments.

Four key events or periods of time emerged from the data: the invasion, the siege, the PLO troop departure and election of Gemayel, and the assassination of the president-elect immediately followed by the massacre. It was found that as the key events triggered subtle changes in the arguments of the editorials, other key terms changed or combined in new ways. Overall, however, the themes held throughout the crisis, and the characterizations of the participants (the four nations/nationalities) was fairly consistent throughout each set of editorials.

Metaphor

How does the use of imagery, metaphor in particular, work to support the main arguments and the characterizations of the key terms?

Although the use of imagery and metaphor to promote the arguments was not systematically analysed, examples were noted throughout. They are found to constitute a varied group, which can be roughly categorized as follows:

(1) military metaphors
(2) images of primitivity
(3) bipolar divisions
(4) familial imagery

I will limit myself to a few examples of each here:

(1) Military metaphors Used in all the editorials, these reduce the nations to 'war machines' that act unconscionably, 'hiding out amongst civilians', or 'rolling the terrorists back', or 'striking a genocidal blow'. They are primarily applied to the actions of the 'enemy', but in the invasion stage are also used by the JP to discuss the initial successes of the Israeli Defence Forces. As applied to the 'enemy', the military metaphors serve to reduce and dehumanize because the nationality or country is portrayed as acting against accepted humanitarian principles. As used by the JP in June, they evince a triumphant pride in the military capability of the IDF to 'crush' the opposition so easily.

(2) Images of primitivity Again, these are used against the 'enemy', who is characterized as 'squatting' and 'shouting out conditions', or treating 'our' side 'brutally and inhumanly'. They are also used to dismiss countries, as when Lebanon is termed 'a quagmire', or a society 'in chaos', carrying out 'vendettas' for centuries.

(3) Bipolar divisions The us's and them's anticipated in the question on underlying ideologies is also found in the imagery. 'We' are presented as honourable, brave, responsible; 'they' are 'terrorists', or 'in a hurry to

harvest [people] before the ploughing and planting really started', or launching a 'beastly invasion'. Nations are portrayed as either strong or weak. The stronger nations have the upper hand and can dictate conditions to the weaker ones, telling them perhaps, what they 'need' to do. The weaker nations must submit; they simply have no other choice.

Another bipolar division is the black-and-white of the political versus the military solution to the crisis at hand. The negotiations and discussions involved in the process of diplomatically resolving the conflict are rarely dealt with in more than cursory detail. Generally, as negotiations (amorphously defined) start to break down, the threat of military action, or more military action, looms. Linguistically this is realized in such sentences as 'the continuing violence in Beirut is lamentable, but it is an unavoidable way to keep the heat on', or 'too much has been invested in it to permit anything less than the complete rout of the terrorists'.

(4) Familial imagery The two most striking examples are, first, the United States-Israel father-son imagery, in which the paternal United States tries to guide the recalcitrant son into better behaviour, through letters ('Dear Menachem') and through official actions 'Yesterday President Reagan gave Israel a slap'; the image of the Lebanese and Palestinians as 'orphans' in the Arab world, abandoned by their Arab family when they are most in need, is the second.

The editorials also utilize new, strikingly vivid metaphors. For example, *Al-Fajr* devotes an entire editorial to extending the meaning of the concept of 'strategic depth' - a term used by Israel euphemistically to refer to the zone in Southern Lebanon under its control. *Al-Fajr* says that the Palestinian people 'have been chosen to play the vital role of strategic depth to the world and Arab conscience - a space over which tanks can roll and bombs explode'. Some metaphors, particularly in the *New York Times'* view of Israel, are contradictory, even in the same editorial. For example, in one editorial Israel is a wounded lion defending her territory and a military machine capable of destroying all in its path.

When used to support the themes, the metaphors consistently create similar images. For example, to support the *Jerusalem Post* theme of the need to get the PLO out of Lebanon, the PLO is seen as a physical body that must be harmed physically. Violent verbs such as 'clobber', 'stamp out', 'knock out', 'break the backbone of', etc. help form the gestalt of the PLO as this kind of body involved in, if anything, a fist fight or a boxing match, and losing. The use of these verbs in a serious editorial (rather than, say, on the Sports page) draws the discourse of sports and fighting on an individual level into the discourse of higher-level political commentary, creating a visceral response in the reader that weaves into his or her intellectual response to the arguments posed.

The editorials are also a rich source of conventional metaphors found by previous researchers using war texts. G. Lakoff (1990) cites, for instance, the following:

(1) Killing enemies is cleansing the land of them.

(2) Our country, the United States, is the father figure for the rest of the world. (In these data, he has only one son: Israel.)

(3) Waging war is a learning experience. (G. Lakoff, 1990, pp. 5-6)

All of these are found in the editorials. The *JP*, for instance, speaks early on about 'the lessons of Israel's war in Lebanon' which 'will be studied for months and years to come', particularly 'the lesson of the superiority of US modern fighter aircraft and missiles'.

Ideology

What underlying propositions concerning war, peace, the control of territory and the justification of nationality are revealed in the use of language, and how do these figure in an overall ideological stance?

Within each set of editorials can be found at least one key concept of what is needed to solve the crisis. These concepts are coherent with the themes and with the characterizations of the major players presented by that newspaper. For instance, the *New York Times* constantly returns to the key concept of 'responsibility', which needs to be taken by powerful nations, particularly the United States, but also, in this case, Israel. Because it has power, the editorials argue, the United States is bound to assume responsibility for negotiations, with some limitations. That responsibility may require 'justification', another favoured term, if too many people start to be killed, and that responsibility should be passed on to the weaker nations eventually. The key concepts for the other newspapers are as follows: *JP* - the need for 'security'; *AF* - the need for 'self-determination'; and *AN* - the need for 'unity'.

All the newspapers agree on some underlying propositions regarding war, peace and the role of nations. Some examples of these are:

(1) War is justified, if not required, under certain circumstances.

(2) Property destruction, displacement of people, injuries and deaths are justified in large numbers if key political goals are achieved.

(3) The massacring of defenceless civilians is wrong.

The *NYT* and *JP*, representing the two powerful nations in this conflict, agree on propositions consistent with their status, such as:

(1) Weak nations are less likely to have peace.

(2) Militarily powerful nations are responsible for deciding when to wage war.

AF and *AN*, on the other hand, representing militarily weaker nations, agree on propositions that are coherent with their world view:

(1) Weak nations are helpless against powerful ones.

(2) Weak nations that are waging a just war are morally superior.

These propositions, and others, I am sure, indicate a deep-seated belief in the power, and the value, of war and/or military options to solve disputes among nations. According to these newspapers, there are times when it is considered appropriate and acceptable to go to war. The conditions for acceptability need to be spelled out, but if they are met, a nation can feel satisfied in moving ahead with weapons of mass destruction, invading, bombing and killing until whatever military objective was intended has been met.

What is of utmost importance, as revealed in this study, is that the nation be preserved as it sees itself. That self-identity may undergo transformation, even very painful transformation, as in the case of Lebanon, but if the nation can manage to establish and obtain agreement (from other nations) on its identity, then the underlying propositions about war pertain. There is a certain irony here. On the one hand, the establishment of the nation as a holistic entity attempts to unify disparate groups; on the other hand, it provides justification for war among these nations.

Conclusion

In the editorials that make up these data, I have found little evidence of a truly peaceful orientation to the resolution of the crisis. Moreover, it has emerged that the way the different nations are characterized in the editorials is crucial to understanding how to resolve the conflict. However, no serious attempt to see the crisis through the eyes of the other participants is made. In those cases when the editorials do discuss and analyse the others' points of view, the interpretations are invariably inconsistent with the actual arguments presented in the corresponding newspaper.

A truly peaceful orientation would require, as a first step, that editorial writers (and governments) actually listen to what is being said by the other side, and how it is being said. Offering up and insisting upon solutions without consulting the parties that will be most affected by them is a sure way to have them rejected. Resorting to violence after only brief forays into political dialogue is at best disingenuous given the extreme danger of warfare in our overly armed world.

The language that is used to argue the main themes in a conflict and to present characterizations of key events, players and concepts is, in fact, the construction itself of how these are understood. Careful comparative study of texts emblematic of the issues in the crisis can reveal how differently those issues are perceived and explained to the constituencies involved. With some further thought, underlying cultural beliefs may be uncovered as well. But this is just a first step. The next one will be to try to step far enough away from one's own position to be able to understand the position of the other. It is not until then that we can begin to reframe our own outlook. As Denise Levertov suggests about peace in her poem, 'Making Peace' (1988):

> A feeling towards it
> Dimly sensing a rhythm, is all we have
> Until we begin to utter its metaphors,
> Learning them as we speak.

Finally, a possible use of a study such as this may be to illuminate a path that can be taken by reading teachers interested in working through comparative texts such as these with their students. It is one thing to pick out a few examples of metaphor or a main argument in one isolated text, as is often attempted by teachers now. A more compelling and potentially far more useful task is to delve more systematically into the analysis of comparator texts - suggested by the students if possible - on a social (environmental, political, community, ...) issue of concern to the class. This would entail making readers researchers of language use which would require that the research process itself be made explicit. For example, it would be important to decide collaboratively what texts to use, what kinds of structures to extract, how to tie imagery to the characterizations of keywords, and finally what kinds of underlying propositions could be brought to the surface. Reading texts with students in this investigative, critical way could prove remarkably rewarding and might stimulate students and teachers alike to look at all the texts that surround them with more care.

Notes

1 'They create desolation and call it peace', *Agricola*, by Tacitus.

2 I am grateful to the Middle East Institute, Columbia University, for a grant to cover the cost of translating the editorials in *An-Nahar*.

3 Because of space constraints, I will omit all but a cursory categorization of some of the literature related to this study. The full study is my dissertation

of the same title (1994, Teachers College, Columbia University, New York).

4 I define an argument as a proposition (linguistic form) that asserts an opinion (sociolinguistic function).

5 This theme contained only a partial reference to the nation in question.

5 The 'Balance' Metaphor in Relation to Peace

CHRISTINA SCHÄFFNER

Introduction

Peace is one of the fundamental principles and aspirations of humankind. Political actions are almost exclusively justified by reference to peace. This was also the case at the time of the Cold War. Both NATO and the Warsaw Pact declared that their main objective was to guarantee peace and security, for which a stable balance of military power was seen as a prerequisite. 'Peace', 'security', 'stability', and 'balance' have for a very long time been used as keywords in political discourse. A question of interest to a linguist is the semantic characterization of such keywords and key concepts. In what follows, a textlinguistic approach was used to identify the recurrent macropropositions that determined the semantic profile of relevant key concepts of the East-West debate during the Cold War. These macropropositions will be presented. Special attention will be given to the cognitive role of the balance metaphor in this context. The discussion concentrates on the debate as reflected in the mass media in the 1980s, mainly related to military aspects.

Methodology

In studies on the lexicon, political words offer a particular challenge. In the more traditional research they have often been described as being empty in meaning, as ideology-bound, or a basic conceptual dictionary meaning was distinguished from politically defined usage (e.g., Schmidt, 1969; Dieckmann, 1981; Fleischer, 1977). However, words never come alone but are embedded in concrete texts to fulfil a particular function. It is in the texts that political words are repeatedly used, and it is, thus, in the texts that their meanings are stabilized, modified, or changed. A textual approach can, therefore, explain the meanings of political keywords in a far more convincing way than the traditional studies which look at words in isolation.

In fact, since the 1970s, the text has increasingly become the primary object of research. There is, however, neither a uniform theory of textlinguistics nor an established methodology. Various aspects of a text have been studied, ranging from text-grammatical features to functional components and to cognitive strategies for text comprehension (for a survey see, e.g., de Beaugrande and Dressler, 1981, Heinemann and Viehweger, 1991). Since I was interested in the semantic profile of political keywords, a semantically oriented methodology for text analysis was chosen as a starting point, i.e., the macrostructure analysis as developed by van Dijk (1980a, 1988b). The basic assumption is that the semantic structure of a text is an ordered sequence of propositions which are represented in specific structures at the text surface in a cohesive way. In comprehending texts, readers reduce and organize the information by applying cognitive operations (i.e., the macrorules of deletion, generalization, construction) to arrive at the semantic macrostructures of the text.

To identify the keywords of the Cold War discourse, leading articles of the British weekly *The Economist* (1979-91), dealing with East-West relations in general and with military aspects in particular were analysed. I have chosen an exemplar of mass media since they obviously play a significant role in the presentation of the world to their readership in that the ways in which the media select and evaluate events is crucial in the production of political knowledge. In other words, these texts are examples of a linguistic representation of politics and also evidence of the underlying conceptualization of politics.

Macropropositions and keywords

Typical macropropositions

After applying van Dijk's macrorules to each leading article to arrive at its macrostructure, the most typical, most relevant and regularly recurring macropropositions were abstracted from the individual texts. There were two main macropropositions (MPs) which dominated the whole discussion in *The Economist* over the period 1979-84, the heyday of the Cold War (in 1979 NATO had agreed on the 'twin track' decision, i.e. to deploy by 1983 new medium-range nuclear missiles in western Europe to counter the Russian SS-20 missiles unless Russia withdrew them; in the autumn of 1983 the first NATO missiles were deployed as a consequence of Russia's refusal to withdraw the SS-20s). These two dominant macropropositions were:

MP 1: Russia has achieved military superiority.

MP 2: The West must restore the balance (to keep the peace).

The whole argumentation centred around these two MPs. On a more functional level, these two MPs correspond to the 'problem' and the 'solution' complex, respectively, of the argumentative texttype of which leading articles are exemplars (Schäffner, Shreve and Wiesemann, 1987). As a next step these macropropositions were reduced to thematic words or thematic collocations which represented the MP as a whole. These words or phrases, then, were arranged in lexical-semantic networks (LSN). The lexical-semantic network for the texts of *The Economist* over the years 1979-84 is presented in Figure 5.1:

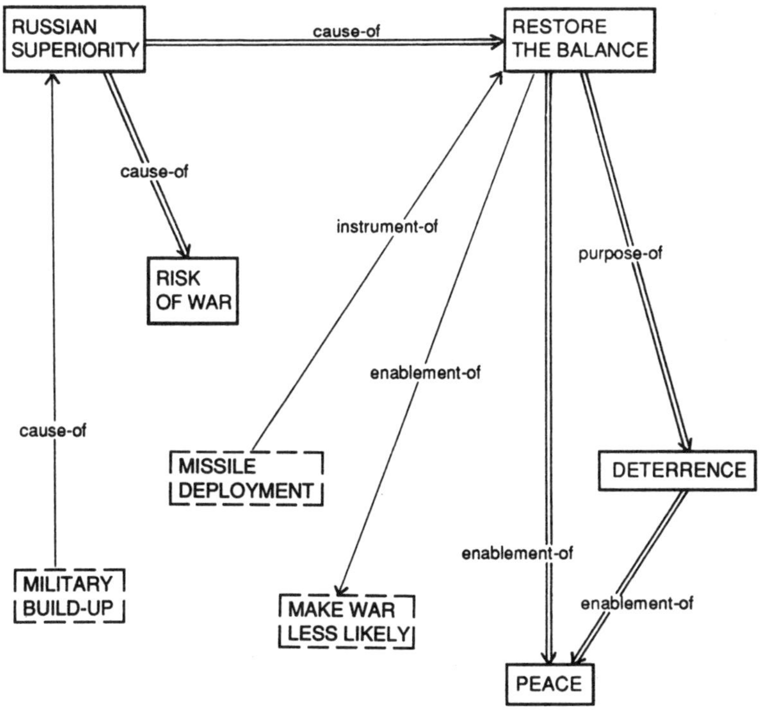

Figure 5.1 Lexical-semantic network for *The Economist* (1979-84)

In these networks the concepts are illustrated as nodes (in capital letters). More often than not these concepts were identical to the thematic words or collocations encountered in the textual surface structures. However, since both the MPs and the LSN were arrived at by abstracting and generalizing from the individual texts, it is the cognitive concepts that have been arranged in the nodes of the LSN. Synonymous expressions were, for example, 'recreate/fix the balance', 'redress the imbalance', or 'missile growth'. In other cases, the concepts were arrived at by abstracting from more explicit descriptions. The primary key concepts of the argumentation in *The Economist* are represented in the solid boxes of the LSN, the secondary concepts (i.e. concepts abstracted from MPs that were in a dependency relation to the dominant MPs) are in the broken-lined boxes. The semantic relations between the concepts are indicated on the links (the typology is based on de Beaugrande and Dressler, 1981, pp. 95-7). Double arrows link primary concepts, simple arrows denote links to secondary concepts. These relations were also abstracted from the texts, i.e. from the MPs. By connecting the nodes via the links, the MPs can be reconstructed. The LSN, thus, represents the conceptual structures underlying the textual surface structures.

Keywords and their semantic profile

Based on the specific textual and macropropositional embeddedness and determination illustrated above, a semantic characterization for the keywords was given. Since this meaning is very specific, holding true only for a particular topic, at a particular time, in a particular paper, I have called it *textword-type* (TWT) (see Schäffner, 1986, 1990).[1]

As can be seen in Figure 5.1, 'balance' is the central concept from which all relations derive. 'Balance' is a keyword for international political relations, and it turned out to be *the* keyword for the discourse on East-West relations (i.e. the Cold War discourse) in the late 1970s/early 1980s. The semantic profile of 'balance', i.e. its TWT (1979-84), is as follows:

> 'balance': a future state in Europe when newly-deployed American nuclear missiles match the Russian/Soviet advantage.

Another example of a specific politically relevant word meaning is the TWT for 'peace' (1979-84):[2]

> 'peace': (future) state between East and West in Europe in which a restored balance, i.e., a high number of nuclear missiles of NATO with a deterrence function, prevents the outbreak of war.

These TWTs clearly reflect the (textually provided) interrelations of the key concepts of the arms control debate between NATO and Russia as reflected in *The Economist*. TWTs are evidence that meaning is not an inherent property of a word, but that it is strongly influenced by the contexts of use. Words like 'balance' develop a politically relevant meaning through their use in political texts. Thus, we cannot speak of a political vocabulary per se, but only of politically relevant meanings. These meanings, i.e. textword-types,

(1) develop in texts,
(2) may be different or valid for only one or a few political groups (for a semantic characterization of 'balance' and 'peace' in *The Guardian* see Schäffner, 1986), and
(3) may be valid for a shorter or longer period of time.

Such a change of a TWT became obvious in the semantic modification of 'balance' caused by the deployment of the American nuclear missiles in Europe (from 1984 to roughly 1990):

'balance': state in Europe which is stabilized by East and West having equal numbers in offensive and defensive missile systems and in which neither side is tempted to attack the other.

Although this modified TWT no longer implies the necessity for a change in the state between East and West in Europe (i.e., by missile deployment), it implicitly calls for a guarantee that this state in Europe will remain stabilized in future. The collocation 'restore the balance' which was typical for the time 1979-84 was later replaced by 'stabilize the balance' or a 'stable balance'. 'Stable balance' was the basis for the development of 'stability' into a keyword, which subsequently became more important in the argumentation than 'balance'. In an LSN for the period 1984-89 'stability' would be in the central position, having replaced 'restore the balance', with 'Russian superiority' having largely disappeared in the argumentation. In such an LSN, 'stability' would be linked, semantically and cognitively, by a purpose-relation to 'deterrence' and by an enablement-relation to 'peace', thus reflecting a certain consistency in the argumentation of *The Economist* on East-West relations following the 1983 deployment of nuclear missiles.

Both keywords, 'balance' and 'stability', had a quantitative dimension during the period 1979 to 1989/90, i.e. a reference to the number of (mainly nuclear) missiles. This quantitative dimension is crucial for these two TWTs. It is via the missiles that the relations between 'balance' and 'deterrence' (i.e., 'deterrence' as the function of the missiles) and between 'balance' and 'peace' (i.e., 'peace' as their purpose) works. The systematic semantic relations between 'balance', 'deterrence', and 'peace' are illustrated both in the lexical-semantic network and in the semantic characterization of the TWTs. These systematic relations also provide the explanation for specific collocations, such as 'nuclear peace', as indicated in excerpt 1. (Thematic words, thematic collocations, and phrases that point to the underlying key concept are italicized.):

> *Excerpt 1*
>
> If Russia can add a nuclear monopoly in Europe to its existing *superiority in non-nuclear weapons* - meanwhile holding the Americans at arm's length with its impending *superiority* in intercontinental missiles - its chances of getting a respectfully subordinate western Europe are excellent. It would probably not have to use its combination of *military superiorities*. The threat would be enough.
> The *nuclear dominance* they would cede to the Soviet Union means, sooner or later, submission to the Soviet will. Non-absolutists will prefer to avoid that, by holding on to a *balance of nuclear power*. Reasoned reflection suggests that *a balance will keep the nuclear peace*. A *nuclear peace* makes it unnecessary to be either red or dead.
> There also remains the need to go on trying to bring more discipline to the production and deployment of these weapons. That includes negotiations with Russia to *fix the nuclear balance at the lowest possible level* ...
> (*The Economist*, 8 August 1981)

The meaning of 'nuclear peace' in excerpt 1 corresponds to the semantic characterization of the TWT given above. It can also be reconstructed by starting from the node PEACE in the LSN (Figure 5.1) and moving along the links to those nodes with which PEACE is connected. Missiles, which are usually instruments of warfare, have been re-interpreted as instruments of peace, and 'nuclear peace' in this way is presented as an instance of a positive peace. This is illustrative of what Mehan and Skelley (1988, p. 43) call a "Pure War Culture" in which "the distinction between peace and war is blurred".

The explanatory value of cognitive metaphors

The balance metaphor

Cognitive semantics (e.g., Lakoff and Johnson, 1980; Lakoff, 1986, 1989; Kövecses, 1986, 1989; Chilton, 1989) explains the cognitive value of metaphors as understanding one domain of experience in terms of another one. Metaphor involves projecting one knowledge domain onto another one, thus mapping the internal structure of the source domain onto the internal structure of the target domain. This mapping refers, first, to the structural elements and units (Lakoff and Kövecses speak of "ontological correspondences", i.e., entities in the source domain correspond systematically to entities in the target domain), and second, to the mapping of all the possible inferences and entailments that are based on this structure ("epistemical correspondences", which permit us to reason about the target domain using the knowledge we use to reason about the source domain) (see Lakoff, 1989, pp. 8-9). Metaphors provide the necessary schemata for producing new thoughts about complex or abstract phenomena. It would seem useful, therefore, to explain East-West (military) relations and, thus, the concept of 'superiority' and the key phrase 'restore the balance' within the framework of a metaphor, i.e. the balance metaphor.

Seen from a metaphorical point of view, 'balance' maps an abstract relationship onto a physical model, enabling the mental models of naive physics to guide the inference process, primarily as an envisionment process (see Carbonell and Minton, 1983, p. 4). The physical analogue, i.e. the source domain for the balance metaphor, is the balancing scales, that is, the two scales and a beam in the middle. These two scales can be in a state of balance ('a stable balance'), or they can be in a state of imbalance as a result of an object with some particular weight having been placed onto one of the balancing scales. In other words, as soon as an object (with a specific weight) is placed onto one of the two scales, the resulting situation can be predicted through reasoning and inferencing processes.

The balance metaphor was introduced in the very first text which opened the debate in *The Economist* (September 1979) and was then consistently referred to in the subsequent texts, thus ensuring both internal coherence in each individual text as well as coherence between the texts (intertextual coherence).

Components of the balance metaphor

When a base conceptual schema is used as the source for a metaphor, not only are all the structural components of that schema transferred to the target domain, but also the actions related to it and their effects. Important aspects of the base conceptual schema underlying the balance metaphor are:

(1) structural components: objects with specific weights, and the two balancing scales (which allow for the ontological correspondences)

(2) actions: to weigh two objects one against the other, to put something onto the scale(s)

(3) effects: end-states (as inferences of actions that are applied to the objects - the weights), i.e. 'balance' versus 'imbalance'; 'stability' versus 'instability'.

This allows for the following inferences (i.e., epistemic correspondences) illustrated in excerpts 2-5 below: if more weight is placed on one scale, then the position of the two scales in relation to each other changes; i.e., one object outweighs the other. In order to achieve balance again, either more weight has to be placed on the other scale, or some weight has to be removed from the first scale.

> *Excerpt 2*
>
> All in all, the first round of the war for peace will probably be won by those who think the *balance of terror* is less terrifying than an *imbalance of terror*. ... The middle-of-the-roaders have to be argued into recognising that an imbalance of terror is more likely to lead to war, including nuclear war, than *a carefully matched pair of nuclear scales*.
> (*The Economist*, 8 October 1983)

> *Excerpt 3*
>
> No sensible agreement for the control of nuclear arms in Europe could be negotiated on the basis of *the present lopsided balance*.
> (*The Economist*, 13 October 1979)

> *Excerpt 4*
>
> Otherwise the Russians will have every incentive to go on spinning words while they also go on doing the things - crushing Afghanistan, *tilting the European nuclear balance*, or whatever - which first led to the crisis. ... In December Nato decided to *restore the balance by starting to build* - a whole decade later - the first Nato missiles capable of hitting Russia from inside western Europe.
> (*The Economist*, 24 May 1980)

> *Excerpt 5*
>
> Obviously, rather than conquer western Europe, the Soviet leaders would prefer to cow it into docility so that it no longer had a disturbingly attractive effect on their east European subjects and no longer *added weight to the Americans' side in the strategic balance*.
> (*The Economist*, 22 August 1981)

In the texts analysed, the objects being placed on the scales were missiles, thus adding a quantitative dimension to the TWT 'balance' in the 1980s. In fact, next to the headline of excerpt 5, there was a cartoon showing balancing scales with a tank on each scale.

Metaphorically based reasoning

Metaphors tell us something about (culture-specific and universal) aspects of thinking and talking, of language and mind, about the fitting of language to what we perceive, experience, and understand. Metaphors are not just a matter of language, but of thought and reason. The language used is a reflection of the mapping (see Lakoff, 1989, pp. 9-10).

The frequently used keywords and collocations found as a result of the textlinguistic analysis show that what is involved is not just conventional language, but a conventional mode of thought. '(Restore the) balance' and 'stable balance' reflect a way of thinking about bilateral political relations in terms of balancing scales. In fact, few different words or phrases referring to the underlying conceptual metaphor, i.e. the balance metaphor, were found. It was mainly the word 'balance' itself that activated the metaphor, suggesting the role keywords play in argumentation.

The whole argumentation around the key concept 'balance' reveals, however, a whole network of metaphorically based reasoning, whereby the balance metaphor is linked via mutual components or inferences to other metaphors. The TWT 'balance' for 1979-84 and also for the years after 1984 was characterized above as a state of mutual relations. Thinking in terms of the mental image of the balancing scales we can say that it is a state achieved by weighing two things one against the other. This has the following consequences which were also textualized and lexicalized:

(1) When two objects are weighed one against the other, it may be found that one object weighs more than the other, the one outweighs the other. More weight means quantitatively more; it, thus, refers to a quantitative dimension. The aspect of being superior and dominant because of sheer quantities is also reflected in two other metaphors: phrases such as 'arms build-up', 'to build up forces' are related to a building metaphor, and the 'growth of the missile force' is related to a growth metaphor (see excerpt 4). It is the inference that 'more is up' (Lakoff and Johnson, 1980) that the balance, building and growth metaphors have in common.

(2) When one object outweighs the other, then this heavier object is superior. Being superior also means having more influence, being dominant; and being dominant implies a risk for the inferior party. This risk was specified in the texts I analysed as 'increased risk of war' and 'danger of a Russian attack' (see excerpts 1 and 3).

(3) The counterweight has an additional function to fulfil in order to reduce the danger emerging from the dominant party: it has to 'deter' (see excerpt 6):

Excerpt 6

Deterrence - the knowledge that a strike by one side would provoke a devastating retaliatory strike by the other - was and still is *the surest way to keep the peace* in a dangerous world. Cuts in the numbers of nuclear

> weapons have come because of carefully negotiated agreements that the superpowers have confidence in. There can be more and deeper cuts. But *stability* is the real problem, not numbers. A test ban would *destabilise the nuclear balance* because neither side could be sure what effect it was having on the other. ... In a nuclear world the sensible aim is a less fragile, *more stable nuclear balance at the lowest level of armaments* on all sides. (*The Economist*, 5 January 1991)

'Deterrence' is another keyword of the Cold War discourse. It can be explained within the fight metaphor. There are two opponents, the two 'sides' (as in excerpt 6), and the one challenges the other. In *The Economist*'s argumentation, the risk of war has increased because of an 'unchallenged Soviet rearmament' (see also Chilton, 1985). The common component of the balance and the fight metaphor is that in each case there are two elements (two scales, two opponents).

Inconsistencies in reasoning in relation to the balance metaphor

What is noticeable here is an interplay of various metaphors which centre around the balance metaphor. This interplay, however, reflects some inconsistencies. For instance, as mentioned above, more weight on one of the balancing scales means quantitatively more. This quantitative dimension is related to the metaphor 'more is up', which brings a vertical dimension into play (see 'come down' versus 'go up' in excerpt 7, 'cut the armouries' in 8, 'a lower balance' and 'accept a lower ceiling on warheads' in 9). Thus, in excerpts 7-9, the balance metaphor has 'faded out' except for excerpt 8 which reflects a mixture of the balancing scales and the vertical dimension.

> *Excerpt 7*
>
> The Russians have an army and an air force in eastern Europe *superior in numbers*, and now at least equal in quality, to the defenders of western Europe.
> ... *re-equalise the military balance of power*: if possible by the Russians *coming down* but, if the Russians won't, by the west *going up*; ...
> (*The Economist*, 28 March 1981)

> *Excerpt 8*
>
> The gross *imbalance between the number and power of the nuclear weapons* that Russia points at Nato Europe, and those Europe can aim at Russia, ... What is not proposed, and would not make sense, is for Nato to put off taking action to *restore the nuclear balance* in Europe while Russia merely talks about possible reductions. ... the alliance is willing to make a serious attempt at *cutting the nuclear armouries* in Europe, so long as the *cutting starts from a basis of equality between the two sides*.
> Salt-2, both its advocates and its enemies agree, should stand on its own. So should Nato's plan to *re-create a balance in Europe*. This should be

> got under way *before the Russians tilt the European nuclear scales even further their way*, and negotiating them out of their lead becomes even more difficult.
> (*The Economist*, 10 November 1989)

Excerpt 9

> The end of the cold war does, however, open the way for *a much lower nuclear balance between the superpowers* ... pushing the Russians to accept a vastly *lower ceiling* on warheads ...
> (*The Economist*, 10 March 1990)

However, when one visualizes the balancing scales, the scale with the heavier weight is not up but down. This image is often made use of in cartoons. Such inconsistencies prove that conceptual metaphors are cognitive patterns that are complex, not necessarily fully conscious, and not always based on the laws of logic (see Opp de Hipt, 1987, p. 109). It is, thus, not, or not always, really the visual(ized) image of the balancing scales which makes the metaphor effective in the texts, but above all its *functional* determination. It is via the *function* of the balancing scales and via 'balance' and 'stability' as the most relevant end-states that the inferences and the interrelation to the other metaphors work. The most fundamental function of the balancing scales, however, is not to achieve an end-state of balance, but to weigh two objects. It is through (a comparison of) the weights that the link to the metaphor 'more is up' is established (the vertical dimension). This again accounts for the inference that up means having more weight, being superior, being dominant.

Bipolar versus multipolar world

One aspect which unites the metaphors used in the argumentation, i.e. the weight metaphor, the balance metaphor, the fight metaphor, the more is up metaphor, is that it is always *two* objects or *two* sides that are involved. Two things are weighed against each other, a balance is struck between two things, two things are in a stable relationship, two parties fight against each other, two things are compared as to more or less. This points to the aspect of bipolarity, the underlying conception for policy making during the Cold War.

The end of the Cold War, however, can be seen as a "critical discourse moment" (Chilton, 1986, quoted in Mehan and Skelley, 1988, p. 38) in that existing conceptualizations, such as bipolarity, on which policies were based, no longer fit well with the new events. It has also been marked by conflicts of a conceptual kind related to thinking and speaking which has to do with the concept of 'balance'. In political discourse, the rigidly bipolar logic of the Cold War system was often opposed to the uncertainties of a multipolar world (see Schäffner, 1994, and excerpt 10):

Excerpt 10

Europe needs *America as a balancing force* against a still powerfully armed Soviet Union, even if that empire is in the throes of internal upheaval; ... the Europeans are keenly aware of the difficulty of switching from *a clear-cut bipolar system*, in which Western Europe was the first line of defense for the U.S. against the Soviet Union, to *a world of multipolar uncertainties*.
(*Time*, 22 April 1991)

Continuity and change in the argumentation

The end of the Cold War also meant a crisis for NATO, whose argumentation in the New Strategic Concept, adopted in 1991, is that although "Europe's security has substantially improved ... potential risks to security from instability or tension still exist".

I have looked at some NATO documents to find out whether there is continuity in the argumentation on East-West relations and in the use of the concept of 'balance' (see excerpts 11-15). What is striking is that in these documents which are more strategic in character, 'balance' is, firstly, often used in the (quantitative) vertical dimension ('balance at a lower level'), and, secondly, it is closely linked with 'stability' rather than with 'peace'. The purpose of the 'balance' is to achieve or enhance 'stability'. 'Balance' is seen as a prerequisite for 'stability'. The link between 'stability' and 'peace' is established via the semantic links to 'balance' and/or 'deterrence' (see excerpts 13 and 15 below):

Excerpt 11

The Parties to this Treaty reaffirm their faith in the purposes and principles of the Charter of the United Nations and their desire to live in *peace* with all peoples and all governments. ...
They seek to promote *stability* and well-being in the North Atlantic area. They are resolved to unite their efforts for collective defence and for the preservation of *peace and security*.
(Preamble of NATO treaty 1949)

Excerpt 12

We look forward to beginning as soon as possible *conventional stability* negotiations, within the framework of the CSCE process, with the objective of *establishing a secure and stable balance of forces at lower levels*, between the 23 members of the two military alliances in Europe. ...
This implicitly acknowledges our long-held view that *redressing the conventional imbalance is a key to more security and stability in Europe*.
(North Atlantic Council Ministerial Communiqué, December 1988)

Excerpt 13

The basic goal of the Alliance's arms control policy is to *enhance security and stability at the lowest balanced level of forces and armaments consistent with the requirements of the strategy of deterrence.* ...
Alliance security policy aims to *preserve peace* in freedom by both political means and the maintenance of a military capability sufficient to prevent war and to provide for effective defence. ...
The goal of Alliance arms control policy is to *enhance security and stability*. To this end, the Allies' arms control initiatives seek a *balance at a lower level of forces and armaments* through negotiated agreements and, as appropriate, unilateral actions, ...
The Alliance reaffirms that at the negotiations on *conventional stability* it pursues the objectives of:
- the *establishment of a secure and stable balance of conventional forces at lower levels*; ...
(A Comprehensive Concept of Arms Control and Disarmament, Brussels, 29/30 May 1989, *NATO Review*, vol. 37, no. 3, 1989, June)

Excerpt 14

However, prudence requires us to maintain an overall *strategic balance* and to remain ready to meet any potential risks to our *security* which may arise from *instability* or tension.
(Rome Declaration on Peace and Cooperation, 7-8 November 1991, *NATO Review*, vol. 39, no. 6, 1991, December)

Excerpt 15

Implementation of the 1991 START Treaty will lead to *increased stability through substantial and balanced reductions in the field of strategic nuclear arms*. ...
Even in a non-adversial and co-operative relationship, Soviet military capability and build-up potential, including its nuclear dimension, still constitute the most significant factor of which the Alliance has to take account in *maintaining the strategic balance in Europe*. ...
In peace, the role of allied military forces is to guard against risks to the *security* of Alliance members; to contribute towards the *maintenance of stability and balance in Europe*; and to ensure that *peace* is preserved.
(The Alliance's New Strategic Concept, Rome, 7-8 November 1991, *NATO Review*, vol. 39, no. 6, 1991, December)

The excerpts suggest that 'stability' is even more fundamental than 'balance'. It is listed as a fundamental objective in all NATO documents, often in combination with 'security' ('enhance security and stability'; 'increase security and stability'). Moreover, in the context of the politics of peace and security, the concept 'stability' is limited in its use to systems of states that are in conflict with one another, a state of conflict in which none of the countries involved has a possibility of using force of arms in order to achieve its political goals.

A simplified lexical-semantic network for the argumentation in NATO's New Strategic Concept (Rome 1991) is presented in Figure 5.2:

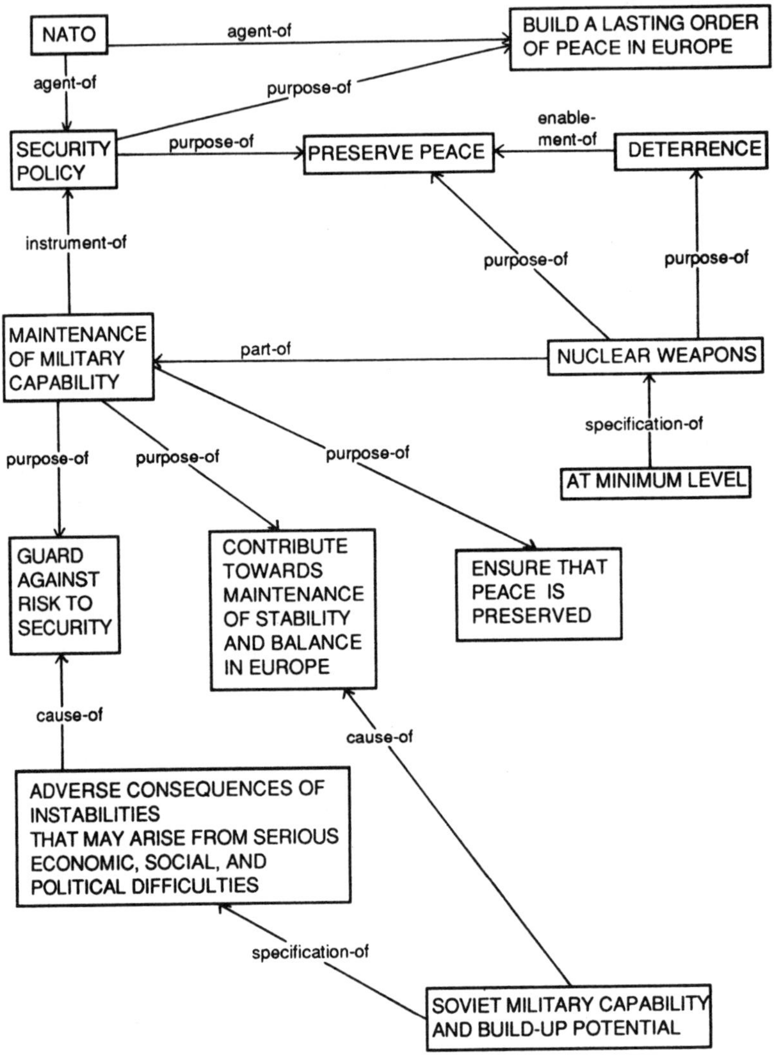

Figure 5.2 Lexical-semantic network for the argumentation in NATO's New Strategic Concept (Rome 1991)

As we can see, in NATO's New Strategic Concept the military dimension remains important. Compared to the Cold War discourse (of which the lexical-semantic network for the argumentation of *The Economist* given before was an illustrative example) there is an obvious continuity in the argumentation that nuclear weapons are a deterrent and, thus, necessary to secure peace. Maintaining the strategic balance in Europe is listed as one of NATO's main tasks. But at a time when the former division of Europe into two antagonistic military blocs has been overcome one would have to ask against whom a balance should be struck? This is another example of the 'critical discourse moment': the traditional reasoning in terms of bipolarity does not fit the new Europe.

During the Cold War, the ultimate aim was a 'balance', i.e. 'a stable balance', or 'stability'. In this case, the concept 'stability' can be explained by referring to the balance metaphor. However, in texts on Europe, especially the united Europe to be built, the concept of 'stability' is also used as part of an architecture metaphor. In this second case, it is related to more structural elements such as 'pillars' or 'foundations' (see excerpt 16). NATO is often referred to as a 'foundation', a 'cornerstone', or a 'security pillar'; the Western European Union is referred to as the 'European pillar of NATO', as a 'defence pillar', and also as a 'bridge between NATO and the EC' (for a more detailed discussion see Schäffner, 1993).[3]

Excerpt 16

NATO remains the *cornerstone* for future European security arrangements, ...

The *new European security architecture* reaches beyond NATO to the CSCE, the European Community, the Western European Union, the Council of Europe, and related organizations. ... We hope the NATO Rome Summit and the EC Maastricht Summit will endorse the development of a European *pillar* within the Alliance, ...

(Speech by the Ambassador of the United States to Germany, Robert M. Kimmitt, delivered before the 7th Annual Conference for Directors of Strategic Studies Institutes, 18 September 1991)

Judging by these findings, the concept of 'stability' seems to allow for two different interpretations. It seems to be a conceptual node that links at least two frames, i.e. metaphorical frames. It accounts for the relative certainty and predictability both of a bipolar world (here we have the relation to the balance metaphor), and to the solidity of structures in the architecture frame. Political metaphors play a role in creating political reality, they are models for comprehending, perceiving, and also structuring the world. In this sense, 'stability' can be characterized as a "world ordering concept" (Mehan and Skelley, 1988, p. 59).

Conclusion

Since the disappearance of a clear-cut bipolar world will affect not only NATO's defence strategy but also decision making by politicians everywhere, it may be predicted that there will be more changes in the conceptual structuring of the discourse on 'security', 'stability', 'balance', and 'peace'. To pinpoint such changes is a challenging task for the applied linguist. In addition to coming up with interesting empirical data, such analyses of text and discourse will also raise (and hopefully answer) questions of relevance for (cognitive) linguistics and communication studies. Some such questions might be: What criteria are decisive for the choice of a particular metaphor and for its textual elaboration once it has been introduced into the argumentation? What is the relationship between the semantic and conceptual representation of concepts and metaphors? Are metaphors, both in their conceptual and lexical structures, culture specific?

The analysis of metaphors reveals that they do indeed represent the ways in which politicians conceptualize the world, and shape their practical politics accordingly. As Lee (1992, p. 90) has pointed out in his discussion of linguistic research into the discourse of nuclear weapons: "In devoting careful analysis to this language, linguists may therefore have made some contribution not only to the study of propaganda but to more fundamental issues concerning the patterns of thought that underlie such discourses."

Moreover, insights gained through linguistic research can be applied not only to education, but also to politics and journalism. Application in the field of education may concern, for instance, the area of foreign language teaching, where culture-overlapping and culture-specific modes of conceptualization and lexicalization may be introduced into a syllabus for intercultural communication. The application to politics and journalism will probably not be so easy to achieve. However, if one aim of discourse analysis is to increase our understanding of how, in our societies, people use language for particular purposes, then attention should also be paid to the relationship between sociocultural and linguistic-cognitive phenomena and to their changes and effects (see van Dijk, 1991b). And if the effects reflect shortcomings or problems in communication or conceptualization, then new questions and problems may be raised for applied linguistics to research, and the application of insights gained in applied linguistics may be useful for society as a whole.

Notes

1 For a more detailed illustration of the macrostructure analysis and of the typical MPs see Schäffner and Neubert, eds, 1986, which also includes a

comparative analysis of typical MPs and TWTs in selected English, German and French newspapers (1979-84).

2 The debate about medium-range missiles also led to an increased awareness of the social responsibility of scholars, also among linguists, especially in Europe (see, for example, the contributions in Chilton, ed., 1985; Burkhardt, Hebel and Hoberg, eds, 1989). In Germany, for example, i.e. the then Federal Republic of Germany, a number of linguists started an initiative "Linguists for Peace" to stimulate research into the discourse on the nuclear debate, including studies on the meaning of the word 'peace' (e.g. Pasierbsky, 1983; Jäger, 1985; and for East Germany, Metzler and Römer, 1990).

3 Interestingly enough, also in the discourse on the united Europe, i.e. the European Union, we find a whole network of interrelated metaphors, particularly container, building and movement metaphors (see Schäffner, in print).

6 Promising to End a War = Language of Peace? The Rhetoric of Allied News Management in the Gulf War 1991

ANDREAS MUSOLFF

Introduction

When and how does a war come to an end? Let us look at the Gulf War of 1991,[1] and see how its *ending* was announced: on 1 March 1991, *The Guardian* quoted political leaders of Great Britain and the United States of America claiming victory for their forces in their campaign against the Iraqi occupation of Kuwait and an imminent ending of the conflict: "Kuwait is liberated and one of the most remarkable military campaigns of all time has been concluded" (British Prime Minister John Major), "This is a victory for the UN, for all mankind, for the rule of law, and for what is right" (US President George Bush). These victory announcements in the final phase of a military campaign that had lasted less than two months refer clearly to the ending of military operations that led to the permanent cease-fire on 2 March 1993, which marked the official cessation of hostilities.

However, these announcements, which suggest that the Western-Iraqi confrontation in the Gulf Region ended in March 1991, may be more problematic than they seem at first sight. That is, though a permanent cease-fire had been declared, Western military forces remained in the Gulf region, and military confrontations with Iraqi forces continued over the UN supervision of Iraq's compliance with the cease-fire conditions. The civil war between Saddam Hussein's regime and Shiite and Kurdish minorities, which had been going on for years before 1991, also continued after the ending of the Gulf War. Moreover, the answer to the question whether the 1991 cease-fire was the 'true' war ending depends upon the political evaluation of the Western 'intervention'. If the war was won as

Major and Bush claimed, what were the achievements of this 'victory'? An armistice, a state of 'peace', or the famous 'New World Order' invoked by President Bush and other Western leaders as one of their central aims of the war?[2] Or did the cease-fire, on the contrary, prove that an Arab country could resist the onslaught of the Western states long enough to negotiate an armistice without being occupied and thus break the power of Western imperialism, as official Iraqi broadcasts claimed?[3]

Thanks to a comprehensive documentation of Western TV media reports on the Gulf War collected for a research project at the Institute of Communications Studies at Leeds University, texts covering the end of the war have become accessible.[4] The following analysis, based on these documents as well as on examples of the print media's coverage of the Gulf War, will focus on the role of media reports from the ground campaign (February 1991) in defining the borderline between war and peace in what is nowadays called 'the Gulf War of 1991'. Specifically, this paper will focus on the two following questions: (1) How did these war reports represent and, therefore, also interpret the beginning and the ending of the war? (2) What motivated their representations?

Defining the beginning of a war

Semantic battles over the definition of the borderline between 'war' and 'non-war' do not only concern the ending of the war, but also the beginning. In fact, in the case of the Gulf War, the question of when it started was a major political issue. According to Iraq's official statements what happened on 2 August 1991 was the rightful 'return' of the nineteenth province to the Iraqi fatherland. Therefore, no invasion of another country (Kuwait) could have taken place, and the starting of hostilities by Allied forces on 16 January 1991 was a unilateral act of aggression. On the other hand, according to the official interpretation of the United Nations (and to the view of the anti-Iraq coalition of Western Allies, led by the United States of America, France and the United Kingdom, and some Arab states, such as Saudi Arabia and Egypt), Iraq had invaded a peaceful neighbouring state on 2 August 1990, breaking international law. Thus, the Allies were not aggressors, but were coming to the defence of the victim of that attack, saving it from the conquest of a brutal tyrant.[5]

This 'timing' of the beginning of the war as the start of the Iraqi invasion ties in with the underlying metaphorical frames for public conceptualization of the war in Western countries analysed by Lakoff (1992) and Chilton (1991b). Chilton, for example, refers to statements by Western politicians which presented a war that sacrificed thousands of lives in terms of stereotypes of TV culture, i.e. "now as a High Noon, now as fist fight between a clean-cut hero and a school yard bully" (Chilton,

1991b, p. 11). Such metaphorical frames derive their political force from their ability to assimilate new experiences to familiar patterns of perception based on well-established stereotypes while, at the same time, reducing the complexity of the semantic content of the issues in question. Metaphors can, thus, be used to exclude problematic aspects of contentious topics from public debate.

The justification of military action is a highly contentious issue, and metaphors and complete metaphorical scenarios have often been employed in attempts to vindicate the guilt of starting a war.[6] Lakoff (1992) summarizes the two metaphorical scenarios that the Bush administration offered to the Western public in order to justify their course of action in the Gulf: the 'Rescue Scenario' with Iraq as villain, the United States as hero, and Kuwait as victim of kidnap and rape, and the alternative 'Self-Defense Scenario', in which "the US and other industrialized nations" were seen as victims of "a threat to economic health" (Lakoff, 1992, p. 467). As this second scenario came close to reducing the aim of the war to "trading lives for oil", it was of less political value than the Rescue imagery, which proved to be the most efficient way of translating the abstract vision of a 'New World Order' into a seemingly concrete situation. Thus, the United States, having selflessly come to the rescue of a victim under attack, would, once again, be allowed to play the role of the defender of the 'Free World'. The 'Rescue Scenario' also made direct military intervention in the Gulf a matter of high urgency at the expense of slower political solutions, such as economic sanctions.

The choice of the 'Rescue Scenario' for justifying military action in the Gulf region also imposed certain obligations on the Allies. It was essential that they emphasize the 'altruistic' aspect of their support for the helpless victim Kuwait and give high priority and status to the role of the Arab Allies in their representation of events in the Gulf region to the Western public.[7] As long as the Allied military fulfilled the obligations and stuck to their agenda of a 'just war', contradictory information from Iraq and from independent media could be glossed over and marginalized. News that did not fit into the official Western perspective, either because of its link to one of these sources or because of discrepancies in Western information management, was denounced as 'unproven allegations' and 'enemy propaganda'. When such news could not be denounced, it was pointed to as evidence of the Allied military's 'tolerance' towards a critically minded press[8] and contrasted to the propagandists of an evil totalitarian system ruled by a dictator, who was often depicted as the modern incarnation of Adolf Hitler.

To some critics of Western military intervention the Saddam Hussein-Hitler comparison was proof of a hidden agenda which extended the aims of the war beyond the UN-sanctioned goals. Namely, it was suspected that the Allies were not willing to make any peace deal with Iraq as long as Saddam Hussein remained in power.[9] Such a view seemed to be corroborated by the encouragement of an internal revolt in Iraq by Western politicians and Allied 'black propaganda' stations in Iraq, posing as representatives of Iraqi opposition groups (see Taylor, 1992, pp. 239-41). However, official statements of Allied leaders, such as President Bush's war announcement, were never endorsed. Moreover, in the end Allied commander-in-chief, General Schwarzkopf, did negotiate the armistice and could, thus, claim to have achieved the official Western war aims, i.e. the liberation of Kuwait and Iraq's declaration to comply with all relevant UN resolutions. The comparison with Hitler and similar hard-line interpretations turned out to have been not much more than a handy tool to justify military intervention and to silence the critics of the war. After it had served these functions, the comparison to Hitler was used much less as a 1945-style defeat of the Iraqi dictator by the Western Allies, which might have proved unfulfillable, was out of the question. In contrast to a World War II model for victory, a victory along the lines of the 'Rescue Scenario' matched the Western war-agenda perfectly. The liberation of Kuwait and the restitution of its government could be presented as the victory of a US-led army of the United Nations. At the same time, it might reduce the trauma of the ignominious defeat suffered by the US forces in Vietnam[10] and re-establish the authority of the United States as the world policeman.

The representation of the ending of the Gulf War was, thus, dependent on the interpretations of its beginning and of its course. If, as the official Iraqi propaganda would have it, the Western Allies had started an aggressive onslaught on a peaceful ('reunited') Iraq in January 1991, the March cease-fire would have meant an acknowledgement of a successful Iraqi defence. As the Western Allies could not aim for the 'total' victory of a World War II, they were faced with the dilemma of how to represent their victory. They foresaw that they would have to negotiate an armistice with a Saddam Hussein who was still in power while still appearing to be the clear winners of the war. If they were not able to convince the world that what they called the 'liberation' of Kuwait was the victory that they had sought, they would appear to have lost the war despite a military 'success'. It was, therefore, of great importance for them to demonstrate their full control of the region after having gained a decisive victory over the enemy. From the Allies' leaders' point of view, the war ending had to be presented as fulfilling their main political promises concerning the 'fruits of victory', i.e. peace and stability in the Gulf region, especially in Kuwait, and new initiatives in Western-Arab relationships.

Defining the ending of a war

How can we assess the relationship between a political promise and the subsequent presentation of the object of that promise? An analysis based on speech act theory suggests a possible approach. If we regard the public presentation of political actions as a complex utterance or speech act in a sense similar to that proposed by Austin (1962) in his theory of *How to do things with words,* the conditions of success of such a presentation suggest a means of analysing its characteristic features. Austin describes these conditions ex negativo by referring to the 'Infelicities', i.e. "the things that can be and go wrong". These can be subdivided into two classes. On the one hand there are 'Misfires', which are "Acts purported but void", and on the other, 'Abuses', which are "Acts professed but hollow" (Austin, 1962, p. 14, pp. 17-18). The 'Happiness/Unhappiness' dimension governing pragmatic 'Felicity' conditions is one of the fundaments of Austin's concept of a theory that aims to treat "the total speech act in the total speech situation" as "the *only actual* phenomenon which, in the last resort, we are engaged in elucidating" (Austin, 1962, p. 148).

However, in order to make political discourse, in this case a political promise, amenable to an analysis modelled on speech act theory, an idealization that highlights those structural aspects that are relevant for the success of the linguistic-political strategies in a public debate must be introduced. Such strategies organize a series of interrelated speech acts into a greater whole by outlining a specific goal for the initial act of promising so that every single part of the 'story' contributes to fulfilling that promise.[11] In the case of the Gulf War, the promise was represented by the publicly stated war aims that had to be achieved in the course of the war and especially at its end point. One of the most explicit formulations of the Western war promise can be seen in President Bush's war announcement on 17 January 1991:

> Our objectives are clear. Saddam Hussein's forces will leave Kuwait. The legitimate government of Kuwait will be restored to its rightful place ... Iraq will eventually comply with all relevant United Nations resolutions and then when peace is restored, it is our hope that Iraq will live as a peaceful and co-operative member of the family of nations ... Our goal is not the conquest of Iraq. It is the liberation of Kuwait.[12]

Within Austin's system of Happiness/Unhappiness conditions, such a commitment would fall into the category of promises which, if 'infelicitous', can be misused, i.e., they can be given in a 'technically' correct, but not honest or truthful manner. The war critics' accusation that the Allies had a 'hidden agenda' (i.e. to conquer Iraq and oust Saddam Hussein) which contradicted their self-professed claims, was an expression of their fears that an abuse of public confidence, an 'Abuse', in Austin's sense, of the official promise had taken or was taking place.

Austin describes the happiness conditions for 'commissive' speech acts (e.g. promises) as stating that

> where ... the procedure is designed for use by persons having certain thoughts, feelings, or intentions, or for the inauguration of certain consequential conduct on the part of any participant, then a person participating and so invoking the procedure must in fact have those thoughts, feelings and intentions, and the participants must intend so to conduct themselves ... [and] must so conduct themselves subsequently. (Austin, 1962, p. 39).

The fact that the 'happiness' of commissives is not only a function of the speakers' inner commitment, but also of their subsequent 'external' behaviour is of particular relevance for the analysis of the Allies' version of the war-ending. At the beginning of the war, the Rescue Scenario demanded that the Allies' public representatives show their honesty and sincerity by stressing the earnestness of their attempts to negotiate a peaceful solution, for example. Further, when the war had started they had to follow it up with appropriate actions, and they had to terminate the whole course of actions with a 'proper' ending. That is, their main public relations task in the presentation of the Gulf War ending was to convince the Western public that they had achieved a victory that justified the scope of their military intervention against Iraq and the risk of high casualties among their own troops, as well as among the Iraqi forces and the civilian population.

In the initial phase of the war, the Allied bombing campaign was the main issue of contention. For instead of exclusively targeting the occupation troops in Kuwait, civilian targets were hit, resulting in civilian casualties, and culminating in the destruction of a civilian shelter in the Amirija district of Baghdad on 13 February 1991, which cost the lives of hundreds of civilians.[13] Allied spokesmen were quick to denounce the free access granted to Western journalists on the occasion of the Amirija bombing as an Iraqi propaganda ploy and insisted that Allied military intelligence had identified the bunker as a command centre and that the civilians killed there had been 'set up' as bomb fodder by Saddam Hussein. Western commentators, however, pointed out that any repetitions of such pictures of mass carnage in a prolonged war would do serious damage to the Allied position in the eyes of the world.[14]

Fulfilling a victory promise

The longer the Allies' bombing campaign lasted, the greater the danger that its military 'advantages' (of destroying the Iraqi command structure, supply lines and combat troops) would be outweighed by an increase in the plausibility of the suspicions that they had a 'hidden agenda'.

Therefore, after the Amirija disaster, the time schedule for the ground war was redrawn so that it could start 'early enough' to avoid political embarrassment for the Allies. At this point, a strange race started between the count-down for the ground campaign and last minute peace efforts motivated by world-wide criticism of the war. These included the diplomatic initiatives of the USSR leadership and Iraqi offers of a conditional withdrawal from Kuwait. Bush dismissed Iraq's offer as a 'cruel hoax' (15 February 1991) and issued an ultimatum for 23 February demanding Iraq's unconditional withdrawal from Kuwait. He could count on Saddam Hussein's defiant determination to trade such a withdrawal for some conditions of his own so as to avoid losing face in the Arab world (Taylor, 1992, p. 232-3). Since, according to US intelligence reports, there had been no sign of withdrawal during the time period set by the ultimatum, the Allies were free, under United Nations law, to launch the ground campaign when the deadline expired. It took them less than a day to do so. On 24 February the land attack was launched.

Once the ground campaign had started, the challenge to the Allies' official version of events by the reporting and broadcasting of Western journalists from inside Iraq was greatly reduced. A news blackout was imposed in the first few hours; afterwards a system of tight military control over most of the media reporting on the war was put into operation. Its main feature was the so-called 'newspool' system: the selection of a few chosen journalists who were allowed to file first-hand reports from the battlefield in groups attached to military units. This arrangement made it easy for the Allied press officers to favour politically friendly media by giving them privileged access to sensational data and to the telecommunication infrastructure needed to transmit reports from Saudi Arabia (see Schwilk, 1992, pp. 65-7). The newspool system did not only ensure that 'classified' information would not be broadcast but also led to an overall homogeneity of reporting that set the general tone for the war debate. Having achieved the harmonization of 'primary' information by combining fine-tuned military press briefings with tight control over newspool reports, the Allied military news managers did not have to bother too much about critical second-hand commentaries from journalists, knowing that in war propaganda, rather than controlling all reports or commentaries, the most important thing is providing the frame of a consistent 'story' into which news items can be fitted in such a way that even critical news or interpretations appear to corroborate one's own version of events. As Taylor puts it, one must conduct "an information campaign across a broad front, in which all the streams are woven credibly and inextricably into the overall impression" (Taylor, 1992, p. 123).

At the start of the ground campaign the Allies' tank forces needed to drive a long way into Iraq in order to 'cut off and kill' the Iraqi troops guarding the supply route north of Kuwait. To ensure silence about this operation, the strategy was very simple: the pool journalists attached to the attacking units were briefed about the battle plan a week before and then ordered to keep quiet about it. The news blackout gave Saddam Hussein an opportunity to claim outright victory to the world only to be forced forty-eight hours later to announce a unilateral 'withdrawal' from Kuwait (see Taylor, 1992, pp. 239-42). Within these two days the Iraqi troops in Kuwait were cut off from the rest of the Iraqi army and decimated in a ground offensive that advanced faster than foreseen even by some Allied military strategists (see Taylor, 1992, pp. 246-7). The speed of the Allied advance was one of the key factors determining the presentation of what Saddam Hussein called "the mother of all battles" as "the mother of all retreats" to the Western public (Taylor, 1992, p. 243).

The greatest challenge to this 'retreat' version of events was Iraq's announcement, on 26 February (local time), that they would withdraw and comply with UN resolution 660, one of the twelve resolutions concerning the invasion of Kuwait. However, when the Iraqi announcement became publicly known in Washington, it was still 25 February there. Moreover, at the beginning of that day the news had come that Iraqi Scud missiles had killed 27 US servicemen and injured 98 others in Dhahran and that some 600 oil wells fired by the retreating Iraqi troops were burning in Kuwait (Taylor, 1992, p. 242). This gave the government of the United States a chance to interpret the Iraqi announcement to withdraw as a cunning propaganda trick. In the first US reaction to the announcement, the White House press spokesman Marlin Fitzwater denied any evidence that the Iraqi troops in Kuwait were withdrawing and defined them as "retreating combat units" (Taylor, 1992, p. 242), and on the next day, President Bush endorsed this version:

> He [Saddam Hussein] is not withdrawing. His defeated forces are retreating. He is trying to claim victory in the midst of a rout, and he is not voluntarily giving up Kuwait. He is trying to save the remnants of power ... Saddam is not interested in peace, but only to regroup and fight another day, and he does not renounce Iraq's claim to Kuwait. (Taylor, 1992, pp. 242-3).

Bush's insistence on calling the Iraqi evacuation of Kuwait a 'retreat', not a 'withdrawal', was not just a legalistic quibble. It pointed to the central purpose of the Rescue Scenario, which Saddam Hussein's tactics aimed at destroying. That is, in order to present the ground campaign as a rescue operation, the West needed to refer to something like a liberation battle for Kuwait, a 'clear-cut', unambiguous victory over the Iraqi invasion forces. However, the liberation of Kuwait City turned out to be a military non-event and could hardly be presented as a victory: the city was abandoned by the Iraqi troops in the morning hours of 26 February. It was not the newspool journalists, but non-pool-aligned, 'unilateral' CBS reporters who arrived there first, shortly after US Marines had reoccupied the embassy of the United States but well before the main Allied troops (Taylor, 1992, pp. 243-4).

On 27 February, Iraq's foreign minister Tariq Aziz sent a letter to the United Nations offering to comply with all its 12 resolutions. Saddam Hussein was trying to save his army and his international reputation by ordering his troops to retreat faster than the Allies could advance and by presenting that retreat as a withdrawal in compliance with the resolutions. This would leave the Allies vulnerable to criticism for overstepping the UN mandate. Such criticism had already been voiced by the USSR leaders as well as by French politicians (who had tried to prevent a ground campaign by way of independent peace initiatives in January 1991), as well as by some Arab states, notably Jordan, and pacifists and war-critics all over the world. Radio Baghdad quickly took advantage of this criticism by claiming that the Allies were going "beyond the resolutions which they made themselves and dictated to the world in the name of the Security Council"; however, at the same time, they threatened "the scoundrel aggressors" saying that Iraq would not "tolerate aggression, humiliation and submissiveness to the aggressor's tyranny" (Radio Baghdad, 27 February 1991, see Taylor, 1992, p. 251).

In the face of such bravado and 'hedging' on the issue of complying with all UN resolutions, Allied leaders had been able to ignore the criticism, dismiss Iraqi withdrawal announcements, and push forward with the attack. However, to do so after the 'liberation' of Kuwait would run the risk of further and more serious public criticism. In order to save the Rescue Scenario, President Bush had no choice but to put an end to the Allied offensive. He announced a victory and declared a temporary cessation of hostilities to begin on 28 February, as preparation for the negotiation of a more permanent cease-fire.

Kuwait had been 'liberated'. However, the victorious liberation battle, so necessary to the Rescue Scenario, was still missing from the war story. The Allies' flanking manoeuvre into Iraq could not be presented as that battle as the release of any pictures of it would have damaged the 'Kuwait only' line. Nor could the liberation of Kuwait City, which, as noted earlier, had turned out to be a military non-event. A battle on Kuwaiti territory, which could be presented as unquestionable evidence of the Allied victory, was needed, preferably without press intervention at the outset. Two such battles did take place, one on the road from Kuwait City to Basra and one on a coastal road. These were in effect the only routes out of Kuwait that retreating Iraqis could take. Both roads were not accessible to Western journalists at the time of the battle.

On 26 and 27 February, most Western journalists were busy catching up with the CBS scoop in Kuwait City, reporting in detail on the effects of the Iraqi invasion on the now liberated city. Particular prominence was given to allegations of systematic torturing and looting committed by Iraqi occupation troops.[15] Meanwhile the two main retreating Iraqi columns were stopped by Allied tank units, engaged, and destroyed from the air by means of cluster and fire bombs. The explosions were such that of the 50 to 60 mile long convoy on the coastal road from Al-Jafrah to Umm-Quasr only 37 corpses were counted by the first Western reporters, who arrived there 10 days after the war had ended. The majority of the Iraqi soldiers had probably been disintegrated by the sheer force of the fire blast.[16]

This was not the great victory battle that the Allies wished to present to the world. Some media had already reported allegations both by Iraqi and Western sources that the Allied military were 'shooting retreating enemy in the back'.[17] In order to counter such criticism, Schwarzkopf called a special press briefing on 27 February, in which he asserted that the Allies were "not in the business of killing" the fleeing Iraqi troops, but were distributing leaflets telling them "over and over again, all you've got to do is get out of your tanks and move off, and you will not be killed" (see Taylor, 1992, p. 252). The Rescue Scenario was in danger of turning into a gory account of the Allies indulging in an unjustifiable mass slaughter.

Searching for victory

In order to 'rescue' their 'peace-as-victory' story and to avoid being exposed as liars, the Allied leaders needed to present the final phase of the ground campaign to the world as the promised victory battle that justified the war effort and ensured that the cease-fire would be seen as a political as well as a military success. Therefore, in the same briefing in which he claimed that Allied troops "were not in the business of killing" fleeing Iraqis, Schwarzkopf insisted there were still fierce 'fights' going on between some Allied units and Saddam Hussein's elite 'Republican Guard'. The General referred to these fights as a "classic tank battle".[18] Other Allied military spokesmen gave more specific hints about "some very genuine armor battles" and stated that the fights near Basra involving 800 US tanks of the 7th Corps and 300 of the Hammuravi division of the Republican Guard constituted the "largest tank battle since the second world war".[19] This was, in fact, the destruction of the other column of Iraqi troops retreating along the North Road from Kuwait to Basra. The first detailed reports of this battle were released from the newspools on 28 February (two days after the event) after having been subjected to the military authorities' censoring procedures.[20] The release of the news was timed to fit into the overall picture of a morally justified and overwhelming victory. It followed upon the reports about the 'liberation' of Kuwait City and a new series of allegations of atrocities committed by the Iraqi occupation troops. It came after the declaration of the first temporary cease-fire on 27 February by President Bush[21] but still preceded the agreement for a permanent cease-fire. As the concluding piece of the military campaign, it provided evidence of the Allied victory necessary for an armistice that would count in the eyes of the Western public as the equivalent of the peace promise.

This hypothesis, that the Mutlah Ridge Battle news was used as the 'proper' end-of-campaign story for the Gulf War, is strengthened further if we look at the contents of the reports. Graphic descriptions of that battle did not become known to the world until 1 March, when the first pictures of the remainders of the Iraqi forces on the Basra road were broadcast by the TV stations. What was evident to the viewers were the effects of Allied cluster bombing, which had left few survivors and not many corpses. What Schwarzkopf had called a 'classic tank battle' turned out to have been a trap from which there was no escape. Western reporters describing the scene used such terms as 'carnage', 'slaughter', or 'massacre'. CNN's reporter, Greg LaMotte, for instance, did little to hide his own horror of the pictures:

> What we're seeing is bodies strewn all over the place ... We've got cars that have been stolen from Kuwaitis as the Iraqis tried to get out of town. They piled the cars full of booty and they simply didn't make it. There's civilian cars all over the place, there's burned out tanks, there's trucks, you name it. ... Some were completely disintegrated, including the people inside of them. What this could be is thousands of people possibly could have died given the number of vehicles involved. The pilots described their mission as shooting fish in a barrel and indeed that's what the case was. It seems that many probably didn't know what hit them given the scenes that we saw.[22]

The pictures from Mutlah Ridge might have worked against the aim of presenting a clean 'rescue' victory of the Allied war propaganda if it had not been for remainders of looted Kuwaiti property in the burnt-out convoy, e.g., civilian cars, household items, TV sets, etc., which were interpreted as pieces of the political-historical 'evidence' supporting the Allies' war scenario. Some reports also mentioned Kuwaiti hostages as part of the convoy who, it was alleged, had been murdered prior to the bombing raid.[23] In the first British TV reports, which were broadcast on early afternoon (GMT) of 1 March, the devastating effect of the cluster bombing was the main feature, but later the emphasis switched to the looting. Still, at a press briefing in Riyadh, a British officer claimed to have no details on the issue of civilian vehicles in the Mutlah Ridge convoy. In the evening, ITN's *News at Ten* gave the Allied military's official version of events:

> The spoils of war were spilling from almost every vehicle - evidence of the Iraqis' orgy of looting. They tried to drive home with all the treasures of Kuwait. There were clothes and children's toys, radios and vacuum cleaners, jewellery and china. A musical card still played 'A Happy New Year'. A stolen Koran: the ultimate sacrilege ... For American Marine General Walter Boomer, the shambles summed up his views on Saddam's

> defeated army: 'In addition to being fairly incompetent, they were thieves as well as murderers'. (Jeremy Thompson, on ITN 22:00 (GMT), quoted in Taylor, 1992, p. 257).

Here we have a classical example of a final victory statement: the defeated enemy is denounced as a criminal who has committed "the ultimate sacrilege", and has deserved his destruction both for his "incompetence" and his evil. According to ITN's source, Lieutenant General Boomer, this interpretation had been the truth right from the outset of the war. In his address to the United States at the beginning of the Allied bombardment in January, President Bush had already quoted this unusually outspoken general as an authority on the moral aspects of the Gulf War: "Listen to one of our great officers out there, Marine Lieutenant General Walter Boomer. He said, 'There are things that are worth fighting for. A world in which brutality and lawlessness are allowed to go unchecked isn't the kind of world we're going to want to live in.'" (Volmert, 1993, p. 225). Listening to General Lieutenant Boomer, the Western public was bound to gain the impression that the initial statements justifying the war as a fight against 'brutality and unlawfulness' were now fully corroborated in the representation of the beaten enemy soldiers as incompetent 'thieves and murderers'. What could have counted only as a hypothetical assumption at the start of the war appeared to be borne out by the 'evidence' of Mutlah Ridge. The result of the battle served as proof of the truthfulness of the Allied leaders' promises to rescue Kuwait, the helpless victim of 'rape', by fighting and winning the war against the evil aggressor.

This vindication of the Allies' publicly stated war commitments was the precondition for making the permanent cease-fire with the Iraqis the official ending point of the war. A war ending without the evidence of a decisive victory would have been 'useless' for the Western leaders as it could not have counted as a fulfilment of the obligations that they had undertaken earlier when they promised liberation and peace. They would have run the risk of appearing to be impostors and liars and of having uttered their commissive speech acts insincerely (in Austin's terminology: of having committed an 'Abuse' through insincerity). The appearance of consistency between war aims and the 'evidence' of victory in the Mutlah Ridge battle ruled out any such criticism for the time being.

The interpretation of the battle scene as a vindication of the Western war effort was not the only view presented by the media either at the time of the first broadcasts or later on the evening of 1 March. BBC 2 *Newsnight* showed a report by Mark Urban that focused on whether or not Kuwaiti refugees had been part of the destroyed convoy. Jeremy Paxman, in his commentary to this report, pointed out that many of the soldiers "who died at allied hands in this engagement were Kurds, Turks and other minorities already victimised by the Party dictatorship" (Taylor, 1992, pp. 258-9).[24]

But what impact could such critical questions have on public opinion? None of the pictures or the commentaries about the massacre, however critical, ever had a chance of being viewed by the world as part of topical 'real-time' news due to Saddam Hussein's propaganda bravado and Schwarzkopf's efficient timing. They were broadcast only after the official interpretations praising the battle news as evidence of 'liberation' and 'victory' had been worked out and established. By then the reports of large scale Iraqi atrocities and of the plundering and torturing in Kuwait City had been reiterated time and again, and since 25 February there had been constant reporting on the firing of almost 600 oil wells in Kuwait by Iraqi troops. Schwarzkopf described a surveillance flight over the burning wells as "flying into hell" (Taylor, 1992, p. 260). Against this background, pictorial and verbal descriptions of the Mutlah Ridge battle were received as confirmation of a 'hard, but just' punishment for those Iraqi 'murderers and thieves', acting on orders of an evil dictator. The critical questions, which the Western media did ask, would only be taken into account by the public later, at a time when the military campaign was over.

But was the military campaign really over? This question is not purely rhetorical: on 1 and 2 March 1991 there were further clashes between Iraqi and US troops that cost hundreds, perhaps even up to 2000 lives (see Taylor, 1992, p. 261). None of these clashes was seen as a continuation of the war. Nor was the extermination campaign of Saddam Hussein's supposedly destroyed army against the uprising of Kurdish and Shiite minorities or the subsequent Western military interventions to secure a partial escape of the survivors to safe havens interpreted as part of that Gulf War. A new rescue scenario of 'safe havens' was established for them.[25] Further US-Iraqi clashes, such as those that followed the imposition of a no-fly zone in southern Iraq by the United States, or that took place during the bombardments by the US airforce in 1993, were presented officially as 'minor incidents'. Alternately, they were criticized as possibly leading towards a 'new' war - but none of them was seen as a 'continuation' of the Gulf War of 1991. Officially, the United States celebrated its Gulf War victory in the parade in June 1991.[26] Viewed against the background of the Allied 'peace' promises it seems that even if there were logical reasons for calling the post March 1991 clashes a 'continuation' of the Gulf War, such an interpretation did not fit the official Allied victory claim and, therefore, had to be discarded.

Conclusion

In conclusion, 'peace', as defined by the Allies in the Gulf War seems to be based on the presupposition of a victorious end battle that would 'settle' the war. Thus, the beginning of the non-war/'peace' period was defined in terms of war events. This appears to me to be a curious and somewhat depressing finding that needs further explanation. Perhaps it points to a more general question, i.e., whether or not there is a stereotypical 'Gestalt' of a 'proper' war scenario that requires such a victory for one side (and a clear-cut defeat for the other) and that is connected with a particular definition of peace.

In other words, a rescue scenario might turn out to be more aggressive than a scenario in which peace results from a compromise between two powers satisfying their selfish interests. More analysis of the language in which wars are being represented is needed to identify the scenarios for 'proper' beginnings, courses and endings of wars that are shared by large parts of the public. Comparative investigation of different war scenarios would clarify whether or not war propagandists rely on the existence of stereotypical perceptions, which they would only have to 'trigger' to enlist public support for a particular campaign and, thus, avoid having to invent new convincing scenarios each time. Applying Austin's claim that commissive speech acts bind the speakers to follow the specific course of action (see Austin, 1962, p. 39) implied by the war stories told to the public, we may come to a better understanding of how supposedly rational peace-promising declarations of war aims become prophecies, which, rather than 'fulfilling' themselves, turn into agendas of aggression.

Notes

1 For a presentation of the 'Second Gulf War' following the 'First Gulf War' (the Iran-Iraq war 1980-88), as a well-defined historical entity see Goldstein, 1992, pp. 135-8.

2 For Bush's application of the *New World Order* notion to the Gulf War in his "address to the nation" see the documentation in Volmert, 1993, pp. 224-5.; for a political assessment of the *New World Order* concept as depending on victory in the Gulf see Chomsky, 1991a, 1991b.

3 See, for example, the interpretation by Baghdad radio of the result of the war as proof of "Iraq's great steadfastness" which "will guide the Arab nation to the road to resuming its civilisational march and to expelling the imperialist and Zionist aggressors" (quoted after Taylor, 1992, p. 264).

4 The texts of TV broadcasts to be analysed are taken from Philipp M. Taylor's *War and the media. Propaganda and persuasion in the Gulf War,* the first survey of material from the University of Leeds project, based on an archive of some 10,500 hours of videotape recordings of the war coverage by the main British and American TV stations as well as a

selection of French, German, Italian and USSR programmes (see Taylor, 1992, pp. viiii-ix).

5 See, for example, President Bush in his address to the nation, announcing the beginning of Allied air strikes on 16 January 1991: "This conflict started August 2nd when the dictator of Iraq invaded a small and helpless neighbor. ... Five months ago, Saddam Hussein started this cruel war against Iraq; tonight the battle has been joined" (quoted after Volmert, 1993, p. 223).

6 See, for example, Krumeich's analysis of the 'metaphorical' justification for the aggressive German policies in the run-up to the First World War by way of creating a 'siege' mentality (Krumeich, 1989).

7 There is evidence that US military newsbriefers exaggerated the part that allied Arab troops played in the battle of Khafji during the early phase of the war and in the liberation of Kuwait City (see Taylor, 1992, pp. 136-40, 157-9, 241-3).

8 For a show of liberal attitude see the analysis of Allied press briefings in Taylor, 1992, pp. 198-205, 216-8. Such pretence of tolerance did not prevent military officials and conservative war commentators from accusing journalists of making propaganda for Saddam Hussein, culminating in the vilification of the BBC as the "Baghdad Broadcasting Corporation" (see Taylor, 1992, pp. 8, 38, 107, 113-4, 148, 164, 223; Miller and Allen, 1991, pp. 73-83; and Hebert, 1991).

9 For a discussion of the ideological implications of the Saddam Hussein-Hitler comparison see, for example, Link, 1991, and Wild, 1991; for an analysis of the impact of this comparison on debates in the German peace movement see Musolff, 1994.

10 See Bush's Gulf war announcement: "I've told the American people before that this will not be another Vietnam. And I repeat this here tonight. Our troops will have the best possible support in the world. And they will not be asked to fight with one hand tied behind their back." (quoted after Volmert, 1993, p. 224).

11 For Austin's classification of different kinds of 'promises' based on interpretations of typically 'commissive' performative verbs, such as 'promise', 'undertake', 'bind myself', 'give my word', 'guarantee', 'swear', 'declare for', 'contemplate', etc. in the final lecture of *How to do things with words*, see Austin, 1962, p. 156.

12 Bush on 16 January 1991; quoted after Volmert, 1993, 223-5. In his provocative interpretation of the war, the French philosopher Jean Baudrillard stated that the Gulf War would and did not take place as a 'proper war', because there was no declaration of war (Baudrillard, 1991; for criticism of this postmodernist interpretation see Norris, 1992, and Jarvis, 1992). On the basis of the speech act interpretation suggested here, Baudrillard's fallacy results from his neglect of the success conditions for such declarations: an official war-declaration was not legally necessary in the case of the Gulf conflict of 1990-91, as the Allied forces did not act as armies of their respective national states, but 'on behalf' of the UN (though they were not UN troops). The 'Gulf War promise' in the sense in which the term 'promise' is used here was not issued to the Iraqis, but to the

Western public; it underscored the aggressive character of the war and highlighted instead visions of a 'just peace' as result of an Allied victory.

13 For analyses of the Amirija bombing coverage by Western media see Taylor, 1992, pp. 187-215; Kellner, 1992, pp. 297-310; Schwilk, 1992, pp. 42-4.

14 For the Western media's reactions to the military's criticism of their coverage of the Amirija bombing see Taylor, 1992, pp. 215-22. How nervous the Allies were about accusations of waging a war against Iraq (instead of concentrating on the liberation campaign for Kuwait, as Bush had promised) can be seen from General Schwarzkopf's admission after the war of having wondered, "how long would the world stand by and watch the United States pound the living hell out of Iraq without saying, 'Wait a minute - enough is enough'." (*Newsweek,* 11 March 1991; quoted after Taylor, 1992, p. 232).

15 For analyses of the 'atrocity campaigns' during the ground war and of their contradictions see Taylor, 1992, pp. 225-7, 245-6; Kellner, 1992, pp. 396-402, and Volmert, 1993, pp. 216-7.

16 See Taylor, 1992, pp. 262-3; reports of this battle were first published in *The Guardian* on 11 March 1991.

17 See *The Guardian,* 28 February 1991, 'Allies accused of shooting retreating enemy in the back'; ibid., 'Humanity loses out as the allied forces have a field day'.

18 See *The Guardian,* 28 February 1991, '"The gates are closed" on fleeing Guard'.

19 See *The Guardian,* 28 February 1991, 'Battle rages in Basra'.

20 See, e.g. *The Guardian,* 28 February 1991, 'Humanity loses out as the allied forces have a field day'; ibid., Ph. Jacobson, 'Stunned and silent soldiers surrender in the rain'; *The Guardian,* 2 March 1991, C. Wills and G. Airs, 'Burnt bodies litter highway after bombing'.

21 Bush's cease-fire declaration on 27 February was the response to the official Iraqi offer to comply with *all* UN resolutions, which had been sent to the United Nations earlier that same day. It came too late to save the Iraqi soldiers' lives at Mutlah Ridge where the battle had taken place on 26 February (see Taylor, 1992, pp. 246-8).

22 See LaMotte, quoted in Taylor, 1992, p. 253; compare also Kate Adie's and Robert Moore's broadcasts on 1 March 1991, ibid., pp. 254-5.

23 See C. Wills and G. Airs, 'Burnt bodies litter highway after bombing', *The Guardian,* 2 March 1991.

24 Some critics pointed out that the continued presence of Saddam Hussein's regime invalidated Allied claims to have scored an epoch-making victory (e.g. *The Guardian,* 1 March 1991, 'Grand victory, or a skirmish?'; M. Gräfin Dönhoff, 'Ein dubioser Sieg', *Die Zeit,* 12 April 1991).

25 *The Guardian,* 9 April 1991, 'West uses UN charter to justify aid but deny military support to Kurds'; 18 April 1991, 'UN moves in to set up havens'.

26 *The Guardian,* 11 June 1991, 'Broadway raises a storm for its heroes'.

Part III

Language and Social Discrimination

7 Establishing Linguistic Markers of Racist Discourse

MICHAEL CLYNE

Introduction

The face of racism is changing. The 'new racism' has departed from an emphasis on the inferiority of other races and expresses 'racial difference' as sufficient justification to close bounds against them and be hostile to them (Barker, 1981; Tucker, 1986; Markus, 1986). Accompanying this change, racist discourse has reappeared in many parts of the world. Some countries are attempting to curtail it through educational campaigns and legislation against racial vilification. However, defining racist discourse is not easy though language is crucial to the dissemination of racist ideologies - whether as a medium of communication, a means of identification, a means of cognitive development or an instrument of action. In some cases, many with racist objectives conceal these, partly by couching them in cautious 'mainstream' discourse. Others, however, are more explicit. This paper illustrates linguistic devices used in both explicit or overt racist discourse and less explicit or covert racist discourse. The research findings are based on texts from American racist newspapers, far-right German pamphlets, a Melbourne suburban newspaper, and tapes of a Sydney talkback radio.

Overt racist discourse

We can differentiate between *overt* and *covert* racist discourse. Overt racist discourse is intended for a homogeneous, sympathetic audience and makes no attempt to conceal its message or the ideology that lies behind it.

Overt racist discourse in the print media

On the basis of the data from racist newspapers and pamphlets, this type of racist discourse can be characterized by some or all of the following:

Us - them antithesis The *Us - them antithesis* creates two worlds by the use of two sets of words, one for the ingroup and one for the outgroup, thereby separating one group from another, e.g.:

(1) Jew, black, hispanic versus white or European
(2) Deutsche versus Ausländer [Germans versus foreigners]

People are seen in terms of their externally determined group affiliations, thus excluding and depriving them of individuality, e.g.:

(1) black (referring to Australian Aborigines, Black South Africans, Papuans)
(2) Asians (including Chinese, Lebanese, Turks, Indians)

Another example is the redefining of 'Wir sind das Volk' ['We are the people'], the catchcry of the East German revolution, in racial terms by members of ultra-right groups.

Collocations of labels of ethnic groups (or places of origin) In such collocations we find adjectives or nouns with a clearly negative meaning, e.g.:

(1) uncivilized black Africans
(2) Asians desiring an unfair share
(3) power hungry Jews

Complex symbols These are general symbols which invoke diverse denotative and connotative components which may solicit an unfavourable attitude towards the outgroup and a favourable one towards the ingroup, e.g.:

(1) overpopulation of non-whites
(2) intellectual inferiority of blacks
(3) white superiority
(4) Jewish power and subversion

Dysphemisms These are words that are selected from the 'strong' end of the lexical field for the victims of racism and euphemisms referring to the work of racists (see Allan and Burridge, 1991), e.g.:

(1) Ausländer/Asylanten raus! ['Foreigners/asylum seekers out!']
(2) Halt infestation! (Used by an American racist newspaper in a headline to express opposition to 'ethnically mixed marriages')
(3) Judenbetreuung im KZ. ['Care of Jews in the concentration camp']

Feminine forms (This applies to English only.) Feminine forms are used only for ethnic labels that are the target of prejudice, e.g. 'Jewess', 'Negress'.

Overt racism in talkback radio

Some examples of overt racism may be found on talkback radio programmes conducted by a Sydney commercial radio announcer found guilty of racial vilification in 1987. Talkback announcers can have enormous power over listeners' thoughts and attitudes. They can intimidate callers by abusing them and putting them down in front of a large audience. They can regulate the callers' turn lengths and terminate their discourse. Announcers aim at developing group solidarity and cultivating networks of like-minded listeners and callers. This is done in a number of ways, including insulting and cutting off those of different opinions. In the first excerpt, the caller raises a superannuation and workers' compensation dispute between coal workers and management, which is not an inter-ethnic matter (2KY talkback programmes, 24 April 1987, 18 February 1988):

Excerpt 1

Caller: Now I've worked in a coal mine for the last twenty-six years and four years on the railway. You know I'm not saying nothing but you I mean know it's gone by the board, but we got a three pronged attack - a three front attack with coal owners. One is unsolved that the superannuation which happened before Christmas. Now we thought that was all settled, we only had to sign the papers when we come back to work. Now that hasn't been settled at all. The coal miners have reneged on that.

Announcer: The coal mine owners.

Caller: The coal owners OK.

After some discussion on the compensation case, the announcer suddenly turns the problems into a racial issue. Using dysphemisms, he blames the Japanese for the worker's situation:

Announcer: Those rotten little bastards that live to the North of us called the Japanese (who) have demanded, because there's a glut of coal production in the world, as you know better than I do, they have demanded a twenty per cent cut in the price of Australian coal those slant-eyed little devils to the north of us (who) screw us down to twenty per cent under what they have been paying us here.

The ingroup becomes the victim and the outgroup the enemy. Australian workers and management are equally threatened by the Japanese. In order to be able to keep on the air and be able to continue with his list of problems, the caller agrees:

> *Caller:* That's right.

The announcer indicates some awareness that he has diverted the argument before offering advice to strike:

> *Announcer:* Now coming back to your problem ...

However, the racist diversion is repeated at the end before he finally cuts his caller off:

> *Announcer:* ... with the Japs screwing us ... Oh goodbye my friend, you bloody idiot, get off.

In the second excerpt, a caller obviously in sympathy with the racist network around the announcer depicts an incident she claims to have occurred at a Chinese restaurant. Unlike the previous call, this one has an 'ethnic conflict' as its theme:

> *Excerpt 2*
>
> *Caller:* Look, my daughter, she went to a restaurant in Chinatown and they had a late dinner. There was herself and three friends, they only brought three meals out. My daughter objected to this. Anyway after ...
>
> *Announcer:* Excuse me, wha- they ordered many different dishes, and they only brought three out?
>
> *Caller:* No, they ordered four meals, and they only brought three out.
>
> *Announcer:* That's no good, yes I see.
>
> *Caller:* Anyway, my daughter was a bit annoyed about this. Anyway they ate their dinner and as she was walking out, she said something to the proprietor or whoever it was at the till, that she would only pay for the three meals. And with that he hit her across the face.
>
> *Announcer*: It does sound as though the Chinese fighters and the Chinese restaurants in Chinatown are ganging up on customers, doesn't it? ... There's plenty of them. ... It makes you feel like getting a dozen or so of your footballing mates together and have a night out down there and test these little bastards right out, doesn't it? ... He's smaller and our weed and we've never lost a war against the Chinese. Why not?

The announcer's discourse stimulates an *us* versus *them* situation by expressions such as 'ganging up'. The common racist complex symbol of over-population is invoked ('There's plenty of them') twice, and there is an explicit incitement to racial violence ('It makes you feel like getting ...'). The 'doesn't it?' and 'why not?' force the caller to agree, which she does. Finally some of the most offensive examples of terms of abuse, such as negative nicknames, come in a so-called satirical advertisement to close the segment, including terms such as 'chinks' and those that refer to physical attributes (e.g. 'slant eyed little chinks'; *italics are mine*):

> *Announcer:* Have a night out folks, go down to Chinatown and eat at the Hooquonfongclonhongdung Restaurant. There you can have not only a fight with the proprietor. You can also have a seven course Chinese banquet, all for twenty dollars. You'll only have to wait three hours for the meal and of course if you're not satisfied, there'll be *a thousand little chinks* come out and kick your guts out. And of course, if you are not satisfied with the way they kick you, these friendly *little slant-eyed people* will of course make sure they complain to the Broadcasting Tribunal.

The latter is a reference to the body which had been monitoring the particular talkback announcer's programmes to ascertain if he is guilty of racial vilification. After the 'advertisement', the caller is invited to express approval:

> *Announcer:* What d'you think of it?

Both announcer and caller are collaborating in solidarity against the authorities who might withdraw the station's licence and against the majority attitude, in the words of the announcer:

> *Announcer:* Those people who wanted Australia to be taken over by Asians.

Covert racist discourse

Covert racist discourse is addressed to heterogeneous groups who are not necessarily supporters of the point of view. The discourse aims at making the audience believe there is a consensus between them and the speaker/author. It usually has pretentions of objectivity and pragmatism and the pretence of the acceptance of a liberal philosophical framework shared between addresser and addressee. Our example here is an editorial, 'Whites must keep control', from a Melbourne suburban news and advertising weekly (*Waverley Gazette*, 25 June 1986) which argues against majority rule in South Africa for the foreseeable future.

Scientific truth and philosophical principles in conflict

The author of the editorial is projected as a moderate balanced person, and those with opposing views as extremists (*italics are mine*):

Excerpt 3

The *sad, cold, hard facts* are that the whites must remain in power in South Africa because if they don't hundreds of thousands of them would probably be butchered by the blacks in a revolution.
The *harsh reality* of South Africa is that the whites must remain in control, and hold that control while promoting an orderly, and it is hoped, a peaceful progression to majority rule.

These words imply a clash between scientific truth on the one hand and philosophical principles based on emotionalism on the other. The main syntactic device employed is modal auxiliaries, e.g.:

(1) The whites *must* remain in power.
(2) The whites *must* remain in control.
(3) It's timely to reflect on what *could* happen.
(4) It is the price that *must* be paid.

As Kress and Hodge (1979, p. 122) have pointed out, English modal auxiliaries reflect an ambiguous attitude between knowledge and power where it is unclear whether the proposition is true or whether the powerful are dictating an opinion to those not in a position to have the information. In that respect, they are similar to agentless passives - passives without a 'doer' (e.g. '... that *must* be paid.').

Words of concession

Words of concession ('but', 'however') feature in covert racist discourse. An important discourse device is the *apparent disclaimer* (van Dijk, 1991a, p. 128), ('We aren't racists, but ...'). What follows 'but' is usually prejudice masquerading as scientific fact. For example, alluding to the peaceful progression referred to above, the newspaper editorial states:

Excerpt 4

That might take another 20 years - but it is the price which must be paid to ensure both black and white people are not murdered in the streets and a once great nation does not become a grimy Third World backwater.

Tolerant talk and covert racist discourse

Van Dijk (1982) has identified 'stereotype talk' where people join in prejudiced discourse for reasons of social co-operation with those whose views they do not share. I would suggest that there is also 'tolerant talk' involving prejudiced people participating in anti-racist discourse to which they would have an ideological objection. Covert racist discourse embeds such 'tolerant talk' in the context of a prejudiced ideological intention.

Beneath the tolerant layer, we find an *us* versus *them* dichotomy as in the editorial cited earlier:

Excerpt 5

And when the whites are ejected, or murdered or both, who would be left to run the country?
South Africa would slip, inexorably, into near anarchy as happened in Uganda and other tinpot African countries.

Complex symbols

Complex symbols represent 'whites' as [victims of violence or murder] [orderly] and [peaceful] and 'blacks', symbolized by Uganda, with the features [aggressor], [murderer] and [tinpot].

'Tribal fighting' is identified with blacks only. The contrast 'once great nation' and 'grimy Third World backwater' assumes two symbols of blacks from overt racism, [-clean], [-progress].

Playing down

Among rhetorical devices discussed by Gruber and Wodak (1992, pp. 14-20) is 'Verharmlosung', playing down the offensiveness of the racism diminishing the racist aspect of a proposition, e.g. by blaming the victim, implying an alliance between aggressor and victim, justifying racism by citing a member of the 'class' of victims rejecting the offence or playing it down, and ironizing it, perhaps by overstatement as in excerpt 6:

Excerpt 6

'Es besteht kein Zweifel, daß bis zu 1,5 Millionen getötet wurden.' Der größte Teil durch Gas. ['There is no doubt that up to 1.5 million were killed.' The majority by gas.] (Gruber and Wodak, 1992, p. 54)

Some comparative remarks on overt and covert racism in discourse

Both overt and covert racism make use of complex symbols such as those mentioned by van Dijk (1982) - fear of numbers, 'they take our jobs and use our social services', unfairness. But the difference lies in the 'apparent objectivity' of covert racist discourse.

In a more concealed way, covert discourse presents the same *us* versus *them* dichotomy as the discourse of overt racism, with complex symbols representing, for instance, 'whites' (as in the editorial) as civilized, orderly and peaceful, and the 'blacks' as backward, dirty, and violent.

While overt racist discourse is intended for the like-minded to strike a note of concord in them, covert racist discourse can have the effect of confusing the uncommitted into accepting a racist position as a rational and broad-minded one.

Conclusion

This paper has raised a small number of issues in reference to one written text and two radio talkback conversations. The field of study is not only a productive one; it is one where linguists can play some role in diminishing impediments to a just and harmonious society. Not only will there be a need for guidance on when a text, whether written or spoken, is racist. There will hopefully also be a demand for educational programmes and policies for the identification and avoidance of racism in discourse.

8 Power and Ideology in Different Discursive Practices

JULIETA HAIDAR AND LIDIA RODRIGUEZ

Introduction

The central issue of this paper is the relationship between discourse, ideology, and power. It is based on the French approach to discourse analysis, which proposes that *discursive practices* go beyond merely accomplishing linguistic rules but also comprise more complex processes, such as the maintenance of power and the reproduction of ideology. Taking into account conditions of discourse production and reception, the paper analyses several discursive devices utilized to reproduce ideology and maintain power in social discourse.

The main objective of the analysis is to define the degree to which these discursive devices support peace or favour violence. That is, do they constitute mechanisms that defend and support *or* that criticize or attack the established power structure and social inequality? Do they lend support to the alternative power of emerging social movements or not? The specific objectives of the analysis are twofold:

(1) To analyse how the dominant ideology is reproduced in discourse, thus preventing participants from becoming aware of the place of subordination or dominance they occupy in the social structure.

(2) To identify different devices that manifest ideology and power in several *discursive practices*.

Source of data

The analysis to be presented in this paper was based on previous research of the following types of discourse:

(1) *Textile Proletariat Trade Union Discourse (TPTD)*

The TPTD was shaped by a series of discussions regarding collective agreements between Puebla's textile industries and the 'Workers' and Peasants' Revolutionary Federation' (FROC) trade union, signed during the 1960s.[1]

(2) *CEU Student Discourse (CSD)*

The CSD consisted of a televised public debate between the University Student Council (CEU) and representatives of the National Autonomous University of Mexico at the beginning of 1987.[2]

(3) The *Subordinated Urban Group Discourse (SUGD)* and the *Dominant Urban Group Discourse (DUGD)*

The SUGD and the DUGD discourses consisted of excerpts taken from interviews conducted as part of an ongoing research project ('El Habla de Monterrey') concerning the crisis experienced in Mexico in 1985 (especially in Monterrey).[3]

Though the four discourse types imply inter-subject relations between the addressers and their interlocutors, here we take into account only the production of the addressers, whom we call 'subjects of discourse'.

Discourse

Our definition of 'discourse' is in accordance with the postulates of the French approach to discourse analysis. That is, we define discourse as every unit of language larger than a sentence that (1) accomplishes syntactic, semantic and pragmatic rules, (2) is ruled by the conditions of its production and reception, and (3) constitutes a distinctive sociocultural practice that is institutionalized to a greater or lesser degree.

Discursive practices

The definition of the term 'discursive practices' is based on the above. That is, *discursive practices* are understood as happenings which essentially fall into the production and reproduction of social, historical, and cultural life manifesting not only linguistic mechanisms but also devices of a different order, such as those that reproduce ideology and contribute to maintaining existing power structures. This conception of *discursive practices* implies at least three other considerations that need to be taken into account in the analysis (Haidar, 1992):

(1) The sharp division between what is said and what is done must be eliminated.[4]

(2) Like all sociocultural practices, *discursive practices* shape addressers and receivers precisely through their participation in the discourse.

(3) *Discursive practices*, considered as encoded and institutionalized social practices that are not only external to but also constitutive elements of discourse, can be rigorously analysed only by taking into account their conditions of production and reception. These conditions impregnate and leave their marks on discourse although these marks may not be directly perceived by the addresser and receiver and may go through long series of mediations (De Ipola, 1982).

In the first section we will describe *discourse conditions of production and reception*, and in the second section, analyse discursive devices of power and ideology.

Discourse conditions of production and reception

The analysis will present results that refer to three ways of understanding *discourse conditions of production and reception*, namely (1) *discourse possibility conditions*, (2) *inter-discursive processes*, and (3) *imaginary formations*.[5]

Discourse possibility conditions

As Foucault (1972, 1980) points out, what is expressed in discourse is nothing more than the repressive presence of what has been excluded from it. In other words, *discourse possibility conditions*, which operate through *rules of exclusion*, determine what can and what cannot be said in a given society or in a given social context. These *rules of exclusion* influenced the selection of topics discussed in the four discourses analysed as follows:

(1) Textile Proletariat Trade Union discourse (TPTD)

In the textile proletariat trade union discourse (TPTD), leaders are not allowed to talk about matters which might lead to worker dissidence. In consequence, any reference to 'worker exploitation' or 'the class struggle' is avoided; instead, there appear euphemisms, such as 'worker-employer conflicts' and 'worker-employer problems', which dissimulate what is being excluded from the discourse. Moreover, objects of discourse are imposed: 'friendly worker-employer relations', 'harmonious worker-employer relations', 'modernization of the textile industry', 'the textile industry crisis'. The requirements of the *rules of exclusion* are imposed on discourse like grammatical rules, shaping the ideology and power devices which operate to support the established power structure.

(2) CEU Student discourse (CSD)

In CEU student discourse (CSD), the forbidden object of discourse is 'politics'; however, the student leaders do not respect that rule of exclusion and include these themes in their discourse. This rhetorical discourse strategy acts against the institutionalized power in the university and favours student petitions. Simultaneously, however, the students' leaders are forced to talk about objects of discourse imposed by the university administration, i.e. academic reforms and excellence, democracy, etc.

(3) Subordinated and Dominant Urban Group Discourse (SUGD and DUGD)

The subjects of the subordinated urban group exclude from their discourse some aspects of the crisis which they know nothing about, such as foreign debt, monetary devaluation, as well as the ascription of any responsibility for the crisis to their employers; subjects of the dominant urban group discourse seem to be the only ones who are able to speak about such matters. On the other hand, neither group refers to 'third world economic dependence' or the Mexican situation within capitalism. The manifestation of these *rules of exclusion* makes evident the operation of ideological devices in, at least, two ways:

(1) subjects of the subordinated group do not question the generally accepted ideology in Monterrey[6] which ascribes only good qualities to the employers, and

(2) subjects of both subordinated and dominant groups reaffirm an ideological position which supports the idea that the only cause of Mexican subordination to international economic power is internal.

Inter-discursive processes

The dialectics of *inter-discursive processes* imply that a previous discourse is present in a later discourse. That is, *discursive practices* are interrelated. Some manifestations of these processes in the discourses analysed are as follows:

(1) CEU Student Discourse (CSD)

In CSD, there is reference to discourses about events that took place in the past, quite some time before the actual discourse, e.g. the discourses of the 1968 student movement, the previous administration and the political parties, PSUM and PRT. There is also reference to discourse that took place at the same time as the student discourse: to the discourse of the present University administration, the trade union and to academic and political party discourses; to discourse produced by the Chancellor and other National Autonomous University authorities, the University Council, the PAN party and other conservative sectors. *Inter-discursive processes* appear more frequently as indirect discourse in the televised debate as well as in its references in the press and less frequently as direct discourse using citation as a discursive strategy.

(2) Subordinated and Dominant Urban Group Discourse

In urban group discourse practices (SUGD and DUGD), diachronic *inter-discursive processes* (referring to past events) are manifested through a continuous comparison of the crisis situation to its historical antecedents. On the other hand, synchronic *inter-discursive processes* (the interweaving into the subjects' discourse of other discourses proceeding from different present time events) are evident in the continuous reference to (1) official and other discourses transmitted by the mass media (e.g. about the Government's Austerity Plan and the possible Mexican entrance to the GATT as ways of dealing with the economic crisis), and (2) the interviewed subjects' daily discourses, in which it is common to include references to public opinion about the same crisis.

The prejudices and stereotypes which appear in both types of *inter-discursive processes* support national, regional and social group ideologies. Subjects of discourse directly maintain these ideologies (through identification operations) and, indirectly, the established power structure, as can be seen in the following two excerpts from the DUGD:

> *Excerpt 1*
>
> You [tú] can't make a comparison between yourself [tú] and the poor people. Many of them are poor because they want to be so, because they don't want to work. Instead of improving their condition, they say they don't need anything. We have heard that they say 'I don't need anything', and their house is falling down; then, you don't understand the way these people think.
>
> *Excerpt 2*
>
> Everyone has the opinion that Mexico should enter the GATT, that the solution is the liberalization of prices, but everyone knows that there is another purpose beyond that. Who is proposing the liberalization of

prices? The private sector. Why do they want to do so? Just to increase prices and to finish plundering our country.

In the first excerpt, group ideologies support the idea that poor people's attitudes are the most important cause of their economic situation and, in the second, national ideologies maintain that the crisis is mainly caused by people in the private sector whose interests are given priority over that of the national economy.

Imaginary formations

In his discussion of discourse conditions of production and reception Pêcheux (1969) refers to imaginary formations, i.e. the representations that the subjects of discourse make about themselves, about their interlocutor, and about the object of discourse. According to Pêcheux, subjects do not perceive themselves as single individuals but in terms of the position they occupy in the social structure. They are similarly perceived by their interlocutors. Through the imaginary formations their individuality is transformed into that of boss, chairman, company manager, chief, worker, employee, etc., enabling the interlocutor to anticipate their responses and plan his/her discursive strategies. Thus, imaginary formations function as ideological devices and must be so analysed.

(1) Textile Union Proletariat Discourse (TPTD)

The following excerpts illustrate the *imaginary formations* that a trade union leader of the working class makes about himself and his interlocutor (subject of the dominant class) in textile proletariat trade union discourse (TPTD):

Excerpt 3

Due to the hard situation proposed by the industrialists, workers have been forced to look for a better way to defend their interests.
(*Resurgimiento*, 9 January 1960).

Excerpt 4

In spite of the willingness shown by the workers to achieve a respectable agreement with the employers to sign a new collective work agreement, the industrialists have refused absolutely and flatly to grant any improvement in wages.
(*Resurgimiento*, 29 June 1968).

The representation of the opposition between the working and the dominant classes in the above excerpts can be analysed as follows:

Working class	*Dominant class*
healthy labour	ill-intentioned resistance
fair goals	evident ill will
spirit of solidarity	negative attitude
goodwill	posture of excessive pride
dignified posture	well-known manoeuvres

While, on the surface, this opposing representation of two social classes suggests that the trade union leader is seeking to achieve the aims of the workers, in fact, it is just a discursive device to trick the workers. It is a strategy to control the workers and to prevent any dissidence, thus favouring both the government and private enterprise. In this way, fetishism processes, which disguise the true intent of the trade union leader, are used to support the established power structure.[7]

(2) CEU Student Discourse

Imaginary formations in the CEU student discourse (Haidar, 1988) are evident in excerpts 5-9, corresponding to three phases of the debate. At the beginning, the CEU discourse appears to be vindictive even though there were some divergences:

Excerpt 5

I exhort you, members of the Student Council, to let the university spirit prevail in the heart of this round-table discussion ... and let us make full use of the rights that our legislation and our customs offer to all the university students.
(university administration's representative, 6 January 1987)

During the days before the strike, there is a significant contrast in the argumentation by the CEU. The discourse was not so vindictive and a more reasoned rebuttal was initiated:

Excerpt 6

I urge you to consider the point that one of the central elements in the critical tradition of this university is change within the institution ... We are not far from the same vision, a university with socially committed researchers, teachers and students.
(university administration's representative, 23 January 1987).

Excerpt 7

What has to be clearly stated is that there are issues that we are not to abandon; we are sick and tired of this university, and not only the students ... The sensitivity that they claim to have had when they made the proposal, which I think doesn't reflect the CEU's position ...
(CEU, 23 January 1987)

On the last day of the debate, some hours before the students' strike, the polemical style of the discourse increased and it was impossible to reach a consensus although the word 'consensus' was continuously repeated:

Excerpt 8

I would like to start my speech by saying clearly that in fact, unfortunately, it was not possible for this special committee to achieve the consent of the two parties. (We would like) to ask the Student Council that, as soon as they have another proposal, to meet with us again to discuss it.
(last participation of the university administration's representative, 28 January 1987)

Excerpt 9

... we shall defend the people's rights, we shall defend to the ultimate consequences the right to be students because the young people of today will be the men of tomorrow. We will defend our University, we will defend our mother country. We are not tired ... We are preparing the strike ... to demonstrate the strength and the consensus the Student Council has. (CEU, 28 January 1987).

In all three phases the opposing *imaginary formations* present in the discourse-power relation can be synthesized as:

CEU Committee	*Administrative Committee*
defiant	conciliatory
challenging	slow
impressive	calm
passionate	neutral
emphatic	hieratic
vigorous	indifferent

(3) Subordinated and Dominant Group Discourse (SUGD and DUGD)

In the urban group discourses (SUGD and DUGD), *imaginary formations* support and manifest attitudes of insecurity (SUGD) and confidence (DUGD). Moreover, they predispose members of each group to support the power structure with members of the subordinated group recognizing their subordination as 'natural' (excerpt 10) and members of the dominant group regarding their dominance as a privilege of their social group (excerpt 11):

Excerpt 10

Well, let me tell you something, I don't know how to write well, right? I never went to school; I don't know, I wouldn't know how to answer your question very well. No, I don't know how things can be improved, do I? Because ... (SUGD)

Excerpt 11

The crisis is going to be worse if we are to continue buying dollars. It is going to be harder. Our currency is losing its value, and it is not the Government who makes the currency valuable, but we, we who look for another currency to take the place of ours, isn't that so ? ... Look I'm a 'priista' [PRI-follower, the party in power in Mexico since 1933] and I believe in the Revolution. It has given us family unity, which is the link within the society. (DUGD)

Discursive devices of power and ideology

Discourse acts and power

A discourse act[8] refers to an action which is accomplished through the enunciation of a discourse. It consists of a sequence of micro-acts which constitute the discourse, render it coherent, and condition the production of certain discourse strategies in distinct *discursive practices*. Table 8.1 exemplifies the macro-act of polemicizing (Haidar, 1980, p. 140). It is comprised of three discourse micro-acts.

Table 8.1
Discourse acts and power

MACRO-ACT OF POLEMICIZING		
POLEMICAL-vindictive	POLEMICAL-directive	POLEMICAL-solidary
↓	↓	↓
Denouncing the adversary 1 (textile bourgeoisie)	Denouncing the adversary 2 (worker dissidence) for maintaining power to accomplish the consensus	Denouncing the adversary 1 (textile bourgeoisie) for supporting the state

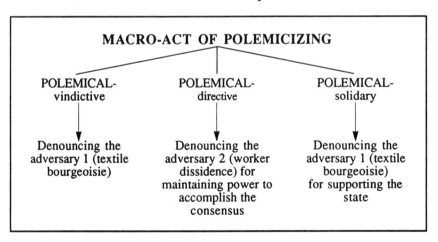

(1) As indicated in Table 8.1, the polemical-vindictive micro-act denounces its adversary. Thus, in excerpt 12, the Puebla textile proletariat denounce the textile bourgeoisie and, at the same time, present petitions before them, thus submitting to their power:

Excerpt 12

At midnight of the tenth day of this month, the textile industrialists' insolent behaviour provoked the placing of placards signalling a strike in all factories controlled by the FROC in the state of Puebla. Since a revision to the agreement was proposed, the employers' representatives have not concealed their perverse intentions of counteracting the good intentions of the workers, who were trying to keep the talks on good terms in order to fix the basis for the new agreement.
(*Resurgimiento*, 24 February 1962)

(2) The polemical-directive micro-act denounces a second adversary so as to maintain the power necessary to reach a consensus. In excerpt 13 worker dissidence is reported by members of the proletariat, who, at the same time, emphatically condemn these actions:

Excerpt 13

... By the legal and moral authority invested in it, ... has condemned without reservation the interference of elements outside the union due to the danger they represent ... because they try to confuse and divide the workers. .... That is why the workers themselves should reject them forcefully and without consideration.
(*Resurgimiento*, 12 August 1967).

(3) The polemical-solidary micro-act is used by the proletariat (represented by its leaders) to submit to the power of the state as in excerpt 14:

Excerpt 14

... President López Mateos answered categorically: 'My government is, within the Constitution, of the left-wing'. ... As for the much criticized term 'left-wing', it has its legal basis in the exact execution of the constitutional ordinances and should not be used to refer to the Russian Revolution nor the present Soviets because, in terms of history, they are from an earlier epoch ... 'Go ahead, Mr. President, because the working class is with you!'
(*Resurgimiento*, 16 August 1960)

Ideological stereotypes

Stereotypes are understood to be an amalgam and conjunction of petrified features that are used by subjects in a discourse to identify themselves and the objects of their discourse, positively or negatively. All stereotypes are a manifestation of power and ideology. The following examples are taken from the trade union discourse.

(1) The slogan of the trade union newspaper, *Resurgimiento*, 'Class struggle is inevitable while there exist the exploited and the

exploiters' is a negative stereotype[9] that hides the real trade union ideology, which is opposed to class struggle.

(2) 'Harmonious worker-employer relations' is a positive stereotype that hides social class antagonism.

(3) 'The alliance between state and working class' is another stereotype; it hides the fact that the trade union does not defend its supposedly allied class, but the bourgeoisie.

These three stereotypes are the result of fetishism processes, which by disguising actual social conditions further serve to maintain the ideological consensus.

Personal pronouns as discursive indicators of power and ideology

Rodríguez (1993, in print) has analysed the use of the pronouns 'yo' [I], 'nosotros' [we], 'tú' [you], 'usted' (respectful formula of address), and 'uno' [one] as manifestations of ideological devices in subordinated urban group discourse (SUGD) and dominant urban group discourse (DUGD). The results are represented in Table 8.2:

Table 8.2
The use of personal pronouns related to ideology and power

Subordinated urban group discourse	*Dominant urban group discourse*
scant use of 'yo' [I] and frequent use of 'uno' [one], an identification operation, by which the subject speaks in the name of the community	frequent use of 'yo' [I], which manifests subjective illusions of originality and discourse freedom
symmetrical respect treatment manifested in the use of 'usted' [you], respectful formula of address, by both the interviewer and the interviewed	asymmetrical respect treatment in the language of power manifested in the use of 'usted' [you], respectful formula of address by the interviewer and 'tú' [you], the familiar formula of address by the interviewed
frequent use of *exclusive* 'nosotros' [we], an identification operation, by which the subjects adhere to their social or family group	frequent use of *inclusive* 'nosotros' [we], an identification operation, by which the subjects share their identity with their interlocutor as Mexicans and Northerners

The use of personal pronouns is a device for the exercise of power. In the following two excerpts (15 and 16) power distance is manifested in the contrast: (1) between the frequent use of 'uno' ('one' - a pronoun used to speak in the name of the group) by subjects of the SUGD and the authoritarian language of the DUGD, marked by the frequent use of 'yo' [I], and (2) between the use of 'tú' [you], a more familiar formula of address by subjects of the DUGD and the respectful formula of address 'usted' [you] by the subjects of the SUGD.

Excerpt 15

To tell the truth, one is ashamed because one doesn't want to earn what one earns there; then one goes back home, and gets a job once in a while, but it is not the same as being there, you ['usted'] see?

Excerpt 16

I think that the crisis is a confidence crisis, confidence in government, because if you ['tú'] have money, the first thing you ['tú'] do most of the time, is buy dollars. This means that the money does not stay here for investment.

In excerpts 17-20, the use of 'nosotros' [we] shows how identification operations are strongly conditioned by ideological differences:

Excerpt 17

Well, on the one hand, it is OK, right? But many times, many people say that the government keeps us this way; we can't rebel because there are lots of children, that is why; because if we were like the ones who lived a long time ago, you ['usted'] would see, there would be other people in the government. However, people are not satisfied.

Excerpt 18

We are all poor because no one has money enough, but there are people who are not as poor, right? We are as in a ladder, our lives are a step. I'm here, and there's someone else underneath, and that one cannot live the way I do, right?

Excerpt 19

We [i.e. all Mexicans] have always liked circus and bread, on which the politics of any state of the world are based.

Excerpt 20

It is not my intention to discriminate, but you can see them [the people from the south of Mexico]; they are brown, small, worse fed than oneself.

In excerpts 17 and 18 (SUGD), the addresser uses the pronoun 'nosotros' [we] to refer only to him/herself and other poor people, without any inclusion of the interlocutor. This preferential use of 'nosotros' [we] in SUGD manifests group ideologies. On the other hand, in excerpt 19 (DUGD) the pronoun 'nosotros' [we] refers to all Mexican people (including the interlocutor); and in excerpt 20 (also from DUGD), the addresser uses the pronoun 'you' [tú] to talk about himself (he is the one who has seen that the Southerners are worse fed, smaller and darker than the Northerners), making it appear that his interlocutor (the receiver) could have the same perception in a similar situation. In both cases (excerpts 18 and 19), with or without realizing or desiring it, the receiver becomes an 'accomplice' of the prejudices expressed by the addresser through this use of 'we' and 'you'. Classified as 'inclusive pronouns', their use in this manner constitutes a very efficacious ideological naturalization device.

Modal verbs

In the present analysis we understand 'modality' to be the subjectivization of discourse, in other words, the way in which the addresser of the discourse manifests his/her view, though in an objective manner. 'Modality' can be used to express a subjective appreciation of facts, through the choice of adverbs (e.g. 'probably' versus 'certainly'), adjectives (e.g. 'wonderful', 'terrible', 'awful'); through the selection of some nouns (e.g. 'disturbances' versus 'riots') or verbs (e.g. 'protest' versus 'scandalize'). To study 'modality', we analysed the use of diction verbs (e.g. 'say', 'affirm', 'argue', 'deny') which refer to a verbal action, and opinion verbs (e.g. 'I think that ...', 'I believe that ...', 'I consider that ...'). Table 8.3 presents a few of the results from Rodríguez (1993):

Table 8.3
Use of modal verbs as a manifestation of power and ideology

Subordinated group discourse	*Dominant group discourse*
scant use of performatives	frequent use of performatives
preference of relic-citations and culture-citations (as proverbs)	use of proof-citations as well as relic-citations and culture-citations
preference for implicit modality	preference for explicit modality
use of lesser adhesion/certitude verbs	use of greater adhesion/certitude verbs

Regarding the use of diction verbs we found that the following three types of discursive devices were used quite differently in SUGD and DUGD:

(1) Utterances in which content performatives (i.e., the enunciation of the verb accomplishes the stated action) are much more frequent in DUGD; for example, 'te aseguro que ...' ['I assure you that ...'], 'yo digo que ...' ['I say that ...'].[10]

(2) Proof-citations (Maingueneau, 1976) ("I saw in some flyers in Guadalajara: 'If you didn't vote, don't complain'") are used more frequently by the subjects in the DUGD, while both groups share the use of culture-citations (e.g. proverbs) and relic-citations (e.g. citations from the Bible).

(3) Indicators of discourse exclusion rules, such as, 'no puedo decir mentiras', ['I can't lie'], 'no quiero decir maldiciones' ['I don't want to say bad words'], appear continuously in DUGD, but not in SUGD.

In respect of opinion verbs, the analysis indicates an evident preference by the subjects in the DUGD for explicit modality marked by the constant use of authoritarian language, indicated in the use of greater adhesion or certitude modality formulae, such as 'tengo entendido que ...' ['I have understood that ...'], 'creo que ...' ['I believe that ...'], in their meaning of conviction, 'pienso que ...' ['I think that ...'], and 'estoy convencido de que ...' ['I am convinced that ...']. On the other hand, subjects in the SUGD show preference for implicit modality and, when explicit, indicate it by the use of lesser adhesion verbs such as 'se me hace que ...' ['It seems to me that ...'], 'siento que ...' ['I feel that ...'], 'creo que ...' ['I believe that ...'], in their meaning of doubt.

These uses of diction verbs and opinion verbs are closely connected to *imaginary formations* which, in turn, are related to the place that subjects of each group occupy in the socio-economic structure.

Although in SUGD and DUGD, the use of personal pronouns (personal deixis) and modality do not have the evident effect shown (to a greater or lesser degree) in political discourses, these discursive devices manifest an ideological process through which social inequality is reaffirmed, supporting the maintenance of the conditions that reproduce power as the privilege of certain groups.

Conclusion

Discourse, considered as a product of codified and institutionalized social practices, can only be rigorously analysed by taking into account its conditions of production and reception, understood not only as external, but also as constitutive elements of discourse. These conditions impregnate and leave their marks on discourse at least in the following ways:

(1) the *exclusion rules* determine the possibility of discourse emergence,

(2) ideologies and power are manifested through references to other discourses, the selection of these references and types of citation, and

(3) the various attitudes expressed in a discourse are determined by the *imaginary formations* that the addresser makes of him/herself, of the interlocutor and of the object of discourse.

As for discursive devices of ideology and power, we have found that they are not only proper to political discourse but can also be identified in *discursive practices* as neutral as the conversations recorded for an interview with a student with merely social aims (e.g. SUGD and DUGD). In the four discourses analysed we have found some differences related to medium of discourse (spoken versus written) and degree of formality, which are manifested:

(1) through the selection of informal versus formal terms,

(2) through repetitions and stammering in spoken discourse versus the formal vocabulary and the previous planning of written discourse,

(3) through the greater use of explicit performatives (e.g. 'I assure you ...', 'I promise you ...', 'I declare ...') in institutional discourses (TPTD and CSD) than in non-institutional discourses (SUGD and DUGD).

At the same time, we have found some similarities in the use of the following discursive strategies:

(1) the manifestation of discourse exclusion rules according to which any reference that can disturb the 'social peace' (a 'peace' supported by inequality and lack of justice) is avoided,

(2) the constitution of addresser and receiver as social subjects,

(3) the addresser's tendency to support his/her disagreements with others and to justify his/her positions by reaffirming the power of some groups and the subordination of others,

(4) the use of *ideological naturalization strategies* (Reboul, 1980), through which prejudices are presented as products of common knowledge.

Since in such different *discursive practices* as trade union discourse and semi-formal and semi-informal research interviews, similar discursive strategies are present, we can infer, firstly, that these similarities are related to the shared socio-political structure; secondly, that similar discursive mechanisms are present in day-to-day conversations; and thirdly, that through all *discursive practices* (and not only in political discourse), the dominant ideology is reinforced and the consensus accomplished.

Through these justifications and ideological rationalizations, subjects of discourse are trapped by established power and become simple repeaters of arguments that implicitly defend inequality, at social as well as national and international levels, indirectly propitiating violence and obstructing peace. As a result, the indispensable premise for obtaining and preserving peace, i.e. the recognition of the equal rights and responsibilities of all human beings, is neither recognized nor applied in this heterogeneous, postmodern world. The recognition of this discourse-power-ideology relation should be an important component of a university education since it provides students with an awareness of their participation in supporting social inequality and, thus, their favouring violence in our unjust social systems.

Notes

1 TPTD is a written and formal discourse subtype analysed for fetishism processes, understood as alienation from and disguise of reality (Haidar, 1980).

2 The main objective of this analysis was to identify discourse strategies used in a polemical situation (Haidar, 1988).

3 These interviews, semi-formal and semi-informal spoken discourse subtypes, were analysed to identify contrasting discursive strategies produced by two socially different groups (Rodríguez, 1993, in print).

4 Common sense admits this in social discourse in general, and particularly in political or in everyday discourse, where it is used as a persuasive strategy.

5 The most well-known conception of *discourse conditions of production and reception* is its relation with conjuncture, perhaps because social sciences emphasize it. This relation is often established externally by the circumstances surrounding its production and reception, i.e. the discourse conjuncture. Conversely, we understand conjuncture to be a constitutive part of discourse determined by the economic-political structure. In our research we have found that conjuncture impregnates the discourses analysed on all the levels of analysis (Robin, 1973, 1976). Therefore, any

synthesis of these results would be insufficient and ambiguous. For this reason, we have not included them in this paper.

6 In Monterrey, the city where the groups interviewed live, employers protected their workers even before it was required under law and far beyond what was required (contrary to the rest of Mexico). Consequently, people in the city ascribe only good qualities to their employers and fail to perceive their responsibility for social inequality in Monterrey, which was the greatest in all of Latin America (Vellinga, 1988a, 1988b) at the time the interviews were conducted (i.e., in 1985).

7 This complex control mechanism is explained if it is taken into account that leaders of all Mexican trade unions can only be affiliated to the official party (PRI) which works in favour of employers. Moreover, it is noted that trade unions in other countries use similar control mechanisms to support 'social peace' based on social inequality.

8 This category results from a theoretical development from Austin's (1962) and Searle's (1969) category of 'speech acts' and the pragmatic proposal of language acts as well as van Dijk's (1980b) category of 'speech acts'.

9 This remains a slogan since it is not thematically developed in *Resurgimiento* during the entire decade under study. Its function is obstructed at the level of the trade union discursive practice itself.

10 Following Ducrot (1979, 1981) we point out that the performative value is presented, not only in the pronoun 'I', the first person of the statement, but also every time the subject carries out the stated action, as in "then you say, 'what a shame!'". In this case, although the statement is expressed in the generic second person pronoun ('you'), the performative value is accomplished since the subject is actually doing what she stated through the pronunciation of the verb 'to say'.

9 The Role of Language in European Nationalist Ideologies[1]

JAN BLOMMAERT AND JEF VERSCHUEREN

Introduction

In his book on *Nations and nationalism since 1780*, Hobsbawm (1990, p. 183) concludes that "the phenomenon [of nationalism] is past its peak". Before he gets to this conclusion (apparently written some time in 1989, still before German reunification became a realistic possibility and before the process of fragmentation in some countries of the old communist bloc had gained momentum) he shows quite convincingly, and almost prophetically, that a new 'Europe of nations' in the Wilsonian sense (with independent entities such as Catalonia, Corsica, Slovenia, Estonia, etc.) could not produce "a stable or lasting political system" (p. 177). For one thing, "the first thing most such hypothetical new European states would do is, almost certainly, apply for admission to the European Economic Community, which would once again limit their sovereign rights, ..." (p. 177).

Indeed, nation-states with highly autonomous 'national economies' probably belong to the past. However, it is far from clear that such a confrontation with economic reality, which will no doubt change the historical content and direction of nation-building processes, has any direct influence on nationalism from an ideological perspective. After all, as Hobsbawm demonstrates equally convincingly, the essence of nationalism from the nineteenth century onwards has been the definition of 'imagined communities' along conceptual lines out of touch with 'objective reality' (a theme also developed in Barth, ed., 1982, and by Anderson, 1983).

An assessment of the ideological processes involved requires access to 'the view from below'. But,

> That view from below, i.e. the nation as seen not by governments and the spokesmen and activists of nationalist (or non-nationalist) movements, but by the ordinary persons who are the objects of their action and propaganda, is exceedingly difficult to discover. (Hobsbawm, 1990, p. 11)

This is further complicated by the fact that

> ... national identification and what it is believed to imply, can change and shift in time, even in the course of quite short periods. (Hobsbawm, 1990, p. 11)

Hobsbawm adds that "this is the area of national studies in which thinking and research are most urgently needed today" (p. 11). To counterbalance the remark about the 'exceeding difficulty' of the research in question, he observes:

> Fortunately social historians have learned how to investigate the history of ideas, opinions and feelings at the sub-literary level, so that we are today less likely to confuse, as historians once habitually did, editorials in select newspapers with public opinion. (Hobsbawm, 1990, p. 11)

This paper is intended to contribute (1) to the further exploration of the topic identified in the above quotations, and (2) to the development of an adequate methodology to approach the complexities of ideology research. It is to be situated in the context of a wider research project intended to provide a historical snapshot of mainstream European thinking about nations and national identification. The main data base consists of a comprehensive collection of articles on ethnic conflicts (whether intra- or internationally), separatist and unificational movements, and other topics - such as minority politics - involving issues of group identity associated with 'nationality', from the mainstream daily press in about twelve European countries (both East and West), over a three-month period in 1991. Though the period itself may not be long enough for observable ideological changes to take place, the temporal demarcation will make it possible to draw historical comparisons with well-documented periods from the past; moreover, similar snapshots can be taken at any time in the future.[2]

From a methodological point of view, the nature of the data base might raise some worries directly related to Hobsbawm's remark concerning the earlier habits of historians 'to confuse editorials in select newspapers with public opinion'. There are three ways in which the project avoids this problem.

First, the selection criterion for choosing the newspapers to be investigated has been that they should be mainstream publications which, together, have a maximal readership, but each of which has a different target audience. Small-circulation publications have been avoided because they are most likely to represent the opinions of a few people.[3] In practice, extremist texts (in any direction) have, as a result, rarely entered the corpus, though - depending on one's perspective - extremism of some kind may turn out to be the norm under certain circumstances and in some geographical areas.

Second, the investigation pays equal attention to regular news reports and editorials (which are more openly subject to personal interpretation and bias); the character of the texts is fully taken into account whenever conclusions are drawn from examples.

Third, and most importantly, more weight is attached to the implicit frame of reference, the supposedly common world of beliefs in which the reports (or the editorial comments) are anchored, than to the explicit statements made by the reporters (or commentators). This approach is crucial for the investigation of widely shared ideologies. And fortunately modern linguistics, in particular linguistic pragmatics, provides us with fully adequate tools to undertake exactly this kind of study. Briefly, the basic assumptions are:

(1) that the authors, just like any other language user in any other communicative context, are unable to express what they want to communicate in a fully explicit way,

(2) that their texts, therefore, leave implicit most of the assumptions they expect their readers to share with them, and

(3) that a careful analysis of those implicit assumptions will reveal a common frame of reference or 'ideology'.

It follows that isolated examples are never sufficient as evidence: coherence - manifested either as recurrence or as systematic absence - is necessary to warrant conclusions.[4] This article is based on a smaller pilot study in which some West European data[5] were scrutinized in view of the specific role which *language* plays in the overall picture of current nationalist ideologies. It goes without saying that our findings will have to be interpreted in the light of the regional restrictions on the corpus, a remark which should be kept in mind whenever we use the qualification 'European'.

Language as a distinctive feature

The significance of a non-issue

As a surface topic, worthy of an explicit treatment in its own right, language is strikingly absent in our corpus of reports on interethnic conflicts or on issues of 'national' identity or nation-building. But far from undermining any attempt to reveal a specific role for language in current nationalist ideologies from the start, this first observation has turned out to touch the very essence of popular linguistic ideology.

Language is raised to the level of an individual issue almost exclusively when reference is made to societies other than the one in which the report in question is itself to be situated. A case in point is a German report entitled 'Amerika und Einwanderung: Schmelztiegel oder Salatschüssel?' ['America and immigration: Melting pot or salad bowl?'], juxtaposed to an article on a dispute over voting rights at the municipal level for minority members in Germany. Though the physical juxtaposition of the two articles is clearly based on a judgement of topical relatedness, the German issue is phrased exclusively in terms of the sharing of political power and the possible infringement of ethnic German rights, whereas language is explicitly focused on as an issue in the United States:

> Heute schon spielen sich harte Kämpfe um die Sprache, um die Dominanz des Englischen ab, das vorläufig noch eine verbindende Kraft darstellt. (*Die Zeit*, 9 November 1990) ['Already today difficult battles are fought over language, the dominance of English, which - for the time being - still presents a unifying force.']

The Official English movement is indeed a sufficiently interesting phenomenon to deserve special mention in connection with the multi-ethnicity of the United States.[6] But implicit in this German report is the idea that the coherence of a society strongly benefits from the existence of just one language. It is not accidental that the quoted sentence follows an explicit statement to the effect that:

> Die ethnisch-rassische Koexistenz scheint zu gelingen solange die Wirtschaft einigermaßen floriert. ['Ethnic-racial coexistence seems to work as long as the economy is somewhat successful.']

Linguistic strife is presented as an important force towards social disintegration, triggered by a worsening economy. Because of the need for linguistic coherence, German as the only language of Germany is taken for granted. The issue, which is in reality as acute as in the American case (though there is not one single 'threatening' alternative such as Spanish in the United States), does not need to be mentioned. Thus, treating language as a non-issue in relation to German minority problems, only reveals how much is really taken for granted.

Language: A marker of identity

That language is seen as a unifying force should be clear from the above. Language assumes the character of a clear identity marker. Thus it appears prominently in an article on Spanish Basque nationalism (entitled

'Der Heimat bewußt: Die Basken - gastfreundlich aber nicht servil' ['Conscious of the 'Heimat': The Basques: hospitable but not humble']):

> Was steckt dahinter? Eine lange Geschichte der allerdings militanten Selbstbehauptung eines Volkes, dessen Herkunft ebenso wie die Herkunft seiner Sprache, des Euskara, den Ethnologen und Linguisten bis heute Rätsel aufgibt. ... Diese Ursprache ..."
> (*Die Zeit*, 16 November 1990) ['What's behind it (i.e. behind Basque nationalism)? A long history of clearly militant self-preservation of a people, of which the origin, as well as the origin of its language, Euskara, has until today been a mystery for ethnologists and linguists. ... This ancient language ...']

The language of the Basques, of which not enough may be known to designate it as 'Ursprache' (if such a designation has any meaning at all), becomes the romantic focus of the identity of the Basque people in a description which is reminiscent of nineteenth-century scholarship.

Natural discontinuities

Nevertheless, language is only one identity marker among others. Descent, history, culture, religion, and language are treated as a *feature cluster*. Their identificational function implies separability, a natural discontinuity in the real world. These discontinuities are 'nations' or 'peoples', i.e. natural groups, the folk perceptions of which conceptualize them in much the same way as species in the animal kingdom. Just as feathers are predictive of beaks, eggs, and an ability to fly, so is a specific language predictive of a distinct history and culture.[7]

Thus the absence of the feature 'distinct language' tends to cast doubts on the legitimacy of claims to nationhood. Consider the following statements from an article on the Ukraine, made in the context of references to the 'russification' of the republic:

> The poor old Ukraine has had a bad press. Both the Poles, who dominated the towns of the western part, and the Russians, who dominated those of the east and south, looked down on the Ukrainians as peasants, speaking jargon. The language itself varied greatly from region to region - in the west quite close to Polish, in the east sometimes indistinguishable from Russian. ... Politically, the Ukraine was underdeveloped ...
> (*The Guardian Weekly*, 4 November 1990)

Here the lack of a clearly distinct language is the first item in a list of indicators of cultural erosion or underdevelopment.

In some cases, language is offered as the only distinctive trait of a 'group'; others are not really needed since a distinctive language is predictive of a distinct group identity. This strategy is typically used when little-known ethnic groups are talked about. A case in point is the reporting on the Gagauz people in Moldavia:

> ... the defiant Turkish-speaking Gagauz districts [of Moldavia] ...
> (*Guardian Weekly*, 4 November 1990)
>
> ... the Turkish-speaking separatist Gagauz minority ...
> (*Guardian Weekly*, 11 November 1990)
>
> ... the Turkish-speaking Gagauz ...
> (*The Guardian*, 1 November 1990; *The Guardian*, 12 November 1990)
>
> ... de Gagaoezen, een Turkstalige minderheid ...
> (*NRC Handelsblad*, 2 November 1990) ['... the Gagauz, a Turkish-speaking minority ...']

The feature clustering underlying group identification is such a powerful cognitive mechanism that knowledge about one feature is assumed to be enough, especially when it concerns language. As a result, groups that are distinguished solely on the basis of a distinct language are often treated as 'real' ethnic groups. And as such, they can be presented as being involved in inter-*ethnic* conflicts, even if their unity along the other parameters of the expected feature cluster does not stand up to scrutiny:

> Les violences entre Moldaves et russophones ...
> (*Le Monde*, 6 November 1990) ['The violence between Moldavians and Russian-speakers ...']

In this report, 'Russian-speakers' (referred to alternatingly as 'minorité russe' or 'minorité russophone') are placed on a par with the Moldavians and the Gagauz. Here we see the dynamics of feature clustering at work. Though 'Russians' (the least-preferred denominator in this report) could be reasonably assumed to share some common aspects of ethnicity, 'Russian-speakers' can obviously be no more than a residual category, an extremely heterogeneous group of people who may come from all over the Soviet Union, united only by the fact that they speak Russian (though it is certain that not all of them speak it as their mother tongue, and though even this feature does not clearly distinguish them from the other groups, as will be shown below), and by the fact that they *cannot* be labelled as ethnic Moldavians or Gagauz. But nevertheless the 'Russian-speakers' are presented, in direct opposition with Moldavians and Gagauz, as an equally solid ethnic unit.

This misrepresentation of the social formations involved in the conflict clearly hampers a fair understanding of what goes on in Moldavia: by applying familiar categories, the impression of clear understanding is created while, in fact, neither the authors nor the readers of the articles have any familiarity with the people talked about. This is further illustrated by another characteristic of our data: after language has been introduced as a categorizing criterion, distinctive features other than language may be dragged in as soon as they are known, irrespective of whether in reality they play an identifying or distinguishing role or not. This leads to strange descriptions such as the following:

> ... de Gagaoezen - een aan de Turken verwante christelijke minderheid - ... (*NRC Handelsblad*, 5 November 1990) ['... the Gagauz - a Christian minority related to the Turks - ...']

Thus our data show the emergence of religion as a further identifying feature of the Gagauz a few days after the first reports, though Christianity in itself is precisely *not* a minority trait in Moldavia.

It may even be more surprising that this language-based identification is maintained though the distinguishing trait is almost in the same breath denied or downplayed:

> They [the Moldavians] claim the Gagauz are strongly Russianised; most speak Russian rather than Turkish and support Russian interests.
> (*The Guardian*, 1 November 1990)

Though this again casts doubt on the legitimacy of a movement (centred around people who have betrayed themselves by adopting another language), we will come back to this example below to demonstrate further aspects of the linguistic framing of nationalism.

Before going on, let us briefly point out that the clustering of language, descent, history, culture and religion, the strength of which we have been trying to demonstrate, is even extended to economic position. Remember the following quote:

> Die ethnisch-rassische Koexistenz scheint zu gelingen solange die Wirtschaft einigermaßen floriert.
> (*Die Zeit*, 9 November 1990) ['Ethnic-racial coexistence seems to work as long as the economy is somewhat successful.']

The relationship between (multi-)ethnicity and economic prosperity is a topic which deserves more than the few lines we can spend here. In general, there seems to be an intuitive, almost automatic, association between the rise of nationalism and economic problems. Thus a weak economy is a much favoured excuse for manifestations of racism. But if economic factors can trigger interethnic conflicts, ethnic groups must be seen as socio-economically undifferentiated wholes which act and react 'en masse' under economic pressure.[8] The economy, which may soothe slumbering interethnic conflicts in times of general prosperity, is seen as flexible and unstable, whereas ethnicity is seen as a stable and timeless element of social stratification, a stratification which largely coincides with socio-economic differences.

The different faces of homogeneism

Since the discontinuities - to pursue the lexical semantics metaphor further - are defined in terms of necessary and sufficient conditions which are so strongly clustered that even one of them may be sufficient to characterize a group entity, *homogeneity* (emphasizing the necessity of the necessary and sufficient conditions) is the norm *within the discontinuities* (i.e. the 'nations' or 'peoples') thus defined. Since such a view is so obviously naive, authors of most of the reports discussed would passionately deny adherence to it when challenged about this. But here we touch upon a deeply engrained dogma which is very coherently - though mostly implicitly - present in discourse about interethnic conflicts. Elsewhere (in Blommaert and Verschueren, 1991) we have called it the dogma of *homogeneism*: a view of society in which differences are seen as dangerous and centrifugal, and in which the 'best' society is suggested to be one without intergroup differences.

In other words, the ideal model of society is mono-lingual, mono-ethnic, mono-religious, mono-ideological. Nationalism, interpreted as the struggle to keep groups as 'pure' and homogeneous as possible, is considered to be a positive attitude within the dogma of homogeneism. Pluri-ethnic or pluri-lingual societies are seen as problem-prone, because they require forms of state organization that run counter to the 'natural' characteristics of groupings of people. This dogma appears to dominate Belgian (and European) immigrant policies (again, see Blommaert and Verschueren, 1991), and - as will be further demonstrated below - it is used as an interpretive frame (with the Soviet Union as evidence and example) even for situations outside of Europe in our corpus:

> Wie in der Sowjetunion stellt sich auch in Indien die Frage, ob ein Riesenreich, das aus derartig vielen ethnischen, religiösen, sprachlichen und kulturellen Splittern zusammengesetzt ist, zusammengehalten werden kann.
> (*Die Zeit*, 16 November 1990) ['As in the Soviet Union, the question also poses itself for India whether a giant empire consisting of such a plethora of ethnic, religious, linguistic and cultural fragments can be held together.']

The conceptual systematicity with which the norm of homogeneity turns language itself into an interethnic battlefield will be discussed in the section **Language in the Empire** below.

Though the norm of homogeneity is demonstrably present across Europe, the criteria along which homogeneous nations are defined differ substantially. Let us briefly look at some of the different forms of expression the norm can take. We find it in its purest ethnic form in the German press, where 'das Volk' is systematically contrasted with 'die Bevölkerung': 'the people' versus 'the population'. For instance, the caption accompanying a picture with Turkish immigrants reads:

> Soll nur das Volk oder die Bevölkerung auf kommunaler Ebene politisch mitentscheiden dürfen? Türken auf einem SPD-Fest in Berlin-Kreuzberg. (*Die Zeit*, 9 November 1990) ['Should only the people or the population participate in political decisions at the municipal level? Turks at an SPD-meeting in Berlin-Kreuzberg.']

Overtly, a clear position of tolerance is advocated:

> Deutschland wird, wie in der Geschichte schon oft, die Ausländer, die gekommen sind und bleiben wollen, 'integrieren'.
> (*Frankfurter Allgemeine*, 2 November 1990) ['Germany will, as often before in history, 'integrate' foreigners who have come and want to stay.']

Yet this claim is embedded in a plea for preserving voting rights at the municipal level for 'Staatsbürger' ['citizens'] and against giving them to 'Bewohner' or 'Einwohner' ['inhabitants']. That the plea is not so much intended to protect all those who have acquired German citizenship, but mostly ethnic Germans, is made abundantly - if unwittingly - clear:

> Mithin ist es konsequent, daß in Deutschland namens des Begriffs der Demokratie ... Versuche abgewehrt worden sind, die Begriffe Nation und Staat voneinander zu trennen und sie damit aufzulösen.
> (*Frankfurter Allgemeine*, 2 November 1990) ['Therefore it is logical that in Germany, in the name of democracy ... attempts have been thwarted to tear the notions nation and state apart and hence to annihilate them.']

The author continues:

> Bisher ist nichts Überzeugendes gesagt worden darüber, daß die Verwischung des Begriffs der über die Staatsbürgerschaft verfügenden Angehörigen einer Nation, die in der Handlungseinheit Staat über sich selbst bestimmen, irgendwelche Vorteile habe. ... Demokratie braucht fest umrissene Einheiten.
> (*Frankfurter Allgemeine*, 2 November 1990) ['So far, nothing convincing has been said to justify blurring the concept of a 'nation' constituted of dependents with a common citizenship who determine their own fate within the action unit 'state'. Democracy needs clearly defined units.']

In the context of this article, the author does not leave any doubt that those 'fest umrissene Einheiten' are nation-states, the homogeneity of which should not be broken: to the extent that immigrants are tolerable as participants in social and political life, they have to be 'integrated'.

But it is exactly at this juncture that the paradox - or the deadly logic - of a nationalist ideology becomes clear. As much as it requires 'integration', the definition of 'das Volk' in terms of a feature cluster makes that very process impossible. As soon as an 'Einwohner' or member of the 'Bevölkerung' has adapted to one parameter of Germanhood, any other feature may be arbitrarily focused on to preserve the difference. Thus, language is only one feature in the cluster. Just as

German Jews (even if indistinguishable in other respects) lacked the proper genetics, any migrant worker fluent in German and respecting all German laws and rules of public life, may still be stuck with the wrong descent, historical background, looks, religion: he or she cannot become a member of 'das Volk'; his or her presence inevitably breaks the 'natural groupings' of people, the homogeneity of nations, the strictly separable units needed for democracy. Just consider the categories introduced in the following sentence:

> Nur gebürtige Deutsche und diejenigen, die ihnen kraft 'Volkszugehörigkeit' oder durch späteren Erwerb der Staatsangehörigkeit gleichgestellt sind, dürfen wählen - ...
> (*Die Zeit*, 9 November 1990) ['Only those born as Germans and those who have been given the same rights on the basis of their 'membership in the people' or later naturalization, are allowed to vote - ...']

Of the two categories who have to be 'given' the rights which those born as Germans have 'naturally', the first group (including the 'Aussiedler', descendants of earlier German emigrants) are immediately defined as belonging to 'das Volk'. The second group will probably never make it: their children will be second-generation immigrants, not really 'gebürtige Deutsche'.

In contrast to the German emphasis on an ethnic definition of 'das Volk' (in terms of language, descent, culture, etc.), the French version of homogeneism stresses the importance of territoriality. The difference in emphasis has clear historical roots. The German quest for a nation-state was considerably facilitated by the spread of German dialects across a large part of Europe. Though only few people actively used a common language of culture, politically the geographical area in question had been so fragmented that language was not only a useful, but virtually the only possible, focus for unity. Moreover, by the time of German unification in the second half of the nineteenth century, European nationalism was taking a linguistic turn (expressed, inter alia, in the insertion of a language question in national censuses). By contrast, when France needed to identify 'le peuple' after the French revolution, the French language was no more than an administrative means for state-wide communication, a language which was shared (even in its dialectal variants) by less than 50 per cent of the population. As a result, the search for self-identification led to a reification of France itself as a natural and indivisible entity, the French 'people' consisting of everyone living in its territory. Though from the mid-nineteenth century onwards France has been 'successful' in imposing the French language and reducing the size of all its linguistic minorities, even today 'linguistic nationalism' is seen as a distinct type of nationalism with which the French do not ideologically associate themselves. Thus a sense of bemusement is hardly suppressed in an article on 'Les forcenés du nationalisme linguistique slovaque' ['The fanatics of Slovak linguistic nationalism']:

> Grévistes de la faim, ils campent devant le Conseil national slovaque depuis le vote, jeudi 25 octobre, d'une loi érigeant le slovaque en langue officielle de la Slovaquie.
> (*Le Monde*, 1 November 1990) ['These hunger strikers have been camping outside the Slovak national Council since the vote, on Thursday, 25 October, which made Slovak the official language of Slovakia.']

Thus having introduced the event ambiguously, leaving open the interpretation that the 'plusieurs dizaines de jeunes' ['several dozens of young people'] who are conducting a hunger strike, are protesting the new law passed by the 'forcenés' ['fanatics'] of linguistic nationalism, the author then catches the reader by surprise:

> Pour eux, cette loi est trop laxiste: ... ['For them, this law is too permissive: ...']

The hunger strikers are themselves the fanatics. They do not only want Slovak to be the official language, they want to take away any linguistic rights that the Hungarian, Gypsy, Polish, Ukrainian and German minorities within Slovakia might have.

In spite of this expression of astonishment concerning the lack of tolerance for linguistic discontinuity in the Slovak case, the territorially based French version of nationalism has as much trouble accepting discontinuities: within its borders, France is one. This is clearly expressed in the debate over Corsican separatism, and in particular the official acceptance of the very notion of a 'Corsican people'. That a debate over the fact that 'Le gouvernement reconnaît l'existence d'un "peuple corse"' (*Le Monde*, 2 November 1990) ['The government recognizes the existence of a 'Corsican people''] is at all necessary, and is treated as front-page news, is already significant. But the phrasing of that recognition is symptomatic of the French version of homogeneism:

> M. Mitterrand est intervenu pour que la notion de 'peuple corse' soit retenue en tant que 'composante du peuple français'.
> (*Le Monde*, 2 November 1990) ['M. Mitterrand has defended the acceptance of the notion of a 'Corsican people' as a 'component of the French people'.']

In spite of this rhetorical attempt to avert discontinuity, questions are raised about the constitutionality of the government decision, and even about its logical possibility; and it is ridiculed as 'le modèle polynésien' ['the Polynesian model'], with reference to earlier decisions concerning French Polynesia. The French press avoids any reference to what the German press identifies as an underlying problem for those who are disturbed by the decision:

> Sie sehen voraus, daß wo ein Volk ist, auch ein Staat sein müsse, und sie befürchten, daß nach dem korsischen auch ein 'bretonisches', ein 'baskisches' oder sogar ein 'elsässisches Volk' Ansprüche erheben könnte.
> (*Frankfurter Allgemeine*, 2 November 1990) ['They anticipate that where there is a people, there must also be a state, and they fear that after the Corsican also a 'Bretonic', a 'Basque' or even an 'Alsatian people' could be making demands.']

Corsican nationalists are reportedly satisfied, while the most avid opposition comes from Le Pen's *Front national (italics in the original)*:

> Le Front national "*souligne les responsabilité [sic] que prendraient les parlementaires, les fonctionnaires ou, même, les citoyens qui attenteraient aux liens institutionnels qui placent la Corse dans la République et aux droits historiques et moraux de la patrie française en Corse.*"
> (*Le Monde*, 3 November 1990) ['The Front national "*emphasizes the responsibilities that would be taken by those representatives, functionaries or even citizens who would make an attempt on the institutional ties which place Corsica within the Republic and on the historical and moral rights of the French fatherland in Corsica.*"']

Here again we find a fundamental paradox of nationalism: though grounded in the observation of 'existing' differences, once a separate entity has been defined, nationalism is unable to recognize the legitimacy of any smaller-scale (or larger) group identities.[9]

The data from the British press contain remarkably few references to ethnic or linguistic diversity within Britain. Still, one small article in *The Guardian* (entitled 'Welsh militants urge supporters to breed children "for the cause"') tells a lot. In this article, a meeting of Welsh nationalists is reported. One of their leaders is said to have pleaded for Welshmen to have as many children as possible, so as to perpetuate the Welsh language, in the following terms:

> If you cannot speak Welsh, you carry the mark of the Englishman with you every day. That is the unpleasant truth.
> (*The Guardian*, 12 November 1990)

Objectively, this is a strong radical statement, revealing a degree of fanaticism mostly associated with radical nationalists. The meeting could, therefore, easily be taken seriously. But the opposite happens. The tone of the entire article is mildly ironical. The proposal to breed children in order to perpetuate the Welsh language is ridiculed. Moreover, the article ends with the suggestion that this proposal is reminiscent of the German Nazi 'Mutterkreuz' - a suggestion which is strongly rejected by the speaker. But even this comparison, grave as it may sound on the surface, is basically ironic. Nationalism (or even more generally, ethnic diversity), at least within the United Kingdom, is treated as folklore: it is not to be taken seriously as a political movement in Britain. Welsh activists are sketched as picturesque, romantic people, who cherish old customs and values in a harmless way - harmless because of the strength of the centralized, English-speaking state.

In Belgium, homogeneism is most manifest in the domain of immigrant politics. That the Flemish and the Walloons run their own business, quite separately, is taken for granted (to the point where even arms sales can become a regional matter). Real problems of diversity (and the resulting destabilization) are caused only by the presence of immigrants of Maghrebine or Mediterranean descent. Although the presence of these foreign elements in Belgian society is officially declared to be a form of 'cultural enrichment' (invoking a suggestion of tolerance and openness from the Belgian side), a detailed analysis (see Blommaert and Verschueren, 1991, 1992, 1993b) reveals that Belgian society wants to be 'enriched' only in domains such as exotic cuisine, exotic music and dance - in sum, folklore. Socially, culturally, and linguistically, if not religiously, immigrants should 'integrate' or de-ethnicize themselves, to the point where, as one government party's policy document on immigrants states, 'Migrants should become Flemish'. An intriguing side-effect, but one which cannot be elaborated within the scope of this paper, is the observation that in the discourse about immigrants in Belgium, the age-old division between Flemish and Walloons seems to vanish. The formulation of an attitude towards immigrant minorities has caused the (re)construction of a common Belgian identity, thus allowing two clearly defined (and supposedly homogeneous) groups to form the core structure of a Belgian immigrant policy: 'Belgians' as opposed to 'Immigrants'. Needless to say that neither is, or has ever been, a homogeneous group. The illusion thus created demonstrates the power of homogeneism: it blanks out intra-societal differences such as age, sex, social status, power etc. and equates homogeneity with social harmony. Thus, language may play different roles at the rhetorical surface. But it is a constant ingredient at a deeper implicit level in all the cases of homogeneism reviewed above.

Of nations and tribes

Very little disagreement seems to exist with regard to the reality of 'nations' in Europe. As demonstrated above, the 'nation' is presented as a natural, objective and almost biological unit. People are divided on the basis of sex, age, and nation. In spite of the general tendency in our data to accept the existence - in 'reality' - of 'nations', explicit statements on the subject are rare in the corpus. Treating this reality as self-evident effectively hides the fact that it rarely stands up to scrutiny. A potentially classical example to disprove the existence of objective criteria of nationhood is a comparison between the Serbs and the Croats on the one hand, and the Flemish and the Dutch on the other. In the Serbian-Croat case, existing linguistic differences (underscored by a different orthography) have become highly symbolic for the discontinuity, whereas in the Flemish-Dutch case (where the linguistic differences are of almost exactly the same type and degree) language is the main symbol of cultural unity. On all other counts, the differences are completely analogous as well: e.g., history (Ottoman rule for Serbia versus Spanish rule for Flanders, resulting in long periods of political separation from Croatia and Holland, respectively); religion (Orthodox versus Catholic in the one case, Catholic versus Protestant/Calvinist in the other). In spite of its obviousness, not a single observation of this kind can be found in the corpus.

Interestingly, in the two explicit statements on the reality of nations which we have been able to find (one inside, and one outside the restricted corpus which is the starting point for the discussion in this article), a comparison is volunteered between nations or peoples in Europe and 'tribes'. Consider the following observation from a Belgian newspaper:

> Tijdens zijn jongste bezoek aan Duitsland heeft President Mitterrand met die Franse hooghartigheid die niet zelden wortelt in een gebrekkige dossierkennis, minachtend gewaarschuwd voor een 'Europe des tribus'. Maar of dat het Franse staatshoofd nu bevalt of niet, het is een feit dat die 'volksstammen' bestààn, erkenning, zeggenschap en een eigen plaats eisen in het Europa dat naar vereniging streeft.
> (*De Standaard*, 27 September 1991) ['During his recent visit to Germany, President Mitterrand, displaying that French sense of superiority which is not rarely based on being ill-informed, has warned with disdain against a 'Europe of tribes'. But whether the French Head of State likes it or not, it is a fact that these 'tribes' exist, that they demand recognition, political participation and a place of their own in the Europe which is trying to reach unity.']

The term 'tribes' has a clear connotation of primitivism and naturalness in this context. And while Mitterrand's use of the term may be seen as ironic, the reaction from the journalist supports the view on nationalism as based on a need for identities analogous to groupings which are supposed to have come about quite naturally and instinctively in the less developed regions of the world. The resurgence of nationalism is therefore normal:

> Overal in Europa zien miljoenen mensen de kans schoon om oude dromen van kultureel zelfbestuur, zelfbeschikking en staatkundige onafhankelijkheid waar te maken. De verdwijning van de loden mantel die de kommunistische regimes over landen en volkeren hadden gelegd, heeft politieke en kulturele krachten vrijgemaakt die de komende decennia de landkaart van het kontinent kunnen hertekenen.

... Lang vergeten haarden van onrust en gevaar blijken nooit helemaal gedoofd te zijn geweest.
(*De Standaard*, 27 September 1991) ['Everywhere in Europe millions of people see the opportunity to realize old dreams of cultural independence, self-determination and state autonomy. The disappearance of the cloak of lead spread out over countries and peoples by the communist regimes, has released cultural and political forces which can redraw the map of the continent in the coming decades. ... Long forgotten centres of unrest and danger seem never to have vanished.']

The author uses history as the ultimate argument for the reality of the nations of Europe. These nations (Lithuania, Ukraine, Moldavia, Croatia, etc.) do not emerge as responses to concrete political or socio-economic situations - they were always there, but they were suppressed by totalitarian state systems (see below). Their reality is historical, and, therefore, objectively real.

The same comparison, though in the opposite direction, is made in the opinion columns of the *NRC Handelsblad* (7 November 1990). The author, a professor of anthropology, argues against the European view of African 'tribes' as homogeneous, traditionalistic groups with rigid group boundaries. An explicit comparison with European nations or 'peoples' is not at all central to this well-taken argument. In the text itself it is introduced only indirectly:

In Europa, zo zeggen Afrikanen, spreekt men van volken; als men het over Afrika heeft gebruikt men het woord stammen. Daarmee is weer bevestigd hoe primitief Afrika is.
(*NRC Handelsblad*, 7 November 1990) ['In Europe, Africans say, peoples are talked about; but as soon as Africa is the subject, the word tribes is used. This serves to reconfirm how primitive Africa is.']

But, maybe as a result of editorial intervention, the comparison is presented as the main focus of attention in the title:

Wat in Afrika stammen heet, wordt in Europa als 'volkeren' getypeerd. ['What is called tribes in Africa, is characterized as 'peoples' in Europe.']

Furthermore, by stressing that the view of African tribes which he argues against, is a decidedly 'European' view, the author implicitly communicates that the properties he rejects for those African tribes are genuine properties of European 'peoples' or 'nations'. Moreover, that similar 'nations' exist in Africa is made abundantly clear by stressing the unity of Tutsi and Hutu in Rwanda, in terms of a familiar feature cluster:

Zij leven door elkaar als leden van één samenleving, bezitten één en dezelfde cultuur en spreken één taal. ['They live together in one society, possess one and the same culture and speak one language.']

Thus again the objective reality of 'nations' is emphasized. Nowhere does it come to mind that groups - wherever they are to be found - have a strongly subjective basis, that 'nations' such as Lithuania or the Ukraine are defined territorially more than ethnically, and that they are, therefore, almost without exception multi-ethnic in population structure.

Obvious universality

Such comparisons between Europe and the rest of the world emphasize the universal validity of a nationalist ideology. When criticism of patriotism or nationalism is voiced and reported on, there are clear markers of distance between the opinions described and a more general public opinion. For example, in a review of Peter Glotz's *Der Irrweg des Nationalstaats* we read:

> [According to Glotz] Das Geschichtsbild müsse europäisiert und Mehrsprachigkeit zum Bildungsprinzip gemacht werden. Kess spricht er von einer 'Hollandisierung Deutschlands' - ein Nationalbewußtsein ohne jeden Bezug zu völkischen, rassischen oder sprachlichen Elementen.
> Schön wär's. Das soll kein Spott sein. Es sind solche Argumente, die Glotz in seinem querköpfigen, anregenden, eigensinnigen Essay auch dazu bringen, für Bonn als Regierungssitz zu plädieren.
> (*Die Zeit*, 9 November 1990) ['Our historical perspective should [according to Glotz] be Europeanized, and multilingualism should be made an educational principle. He speaks boldly of the 'Hollandization of Germany' - a national consciousness without reference to people, race or linguistic elements.
> Wouldn't that be nice! And this is not even meant ironically. It is this type of argument that also leads Glotz, in his provocative, stimulating and idiosyncratic essay, to a plea for Bonn as capital.']

Implicit in this is a perception of Holland as a nation untrue to itself because of lack of attention to real national identity and language. Strangely enough, Belgians tend to share this perception with the Germans. Thus the Antwerp mayor, Cools, takes every possible opportunity to explain that Dutch would have been taken over by French by now if it had not been for the Flemish. And after a recent colloquium on 'Dutch in the World', a prominent linguist writes the following in an opinion article in *De Standaard*:

> Voor zijn taal*kultuur* zal Vlaanderen zich nu en in de toekomst moeten blijven richten naar het noorden: 15 miljoen geeft meer gewicht dan 5 miljoen. Maar voor de taal*politiek* is het anders. Daar zal Vlaanderen de bescheiden voortrekkersrol ... zonder meer naar zich toe moeten trekken. In Vlaanderen ziet men de noodzaak in van de ... instandhouding en verbreiding [van het Nederlands], voor Nederland is dat nog altijd een dubieuze zaak.
> (*De Standaard*, 22 October 1991) ['For its language *culture*, Flanders has to look to the north now and in the future: 15 million carries more weight than 5 million. But for language *policies* the situation is different. There Flanders will

> simply have to assume its modest pioneering role. In Flanders one sees the need for the preservation and spread (of Dutch), for Holland this is still a dubious matter.']

Needless to say that the perception that is reflected in the above German and Belgian texts bears only on Dutch official rhetoric. Our data show that 'the view from below' is not so different after all, and that the Germans and the Belgians can rest assured that nothing emanating from Holland will disturb their universally valid principles of social and political organization. Unfortunately, this cannot be meant ironically either.

Language in the Empire

Language as a battlefield

Our data indicate that language creates identity and discontinuity. It unites and it divides. In the context of conflicts involving nationalist groups in Europe (and elsewhere), these opposite tendencies turn language into the target and the battlefield of interethnic strife. Since language is a distinctive feature of 'natural' groups, and since it is an element of divisiveness between such groups, language can also be used as an object of oppression and discrimination in contexts where interethnic differences are not (or no longer) tolerated.

Dominant in the framing of this role of language is the metaphor of the 'Empire' in connection with tensions between a central government and 'national', linguistic groups. The 'Empire', in our corpus, mostly refers to the Soviet Union or to state systems based on the Soviet model. In all the examples found in our data, the tensions between the 'Empire' and national or ethnic groups are presented as resulting from the systematic denial by the Empire of legitimate linguistic, cultural, and political rights. These minority groups claim the right to use their own language (or orthography), or to restore or introduce its official status as 'national language'. Since language is seen as a natural characteristic of these groups, such rights are held sacred even if the claims are uncompromising and radical in nature.

Linguistic discrimination by the Soviet Government is evoked as an example in statements such as:

> Their [the Kazakhs'] culture has been so defiled by the Bolshevikhs that many Kazakhs do not even know how to speak any other language than Russian.
> (*Guardian Weekly*, 11 November 1990)

> ... a native Russian, Gennadi Kolbin, a party apparatchik who spoke not a word of the Kazakh language and had never been to the republic [of Kazakhstan].
> (*Guardian Weekly*, 11 November 1990)

Soviet oppression is said to have resulted not only in the loss of local language competence among oppressed peoples in peripheral republics. It also resulted in changes in language attitudes and political partisanship:

> The done thing, in the Soviet Ukraine, was to speak Russian if you became educated.
> (*Guardian Weekly*, 4 November 1990)

> They claim that the Gagauz are strongly Russianized; most speak Russian rather than Turkish and support Russian interests.
> (*The Guardian*, 1 November 1990)

The same pattern occurs in Soviet satellites, or in regimes that have adopted the Soviet model. Serbia's centralist attitude towards the Albanian population of the Kosovo region is such a case:

> The Albanian-language press and radio have been abolished.
> (*International Herald Tribune*, 12 November 1990)

When anti-Soviet nationalist groups, once they have gained autonomy or independence, stretch their nationalist fervour to the point of oppressing other minorities within their (supposedly) national territories, this is explained as a direct consequence of the repression and discrimination they have suffered:

> Moldawiens Hysterie ... ist eine Folge des jahrzehntelangen Moskauer Diktats, das der rumänischen Sprache sogar ein Kyrillisches Alphabet aufzwang.
> (*Die Zeit*, 9 November 1990) ['The Moldavian hysteria is a consequence of the decennia-long Moscow regulation, which even imposed a Cyrillic alphabet on the Romanian language.']

In other words, the radicalism of newly autonomous or independent nationalist governments is not a product of their own ideology, but rather an understandable, yet potentially dangerous, reaction to generations-long oppression by the totalitarian imperial authorities. These hyper-nationalist reactions, however, threaten the possibilities of future collaboration among newly autonomous regions:

> Les violences entre Moldaves et russophones revêtent un aspect potentiellement explosif pour l'ensemble du pays.
> (*Le Monde*, 6 November 1990) ['The violence between Moldavians and Russian-speakers hides a potentially explosive situation for the country as a whole.']

The new forms of oppression often take the shape of legislation in favour of the majority language, banning other languages:

> In return, the republic's [Moldavia's] government would soften a law that made Moldavian the national language and required people in dozens of occupations to pass tests in Moldavian. The language law has stirred resentment among Russian speakers and the Gagauz.
> (*International Herald Tribune*, 5 November 1990)

> Pour eux [the Slovak hunger strikers protesting against a new language law], cette loi est trop laxiste: elle autorise l'usage des langues minoritaires dans les bureaux et services dans les regions ou les diverses minorités de Slovaquie comptent plus de 20% de la population locale.
> (*Le Monde*, 1 November 1990) ['For them, this law is too permissive: it allows the use of minority languages in offices and services in regions where the various minorities in Slovakia make up more than 20 per cent of the local population.']

These new forms of oppression are supported by standard nationalist arguments associating national territory with national language. These arguments are, in our data, always presented as direct quotations:

> Lorsque je rentre dans un magasin dans le Sud [de la Slovaquie], on m'aborde en hongrois. Pourtant, je suis sur ma terre natale.
> (*Le Monde*, 1 November 1990) ['When I enter a shop in the South (of Slovakia), they address me in Hungarian. Yet, I'm on my native land.']

> Maar waarom zijn er op de Israelische televisie wel programma's in het Arabisch en niet in het Russisch? We zijn nu toch in ons eigen land?
> (*NRC Handelsblad*, 7 November 1990) ['But why are there programmes in Arabic on Israeli television and none in Russian? We are in our own country after all? (said by Russian Jewish immigrants in Israel).]

Though the ultimate absurdity of this cycle of oppression is not hidden by the reports, the underlying assumption of the legitimacy of each group's preoccupations is never challenged.

Natural resistance and democracy

At an abstract level, these examples invoke the image of an Empire, consisting of a wide variety of linguistic, ethnic, religious, and cultural groups, most of which are oppressed by the unitarianism of the central state. Because the Empire is oppressive, and because its oppression is directed against features which are absolute, inalienable characteristics of natural groups, the resistance of these groups is seen as necessarily legitimate. Such a struggle can only be conceptualized in terms of liberation or 'freedom' movements.

It is only 'natural' that people revolt when they are deprived of their own language and culture. For the natural, normal and desired society is one in which these forms of oppression are absent: the nation-state in which people sharing one language, culture, religion and history live together within a sovereign state system. Here again, we find homogeneism as the underlying premise.

The argument in favour of homogeneism remains complex and often obscure. In relation to Eastern Europe, it is blended with the discourse of anti-communism. The 'natural resistance' movements are directed against (the remnants of) communist rule. By a remarkable and largely implicit rhetorical twist, which defines communism as against human nature, East European nationalism thus becomes an equivalent of democratization. Because nationalist revolt in the communist Empire is aimed at liberating the 'natural' human group from unnatural communist rule, the linguistic and cultural liberation of the East European peoples is at the core of the political liberation of the communist world.[10]

In other contexts (such as the 'giant Empire' India, or minority problems in Belgium), the argument is stripped of its anticommunist connotations, and reduced to its supposed 'naturalness' or 'normality'. The backbone of the argument is, thus, the sole assumption that different people do not like to live together, and that successful society-building requires as high a degree of similarity as possible among the people.

The conceptual problems involved should be clear. First, homogeneism as a view of society rules out a number of social considerations. Class difference, socio-economic status, or social mobility do not come up as factors contributing to social coherence or conflict, except as properties of complete groups which correspond to the 'natural' criteria for identifying and separating them in the building of a peaceful, harmonious society. This is, to say the least, a partial picture obscured by - admittedly persuasive but necessarily mistaken - monocausalism. Second, the direct association of (homogeneistic) nationalism with democracy and freedom is certainly not warranted by the facts, neither synchronically nor historically. Nationalism has been a notorious cause of conflicts, and has led to some of the worst violations of basic human rights in history. The 'liberated' Moldavians and Kazakhs or Slovaks, as well as the liberated East Germans, also seem to be building a track record of oppression and racism against minorities. Every minority has its own minorities. And for members of minority groups, be they immigrants in Western Europe, or Gagauz people in Moldavia, the 'national' government may be as bad as the Empire, because in both cases very little attention is given to their linguistic, cultural or whatever rights. Only the structural level of the debate has shifted. Nothing has been achieved to guarantee more democracy in a pluralist sense.

Multilingualism and tolerance

Still, nationalism is seen as a 'natural' development anchored in linguistic and ethnic identities, a powerful liberation movement, the excesses of which are based on anger and frustration. Our data suggest an intriguing side-aspect of the role of language in this process. In three articles, two about the Israeli-Palestinian conflict in Israel and one on Serbian nationalism, reference is made to individual multilingualism as the opposite of fanaticism. The intriguing point is that this reference is made in a negative sense: even tolerant individuals who speak several languages fluently become fanatics. The orthodox bishop of Serbia, Amphilochios, a Serbian extremist, is said to speak fluent German (*Frankfurter Allgemeine*, 6 November 1990). So here is an educated polyglot who serves a cause which is mostly associated with lower-class, poorly educated monomaniac masses. The same point is made with reference to some well-educated Palestinian highschool students, and a Jewish businessman who has worked with Arab personnel for years. The schoolboys have participated in the violent demonstrations following the Temple Mountain shootings; the Jewish shopkeeper does not trust his Arab employees anymore:

> Although such vows are extreme, these boys do not look or sound like 'Muslim fanatics'. ... Schooled in an elite institution operated by the Christian Brothers, they are polite and well spoken, able to express themselves in English, French and Arabic.
> (*International Herald Tribune*, 6 November 1990)

> Mr. Samar was born in Tel Aviv to parents who came from Iraq and he speaks fluent Arabic. In the last election he voted for a centrist party. (*International Herald Tribune*, 2 November 1990).

The picture that emerges here is the following. The struggle for legitimate national rights is such a central human interest that it eclipses even 'intelligent' and practical solutions, such as learning the language of one's counterpart. That means that a conflict between people based upon nationalist feelings is a fundamental conflict, one which cannot be remedied by slight forms of accommodation between the parties involved. In these references to the failure of individual multilingualism as a solution to interethnic conflicts resides a powerful suggestion about the nature of nationalism. It appears as both an emotional irrational matter and as a respectable phenomenon. The shortcomings of language learning, or education at large, as potential solutions for interethnic conflicts demonstrate that nationalism is based on the fundamental, natural, need for a homogeneous society. Man's political instinct, so to speak, directs him towards homogeneism. *Quod erat demonstrandum.*

Conclusion

Our corpus displays a remarkable consistency with regard to these assumptions. Homogeneism seems to be a widespread ideological premise, underlying much of the opinions reflected in or guided by the European newspaper press. We find a primitive political theory underlying seemingly trivial statements and suggestions about the role of language in nationalism. This theory revolves around the impossibility of heterogeneous communities, and the naturalness of homogeneous communities, the 'Volk'. This theory also rationalizes anticommunism, not in terms of an ideological critique, not even in terms of an economic critique, but in terms of the supposedly unnatural character of the communist system. Nationalism, thus, provides the ultimate evidence for the just cause of the Cold War. The Cold War did not concern political-economic details, it was about fundamental, natural rights such as the right to use one's mother tongue.

The way in which the role of language in nationalist ideology is presented is largely political. The role of language as an element in feature clusters, corresponding to 'natural', objective political units, which makes it a mobilizing force in interethnic conflicts, obliterates the primarily social dimension of language. Within any ethnic group, linguistic resources may be unevenly distributed along social lines, as so much empirical sociolinguistic work has demonstrated. But the feature cluster of 'culture' or 'ethnicity' functions as a powerful frame of reference, with language as a major property treated as if it could equally characterize each and every member of an ethnic group. Less romantic (and maybe less easily accessible) factors virtually disappear from the picture, or their relevance is gravely downplayed.

The way in which language is presented in the overall reporting on nationalist ideologies in Europe reveals a decidedly unsophisticated folk view. Although our analysis in this paper was based on a relatively small set of data, we believe to have demonstrated the usefulness of a systematic search for the 'view from below' by means of a pragmatic analysis of patterns of wording. If applied with methodological rigour to larger sets of data, we believe that this type of analysis can provide an empirical tool for the investigation of elusive phenomena such as ideologies, public opinion, and ideas.

If nothing else, this brief study may have revealed a significant discrepancy between an aspect of popular language ideology and the way in which language is used in multilingual societies. As demonstrated by Woolard (1989) in connection with bilingualism in Catalonia, language choice is highly symbolic and language shift is often motivated by the dynamics of social mobility. In popular ideology (not to be confused with public ideology) however, language tends to be a much more fundamental, even natural and inalienable, aspect of ethnicity or group identity in general.

Notes

1 This paper was written in the context of a research programme supported by the Belgian National Fund for Scientific Research (NFWO/FKFO), the Belgian National Lottery and a Belgian government grant (IUAP-II, contract number 27). Thanks are due to Gino Eelen, who collected the data we needed, to Louis Goossens, Johan van der Auwera, Michael Meeuwis, Luisa Martín Rojo, Susan Philips, Bambi Schieffelin, Kit Woolard and Paul Kroskrity for comments on an earlier version, which appeared in *Pragmatics: Quarterly Publication of the International Pragmatics Association* vol. 2, no. 3, 1992, pp. 355-75.

2 For other preliminary reports on this project, see Blommaert and Verschueren (1993a) and Meeuwis (1993).

3 This statement can be correct only for a free-press tradition in which a wide range of publications is available. By now this is the case in most of Europe, though in the countries of the old communist bloc the situation is less stable than in the rest of Europe, and hence future repetitions of the same research design may reveal more rapid historical change there.

4 Further justification for this approach is to be found in Blommaert and Verschueren (1991, 1993b), and a full-length theoretical and methodological explanation is provided in Verschueren (forthcoming).

5 Most of the data used for this specific study date back to the first weeks of November 1990, but they are not strictly confined to that period. The investigated publications are: *Die Zeit, Zeit Magazin, Der Spiegel, Frankfurter Allgemeine, Frankfurter Allgemeine Magazin; The Guardian, The Guardian Weekly; NRC Handelsblad; Le Monde, Le Nouvel Observateur; De Standaard.* For the sake of comparison, one non-European source (though clearly 'Western' if not specifically American, and widely read in Europe), *The International Herald Tribune*, was studied for the same period. As will be clear from the examples, the general tendency turned out to be very similar.

6 For further discussions of this particular movement which strongly relates national identity to language, see Adams and Brink (eds), (1990).

7 Exactly the same ideological phenomenon is observed by Windisch (1990) in his study of Swiss nationalism and xenophobia. He calls it 'essentialism' and describes it as follows: "Every system of political and social representation is organised around essences, natures or noumena which are regarded as, by nature, transcendent, unalterable and historical" (Windisch, 1990, p. 40). What we call feature clustering is identified by Windisch as follows: "This very common mechanism results in the creation of systems of objects, properties and values which can be defined as 'crystallised', as

each element in the system is linked to another by ideological association" (p. 47).

8 The main exception to this rule seems to be the attempt, in official European rhetoric, to explain away racism and to preserve the European self-image of tolerance by demonstrating that expressions of racism are restricted to the lower socio-economic classes and that a weak socio-economic status is itself the *cause*. (See Blommaert and Verschueren, 1991.) But this is just one manifestation of another rule: that it is easier to perceive significant distinctions in one's own group than in other groups. The phenomenon indicated here also explains the occurrence, in our restricted corpus, of a long article ('Wider die falschen Apostel', *Die Zeit*, 9 November 1990) in which an attempt is made to define 'normal nationalism', and in which economic problems are presented as a risk factor which may transform normal nationalism into xenophobia.

9 Windisch (1990) reports that Swiss nationalism has the same profile as French nationalism, being based necessarily - because of the diversity of the people living in the country - on territoriality. Thus, Swiss nationalists cannot understand Jura separatism because "The only sociological division they recognise is that based on national frontiers: '[within Switzerland] there aren't any frontiers, we're all Swiss'" (Windisch, 1990, p. 57).

10 Some recent scholarship about the Soviet Union shares the same assumptions. Thus Diuk and Karatnycky (1990, p. 16) say: "Yet all these current tensions [in the Soviet Union] arise from a common source - the imperial nature of the Soviet Union". Their book is a perfect example of unshakable belief in the fundamental reality of the Soviet Union's separable and authentic 'hidden nations'. Their holy rights to self-determination are strongly advocated and "the idea that the non-Russian national movements are anti-democratic and xenophobic" (p. 39) is discarded as a new Western myth-in-the-making. How could they be?

10 Language and the Institutionalization of Ethnic Inequality: Malay and English in Malaysia

PETER LOWENBERG

Introduction

A factor that tends to correlate highly with instances of racism and violence in multilingual, multiethnic countries is the relative status accorded the languages of each ethnic group. The status of French and French speakers in Canada and Belgium are familiar examples of this linkage between language and ethnic strife in Western nations. For this reason, in many multilingual non-Western nations previously colonized by Britain or the United States, such as Nigeria, India, and the Philippines, the former colonial language, English, has been retained, not only because of its international currency but also because of its assumed *neutrality* in that it is not the primary language of any of several often conflicting ethnic groups. This paper challenges that assumption. Examination of samples of English in use from one such country, Malaysia, reveals that through lexical transfer from another, politically more dominant language, English can be *deneutralized* and can actually contribute to institutionalizing inequalities among competing ethnic groups.

The paper begins by tracing how, during Malaysia's often turbulent colonial and post-colonial history, the ethnic Malays and their Malay language have gained political dominance over the almost 50 per cent of Malaysia's population of Chinese, South Asian, or other ethnic backgrounds. Examples are, then, provided from Malaysia's leading English-language newspapers of how the English-speaking ethnic Malay elites are institutionalizing their dominance through English, which is the native language of very few Malaysians but is still the principal code for communication among Malaysia's multi-ethnic elites (Augustin, 1982).[1] Analysis of this primary journalistic data will demonstrate that a major way that this occurs is by replacement of English words with denotatively equivalent terms from Malay, resulting in what Clyne (this volume) has termed the 'covert' expression of racism and the institutionalization of inequality.

Historical and sociolinguistic context of English and Malay

The sociolinguistic setting of contemporary Malaysian English began to develop during the British colonization of the Malay Peninsula and the western half of the island of Borneo (from the late eighteenth until the mid-twentieth centuries). When the British arrived, the population of the region was primarily Malay though other ethnic groups had long been present, including at least 3,000 Chinese in Penang (Hirschman, 1985). During the initial colonial period, the British developed commercial centres in Penang (1786) and Singapore (1819) and took over control of Malacca from the Dutch (1824) in order to support the British East India Company's tea trade with China. This era was marked by large-scale immigration of Hokkien-speaking southern Chinese to these centres on the west coast of the Malay Peninsula, where they soon became the majority populations of Penang and Singapore (Platt and Weber, 1980; Platt, Weber and Lian Ho, 1983). In the 1870s, the British began to expand their influence more vigorously in the region, and by the early twentieth century, they administered with varying degrees of direct control all of the Malay Peninsula and the crown colonies of Sarawak, Sabah, and Brunei on Borneo (Vreeland et al., 1977). Concurrent with this increasing British involvement was the immigration of large numbers of Chinese and South Asians from India and Ceylon (present-day Sri Lanka) who came to fill a growing need for labour for which the Malay population was insufficient (Thomas, 1983). Though these Chinese came principally to work in tin mines being opened in the interior of the Malay Peninsula and the South Asians primarily to develop rubber and coffee plantations and to construct a railroad (Parmer, 1959; Hua, 1983), over time, large numbers of both these populations migrated to the trading centres in the coastal cities (Platt and Weber, 1980).

Thus, by the time of its first census in 1911, the colony of Malaya was an extremely multi-ethnic society of over 2.5 million, including about 55 per cent indigenous peoples (mostly Malay), 35 per cent Chinese, and 10 per cent South Asians (based on Vreeland et al., 1977). Eighty years later, in 1991, though Malaysia's population had increased to an estimated 18.2 million, the relative proportions of the major ethnic groups remained remarkably close to those of 1911: over 61 per cent were indigenous ethnic groups, predominantly Malay, 30 per cent were Chinese, and 8 per cent were South Asian (*Britannica Book of the Year*, 1992).

The dominant languages spoken by this diverse population have likewise remained constant: Hokkien, Cantonese, Hakka, and Hainanese are the primary Chinese languages; Tamil is the most widely used South Asian language, in addition to Malayalam, Telugu, and Punjabi; and Malay is the primary language of the ethnic Malays (Le Page, 1962; Platt and Weber, 1980; Asmah, 1985).

In addition to these languages, English became the medium for transacting government and business affairs. As their colonial interests expanded, the British began to need a cadre of English-educated non-Europeans to function as an infrastructure of officials, business agents, and clerks. Hence, as early as the beginning of the nineteenth century, the colonial government authorized the establishment of private secular and mission-supported religious schools in the urban centres, where English was taught and then used as the medium of instruction and other school activities. The students in these schools came from the more prosperous and prestigious families of all ethnic groups, but there was a larger number of Chinese and South Asians sent by their parents to prepare them for entry into government service, positions in trade and commerce, and the professions (Vreeland et al., 1977; Platt and Weber, 1980).

Largely as a result of these English-medium schools, English became the dominant language of power among an urban, multi-ethnic, non-European elite who became integrally involved in the day-to-day administration and commerce of the colony. English was the primary language of the legal system and revenue collection; of postal, telephone, and telegraph communications; and of transportation, including the railroads, harbour facilities, and just prior to Malaya's independence, air transport. In commerce, English was the language of shipping agents, banking, insurance, and transactions with British and other European firms in Malaya and abroad. Moreover, it was the principal language used in the spoken and written mass media and in films imported for the entertainment of the elites (Platt and Weber, 1980; Platt, Weber and Ho, 1983; Hirschman, 1985). As Le Page has observed (1962, p. 133), by the end of the colonial era, English had become "a lingua franca among the more educated sections of the community."

However, at the time of its independence in 1957, the Federation of Malaya, consisting of the Malay Peninsula except for Singapore, established as official languages not only English, but also Malay, which concurrently became the single national language. The official rationale for this policy was "to unify the cultural and national aspirations of Malaya" (Le Page, 1962, p. 138; see also Hassan, 1975). Malay was the logical candidate for national and official language since it was the language of the majority indigenous population. It had also been the language of the Sultans through whom the British had ruled much of colonial Malaya,[2] and it had been widely used for over a millennium as the primary link language of insular Southeast Asia (Lowenberg, 1988; Davey, 1990).

An equally important and explicit reason for selecting Malay was to improve the status of the Malays, the largest and politically most powerful ethnic group, in their economic competition with the descendants of the Chinese and South Asian immigrants (Le Page, 1962; Hua, 1983; Davey, 1990). Many of these non-Malays, especially the Chinese, had gained a significant economic advantage over the Malays during the colonial period, in part due to their concentrations in the urban coastal commercial centres, where they had access to the English-medium schools (Hirschman, 1985).[3]

Nonetheless, despite their emphasis on Malay, the formulators of this language policy also recognized the importance of English as a legacy of the colonial era in Malaya due to (1) its being the only language in post-World War II Malaya that was linguistically equipped to administer the myriad functions of a modern nation, and (2) the availability in Malaya of the English-educated multi-ethnic elites as the only non-Europeans who had the training and experience to administer the new nation. Hence, a policy was devised for both Malay and English to have official status until 1967, a ten-year transition period during which Malay was to be taught intensively and modernized to gradually assume prominence in the major domains of language use (Platt and Weber, 1980; Vreeland et al., 1977).

At the conclusion of that ten-year period, the National Language Act of 1967 established Malay as the sole official language in the expanded nation of *Malaysia*, formed in 1963 and consisting of the previous Federation of Malaya plus Sabah and Sarawak on Borneo.[4] Further policies in support of Malay resulted from economic tensions on the Malay Peninsula between the Chinese and Malays, which culminated in violent confrontations in May 1969. In order both to appease the Malay majority in the population and to diffuse ethnic tensions by promoting a Malaysian identity, the government began to take more determined steps to strengthen the position of the Malay language, which was now renamed a more ethnically neutral *Bahasa Malaysia* (literally, the 'Malaysian language'). The most significant of these steps was a policy initiated by the Ministry of Education in 1969 whereby all state-supported English-medium schools were to become Malay-medium, a process which by the 1980s had been completed nation-wide at the primary through tertiary levels of education (Le Page, 1984; Watson, 1984).

Advocates of this language policy claim that it has met with considerable success, pointing out that whereas in 1970 only 44 per cent of the Malaysian population could speak Bahasa Malaysia (Llamzon, 1978), most Malaysians of all ethnicities now have some proficiency in it (Asmah, 1985). However, among the significant portions of the Malaysian population who are not ethnic Malays, there appears to be less than wholehearted acceptance of Bahasa Malaysia. The renowned Malaysian linguist Asmah Haji Omar has noted (1979, p. 30, quoted in Davey, 1990, p. 96) that:

> The choice of Malay to be the national and official language as well as the main medium of instruction means the choice of a language of one

> particular ethnic group. Although all factors, be they historical, cultural, or linguistic, go to show that the choice was the most feasible, it is not easy to offset prejudices which are, in general, ethnic flavoured.

More specifically, it has been observed by another prominent Southeast Asian linguist, Teodoro Llamzon (1978, p. 90), that:

> the feeling is prevalent, though frequently unexpressed, that the language is still very much identified with a group; that Bahasa Malaysia is unable to transcend the narrow confines of its ethnic identity; that the propagation of the language is nothing more than an attempt on the part of its native speakers to assert their superiority and heighten rivalry and competition by placing the other groups in the country at a disadvantage.

Evidence of these sentiments appears in the Borneo states of Sabah and Sarawak, which were much slower than their sister states on the Malay Peninsula to switch totally from English to Bahasa Malaysia. Though partially due to logistical problems (Noss, 1984), this delay also resulted from the view long held in these largely non-Malay states that English is an ethnically more neutral language than Bahasa Malaysia, the latter being perceived in these states as a tool for political domination by the Malay majority on the Malay Peninsula (Le Page, 1962; Vreeland et al., 1977).

For such reasons, but even more because of its importance as an international language, English has been retained nation-wide in Malaysia as a compulsory second language throughout all levels of primary and secondary school, and it still figures prominently as a reading language in higher education (Platt and Weber, 1980; Augustin, 1982; Le Page, 1984). English is also still widely used by the current Malaysian elites, who were educated in English-medium schools during the colonial or early post-colonial periods and are still quite proficient in it. For example, Augustin (1982) reported in the early 1980s that of 1.1 million Malaysians who had completed secondary school between 1956 and 1970, 69.8 per cent had received an English-medium education. As a result, he observed, "the educated peninsular Malaysians (who are) now in the prime of life and who play leadership roles in government and trade are fairly competent in the use of English...". These English-educated elites are concentrated in the urban centres, where approximately 25 per cent of the population (about one million people) use English "extensively" for interethnic communication (Augustin, 1982, pp. 251-2).

However, as will now be discussed, the traditional ethnic neutrality of English in the region is being eroded; the increasing use and status of Bahasa Malaysia and other government policies intended to favour the ethnic Malays are having a marked impact on patterns of language usage in Malaysian English. This influence is particularly evident in lexical transfer from Bahasa Malaysia into Standard Malaysian English, the prestige variety taught in the schools and used in government, large-scale commerce, and the mass media.

Forms and functions of lexical transfer from Malay to English

Lexical transfer from Malay has been noted in most analyses of Standard Malaysian English (Tongue, 1979; Platt and Weber, 1980; Wong, 1983), but it has generally been attributed to the filling of "lexical gaps" (Richards, 1979, p. 14), for which other varieties of English have no denotatively equivalent terms. Such borrowings occur in excerpts 1, 2, and 3:[5]

Excerpt 1

The residents will repair the roofs on a *gotong-royong* basis.
(*The Malay Mail*, 1 December 1988)

Excerpt 2

I have often been criticised by my friends for easily bowing down to apologise, but I will always do so - it is required by both our religion and *adat*.
(quote from a political speech, *New Straits Times*, 27 April 1987)

Excerpt 3

A carpenter was jailed for five years and ordered to be given six strokes of the *rotan* by the Sessions Court today for possession of heroin.
(*New Straits Times*, 3 May 1987)

All of the borrowed terms in these sentences refer to institutions unique to Malay-speaking Southeast Asia: 'gotong-royong' is a form of communal cooperation, 'adat' is a body of traditional law, and the 'rotan' is a rattan cane used in officially sanctioned and administered punishments.

However, the impact on English of the ascending status of the ethnic Malays and Bahasa Malaysia is more evident in "lexical shifts" (Richards, 1979, p. 14), where Malay words replace English words or phrases which are denotatively, but not connotatively, equivalent. The most striking of these lexical shifts are what Paine (1981, p. 14) has called "banner words": "single words or phrases ... that are likely to induce a proposition by inference." Examples of such banner words in American English are 'democracy' and 'freedom'. These terms trigger in most Americans complex schemata of values and associations that politicians repeatedly appeal to when seeking popular support (Parkin, 1984; Geis, 1987a). The invocation of such words by a speaker or writer is intended to and generally does discourage controversy or debate over any issues being discussed.

In Malaysian English, such banner words tend to be lexical items transferred from Bahasa Malaysia. An example occurs in excerpt 4, where the Malay word 'Merdeka' signifies the achievement of independence from colonial rule on 31 August 1957.

> *Excerpt 4*
>
> Earlier, speaking at the opening of the Sekolah Kebangsaan Lumut, he suggested that certain old schools built before *Merdeka* be turned into museums to motivate pupils.
> (*New Straits Times*, 20 March 1989)

This use of 'Merdeka' instead of its English equivalent 'independence' tends to associate the entire concept of Malaysian nationhood with the language of the ethnic Malays. In contrast, English 'independence' would denote the same concept without marking any group or their language as dominant.

A more striking and politically significant use of a Malay banner word transferred to English is the frequently occurring term 'Bumiputera', which literally means 'sons of the soil'. This borrowing refers to people considered indigenous to Malaysia, predominantly the ethnic Malays, but also officially including other ethnic groups, especially in Sabah and Sarawak, who are neither Malays nor descendants of Chinese, South Asian or other immigrants. Continuing a policy initiated by the British colonizers to appease local Malay rulers (Watson, 1984), 'Bumiputera' is today most often used in the context of a large number of land tenure, political, employment, investment, and educational programmes which, as part of Malaysia's New Economic Policy, deliberately and systematically favour these indigenous peoples in order to elevate their economic status to parity with the wealthier urban Chinese and South Asian Malaysians (Asmah, 1982; Clutterbuck, 1985; Davey, 1990; Means, 1991). For example, large quotas of spaces in most Malaysian universities are reserved exclusively for 'Bumiputeras', who also receive special concessions concerning university entrance requirements (Noss, 1984). According to amendments in 1971 to the national Sedition Ordinance, the mass media are prohibited from any discussion of these special rights of 'Bumiputeras' (Means, 1991).[6] The word 'Bumiputera's' roots in Sanskrit, long considered the most classical and scholarly language of the Malay Archipelago (Alisjahbana, 1976), tend to neutralize this deliberate inequity in official policy while at the same time lending it nationalistic legitimacy.[7]

The frequency with which 'Bumiputera' is used is demonstrated in excerpts 5 to 8: four occurrences in the *New Straits Times* during one six-day period in March, 1989. Exerpt 5 is a news report, 6 and 7 are employment advertisements, and 8 is an announcement of scholarship opportunities.[8]

Excerpt 5

In addition, *Bumiputera* equity participation in the corporate sector increased from 4.3 per cent in 1971 to 17.8 in 1985, although half of it was held through Government agencies and trustees ...
(*New Straits Times*, 22 March 1989)

Excerpt 6

OFFICE COORDINATOR wanted. Varsity/college graduate (any discipline). Male/female. *Bumiputera.* Sociable, able to mix well with people, fluent in English ...
(*New Straits Times*, 25 March 1989; parentheses in original)

Excerpt 7

PRECISION TUBE PRODUCT requires ... *Bumiputera* female Secretary with secretarial qualifications. 2 years experience and fluent in English.
(*New Straits Times*, 20 March 1989)

Excerpt 8

Bumiputera students, including those who are pursuing Matriculation Courses in any local Universities, are encouraged to apply.
(*New Straits Times*, 25 March 1989)

The degree to which 'Bumiputera' has become a part of Malaysian English is reflected in excerpt 9 by the creation of a clipped form with a plural morpheme not found in Bahasa Malaysia or any other variety of Malay:

Excerpt 9

Bumis need to have more initiative.
(*New Straits Times*, 12 May 1985).

Though, as noted above, 'Bumiputera' officially includes not only Malays but also many other indigenous ethnic groups, its range is, in fact, frequently restricted to just the Malays, as indicated in the political speech reported in excerpt 10:

Excerpt 10

Deputy Prime Minister Ghafar Baba has been appointed the head of a high-powered committee to review the New Economic Policy (NEP) and formulate a new policy to help *Bumiputeras* own 50 per cent of the nation's wealth by the year 2000 ... Encik Ghafar said the new policy was expected to "give *Malays* equality with the other races in the real sense of the word" ... "I need the support and prayers of all *Bumiputeras* in this venture to improve the well-being of *the race*," he added.
(*New Straits Times*, 23 March 1987; parentheses in original)

Equally significant is the explicit exclusion from Bumiputera status of the so-called "immigrant races" (Clutterbuck, 1985, p. 377): Malaysians of Chinese or South Asian descent, many of whose families have lived in the region for several generations if not centuries (Hirschman, 1985). Malaysians with these backgrounds are defined in the New Economic Policy as a single population with fewer rights and privileges than the 'Bumiputeras' by being officially designated 'non-Bumiputeras' (Asmah, 1985, p. 19), as in excerpt 11:

Excerpt 11

Foreign ownership decreased from 61.7 per cent to 25.5 while *non-Bumiputera's* [sic] increased from 34 per cent to 56.7.
(*New Straits Times*, 22 March 1989)

'Bumiputera' and 'non-Bumiputera' thus function to exclude Chinese, South Asian, and at times, as indicated in excerpt 10, even indigenous Malaysians from a number of rights and privileges enjoyed by their Malay compatriots. As Davey (1990, p. 100) observes, "the policies of 'Bumiputera' preference drive a wedge between races", a wedge that through lexical transfer from Bahasa Malaysia has been encoded in Malaysian English.

In contrast to this exclusionary force of 'Bumiputera', another Malay banner word often borrowed in English, 'rakyat', has a more inclusive function, especially in the press. In traditional Malay, 'rakyat' meant the rural ethnic Malay population, but in contemporary Bahasa Malaysia it refers to 'the Malaysian people', as in excerpts 12 and 13:

Excerpt 12

Reaching out and touching the hearts of the *rakyat*.
(*New Straits Times*, 1 June 1983)

Excerpt 13

Victory now belongs to both sides, to the *rakyat* and to the system ...
(*New Straits Times*, 17 December 1983, in Shinn 1985, p. 217)

The use of 'rakyat' rather than the English word 'people' in discourses of this type subtly defines in English the entire multi-ethnic population of Malaysia in terms of the language of the ethnic Malays.

Even when used in its traditional sense of only the rural population, 'rakyat' still attributes a common identity with Malays to large numbers of non-Malays, including the many Chinese who still live and work in the villages of Peninsular Malaysia (Carstens, 1986) and most of the population of Sarawak and Sabah. This is illustrated in excerpt 14, which reports on a political address given by an ethnic Malay official in Sarawak, where in

1979 only 19.8 per cent of the population were Malays (*Europa Year Book*, 1987):

Excerpt 14

Datuk Taib thanked the gathering for supporting him and his policies and urged all to work for the *rakyat* to ensure the Fifth Malaysia Plan was successfully implemented.
(*New Straits Times*, 24 January 1985)

Similar borrowing from Malay occurs in Sabah, where in 1978 only 5.1 per cent of the population were ethnic Malays (*Europa Year Book*, 1987). Though not employing such banner words as 'Bumiputera' and 'rakyat', excerpt 15, from the *Sabah Times*, likewise demonstrates how lexical transfer from Malay to English functions to identify non-Malays in Malay terms:

Excerpt 15

A night to remember. "*Mengalai begitu dong*!" says the expert to one of the *makchiks*. The sporting *neneks* sang and "*mengalaid*" through the night.
(*Sabah Times*, 20 June 1980)

This is the caption to a photo accompanying a feature English-language article in the women's section of a major newspaper in Kota Kinabalu, the capital of Sabah. The article describes an in-service training course for elderly midwives from remote villages in Sabah. The word 'mengalai' is glossed in the article as meaning 'to disco' in this context. 'Mengalai begitu dong' can be translated as 'Dance like this'. Of particular interest here are the words 'nenek' and 'makchik', affectionate Malay terms for 'grandmother' and 'older woman', respectively. In this article, these Malay words refer to women who are not ethnically Malay, thereby defining them in English in the terms of the nationally dominant Malays.

As with 'non-Bumiputera' above, the transfer of banner and other words from Bahasa Malaysia into the English-language press in excerpts 12 to 15 serves to define large non-Malay populations in Malay terms. This use of the language of the politically most powerful group, the Malays, to encode in English the lower relative status of other ethnic groups illustrates an observation by Trömel-Plötz (1981, p. 76, quoted in Kachru, 1986, p. 23) that "only the powerful can define others and make their definitions stick. By having their definitions accepted they appropriate more power."

Conclusion

This exploratory paper has first examined how the selection and elevation of Malay to 'Bahasa Malaysia', Malaysia's single national and official language, has been at least partly related to ethnic communalism and competition. For whether intended or not, "it can be argued that the language policies of Malaysia have produced ethnic tension and have effectively conferred lower status on ethnic minorities" (Davey, 1990, p. 96).

The paper has, then, demonstrated how through selected lexical borrowings from Malay, this lower status of the ethnic minorities has been encoded in English, long considered Malaysia's most ethnically neutral language. This process has occurred most dramatically through the incorporation of powerful ethnic banner words from Malay. To the degree that they function to legitimize the exclusion of non-Malays from opportunities enjoyed by the Malays (for example, 'Bumiputera' and 'non-Bumiputera') and to define non-Malays in Malay terms (as in 'rakyat'), these borrowings from Malay institutionalize in English the politically inferior status of the non-Malays and, as such, are markers of what Clyne (this volume) considers 'covert racism'. Their use in this manner also supports Halliday's contention (1993) that language both *construes* and *enacts* social realities.

Ultimately, these findings have broader implications for the study of the political roles of languages in multilingual, multi-ethnic societies. Discussions of particular languages generally focus on linguistic knowledge shared by largely monolingual native speakers of those languages. However, as Kachru has observed (1985, p. 26), "what is needed is recognition of the fact that traditional bilingual societies cannot be viewed from the perspective of a monolingual society." Rather, analyses of such multilingual societies as Malaysia, would benefit from Ferguson's suggestion (1992, p. xiv) that "in describing a particular language or variety, it is necessary to identify its users and to locate its place in the verbal repertoires of the speech communities in which it is used." The validity of such a perspective for interpreting Malay borrowings in Malaysian English has been demonstrated here; it should prove just as valuable in understanding the complex relationships between language, power, and inequality in other multilingual settings.

Notes

1 The validity of such journalistic data as evidence of language variation and change, if carefully controlled with regard to sources, has been demonstrated in previous linguistic research on other topics (Davis and Walton, 1983; Sinclair, 1985).

2 The British themselves had used Malay for some official purposes, requiring colonial officers to be proficient in Malay and, when necessary, employing interpreters, particularly South Asians, who spoke both English and Malay (Alisjahbana, 1976; Vreeland et al., 1977).

3 At the time of independence, the Chinese comprised over 50 per cent of the population on the west coast of the Malay Peninsula (Le Page, 1962).

4 Singapore, with its predominantly Chinese population - in 1990, 78 per cent Chinese, compared to only 14 per cent Malay and 7 per cent South Asian (*Britannica Book of the Year*, 1992) - was also an original member of Malaysia, but withdrew in 1965 due to political problems resulting from Chinese-Malay ethnic tensions.

5 In all of the excerpts quoted in this paper, the markers of emphasis *(italics)* are mine. All but two of these excerpts are taken from Malaysia's most prestigious English-language newspaper, the *New Straits Times*, which is owned by the dominant political party and is circulated nation-wide (Means, 1991). The exceptions, excerpts 1 and 15, are taken from two other leading English-language newspapers, *The Malay Mail* and the *Sabah Times*, respectively.

6 These amendments to the Sedition Ordinance also prohibit the mass media from discussing the status of Bahasa Malaysia as sole official language (Davey, 1990).

7 Kachru (1992) reports that the word 'Bumiputera' has the same exclusionary function in parts of India. In Malaysia's neighbour Indonesia, another Sanskrit-based word, 'Pribumi' (meaning 'first on the soil'), is used to favour indigenous people over descendants of Chinese and other immigrants in a similar series of economic and educational programmes (Wickman, 1983).

8 Notice that in addition to Bumiputera status, fluency in English is also required in excerpts 6 and 7, the employment advertisements.

Part IV

Language, Education and Peace

11 Doctor-Patient Communication: Training Medical Practitioners for Change

JOSÉ CARLOS GONÇALVES

Introduction

> Perhaps if the goal of medicine is the diagnosis and treatment of disease, the quality of communication between physician and patient makes little difference as long as an adequate medical history can be obtained and the necessary cooperation of the patient in doing or refraining from doing certain things can be assured. But if the goal is more broadly interpreted, if the concern is with the person who is sick and the purpose is to relieve, reassure, and restore him - as would seem to be increasingly the case - the quality of communication assumes instrumental importance and anything that interferes with it needs to be noted, and if possible, removed. (Samora, Saunders and Larson, 1961, p. 86)

Institutionalized discourse is a broad term for a wide variety of discourse genres that share a set of factors and constraining features. Some instances of institutionalized discourse are the interaction between teachers and students, doctor-patient communication and the legal language in the court. This paper focuses on the interaction between physician and patient in the medical interview, one type of communication in the workplace which typically displays the major features of institutionalized discourse. This encounter will be examined to determine the role of language either in facilitating or hindering the achievement of interactional peace between the participants. Concluding comments will suggest how communication between physician and patient and, consequently, the patient's health and life can be enhanced.

Asymmetry in discourse

From the perspective of a descriptive as well as critical conversation analysis, asymmetry in institutionalized discourse is not only a result of the discourse, but also of pre-existing conditions in the real world. At a micro-sociolinguistic level, asymmetry in doctor-patient communication, for example, results from differences in socio-economic status, roles, objectives and expectations, as well as from their values and attitudes. Discourse reflects, creates, disseminates and perpetuates this asymmetry in and through the speech of the participants. In institutionalized discourse, asymmetry can be measured by interactional, discursive and linguistic parameters. At the interactional level, for instance, there is the control of the tactical organization of the interaction. In the case of the doctor-patient communication, the doctor controls the turn at talk and the structures of participation of the other participants. Thus, not only *who does the talking,* but also *when* and *how the talking is done* is decided by the doctor. At the discursive level, not only *what* is talked about, i.e. the content, but also *in what order something is talked about*, i.e. the topic sequence and discourse organization, is decided by the doctor who has the hegemonic power to steer the interaction. At the linguistic level, the physician's technical expertise and vocabulary may be an extra cause of discrepancy and divergence in communication both at the conceptual and at the lexical level.

In asymmetric communication the participants do not share the same knowledge, interests, goals and conversational strategies. This also applies to doctors and patients who do not share the same sociocultural bases for knowing, saying and understanding. Nonetheless, because face to face communication is reflexive, i.e., mutually constitutive, the participants are jointly responsible for the flow of activities. In the case of doctor-patient communication, as in classroom interactions, doctors operate as discourse directors, keeping the control during the consultation, and steering the interaction by signalling the beginning, middle and end of the different stages or activities as well as the beginning and end of the exchanges. It is within the context of this type of interaction that physician and patient have to *negotiate* meaning, i.e., to make sense of one another, but talk is ambiguous and vague and must be interpreted. Moreover, shared interpretation depends on shared context, mutually constituted by and for the participants and interactionally achieved. Therefore, if the medical consultation is viewed as a context for healing and if we are to understand the meaning such activities hold for the actual participants in the interview, the shared (and unshared) technical or lay knowledge, beliefs, expectations, implicit in the roles of patient and physician, should be examined as part of the systematic investigation of the social activities that constitute that service encounter.

Conflicting frames of reference

In fact, physician and patient approach the medical encounter with conflicting frames of reference. Patients view the interaction from a personalized, experiential, story-telling frame of reference. They subjectify the interview by reporting various kinds of distress, somatic complaints, pains in different parts of the body, disturbances in normal functioning. These vague, diffuse and unfocused lifeworld complaints are requests for help with health and life. Physicians, on the other hand, view the medical interview objectively, as a routine activity. Their primary goal is to obtain enough good information for an accurate diagnosis and treatment. Thus, their attention to organic aspects of a patient's complaints, their technical rephrasings of a patient's accounts, their recurrent use of questions to elicit specific information are strategies whereby the interview is objectified and made to fit the biomedical model of illness.

This detached, objective, 'cautious', clinical or organic approach is the result of the training received by doctors. In their pre-service training they are told that involvement with the patient should not only be avoided but that it is almost forbidden and anti-ethical. Because they will have to face the pain, suffering and death of their patients, they are told that by working within this institutional framework they will be protected from the dangers of involvement and compassion and, thus, remain freer to act and make decisions that sometimes may go against their feelings and emotions. The following brief excerpt from the film *The Doctor*[1] is illustrative:

> *Dr Mackee*: There's a danger in feeling too strong about your patients. It's very dangerous. Surgery is about judgement. And a judge must be detached.
>
> *Student*: Isn't it unnatural not to get involved with your patients?
>
> *Dr Mackee*: There's nothing natural about surgery. Cutting off someone's body, is that natural? One day you will have your hands around someone's heart and it's beating. And you'll think Aho! I shouldn't be here ... If the patient feels sick, a surgeon's job is to cut. You got one shot. You go in, fix it and get out. Caring needs all that time. When you get 30 seconds before some guy bleeds up, I'd rather have you cut straight and care less.

Thus, the danger of emotional involvement and compassion is pointed out. This impersonal approach is a consequence of the view of delivering medical service as a routine bureaucratic activity. That is, the patient is one more patient, in a row of patients, one more illness, in a row of illnesses.[2]

In sum, during the doctor-patient interview, the doctor, who is in interactional control, seeks and requires information from the patient. He approaches the interview within a clinical frame of reference while the patient views it as personalized and experiential, an opportunity to talk about his/her ailments. This mismatch in conversational style and strategies may cause anxiety, frustration and conflict; it may prevent the participants from reaching a consensus on the meaning of the interaction and/or achieving their intended aims. Ultimately, this may lead to misunderstanding and interactional dissatisfaction.

Description of the study

Data and subjects

Against this general background, this study examines the negotiation of the meaning of the interaction by physician and patient from the perspective of a critical conversation analysis. The data reported here are from a discourse analysis study conducted by Gonçalves (1981) in which the objectification and subjectification of the medical interview in the doctor-patient negotiation of illness are analysed. The data for this study are taken from a medical consultation tape-recorded in a public health system outpatient clinic in the State of São Paulo, Brazil.[3]

Objectives

To investigate how meaning is negotiated between doctor and patient in the medical interview, the analysis examines topic management styles and strategies and the structures of participation in the interaction. More specifically, it focuses on the following research questions:

(1) How does the doctor's interactional hegemony affect how the participants in the medical interview negotiate the topic of the conversation in the construction of the discourse of the interview?

(2) How do the conversational strategies used by physician and patient in the interview reflect the participants' different frames of reference, attitudes, goals?

(3) How do convergence and divergence of interest enhance or hinder doctor-patient communication?

Methodology

In the following sections, a qualitative and quantitative analysis of language use in the interview is presented. Conversation topic is the unit of analysis. It is operationally defined as *what occupies the focus of attention of the participants for a given time, i.e., the theme or subject of the talk.* Following Polanyi (1979), the analysis of the *negotiation* of the meaning of the interaction is done by the discussion of *proposals* and *counterproposals*. Roughly speaking, a proposal is the selection of a topic to talk about. A counterproposal, then, is the selection of an alternative topic to be discussed, or another proposal. Schematically, the interview was divided in proposals and counterproposals, by assigning each topic a title, such as *Breathing*, *Smoking*, etc. Next, the linguistic evidence of the discourse devices used to introduce, shift and terminate talk on selected topics was identified together with the linguistic features of evaluation and involvement. (See **Appendix 1** for a literal English translation of the transcript of the interview and Gonçalves, 1981, for a more comprehensive analysis of the data.)

Data analysis

Interactional hegemony

As indicated in Table 11.1, which summarizes the macrostructure of the interview, the whole conversation comprises 22 topics (or proposals and counterproposals).

Table 11.1
Distribution of utterances per topic

	Speaker	*Topics (Proposals and Counterproposals)*	*Utterances comprising each topic*
00	Doctor	Opening	1, 2
01	Patient	Breathing	3, 4, 5, 6, 7, 8, 9, 10, 11, 12, 13, 14, 15, 16
02	Doctor	Age	17, 18
03	Doctor	Duration	19, 20, 28, 29
04	Doctor	Antecedents	30, 31, 32
05	Patient	Breathing	21, 22, 23, 24, 25, 26, 27
06	Patient	Heart	33, 34, 35, 36
07	Doctor	Electrocardiogram	37, 38
08	Doctor	Place	39, 40
09	Doctor	Cough	41, 42, 43
10	Doctor	Work	44, 45, 46, 47, 48, 49, 50, 51, 52, 53, 54
11	Doctor	Physical effort	55, 56, 57, 58
12	Patient	Smoking	59, 60, 61
13	Doctor	Legs	62, 63, 64, 65, 66, 67
14	Patient	Breathing	68, 69
15	Doctor	Time	70, 71, 72, 73
16	Doctor	Pillow	74, 75
17	Doctor	Position	76, 77, 78, 79, 80, 81, 82, 83
18	Patient	Breathing	84, 85, 86, 87, 88, 89, 90, 91, 92, 93
19	Doctor	Other	94, 95
20	Doctor	Intestines	96, 97
21	Doctor	Urine	98, 99
22	Doctor	Closing	100

The analysis first focused on the patterns of topic management, trying to determine dominance and/or participation by the speakers in the interaction. Judging by the number of utterances comprising each topic, it appears that the patient's topics (e.g. 01, 05, 18) are more thoroughly developed and extensively evaluated than the physician's topics.

In contrast, the doctor's topics are generally brief, truncated, as if he were following a pre-established agenda, ticking appropriate boxes on a questionnaire or application form. Because the patient talks more, this could lead us to conclude that he dominates the interaction. However, Table 11.2, which indicates who introduced the topics in the conversation, makes it clear that it is the doctor who dominates the conversation.

Table 11.2
Dominance by topic introduction

D = Doctor, P = Patient

00	01	02	03	04	05	06	07	08	09	10	11	12	13	14	15	16	17	18	19	20	21	22
D	P	D	D	D	P	P	D	D	D	D	D	P	D	P	D	D	D	P	D	D	D	D

Doctor's topics: 19 = 86.3%   Patient's Topics: 3 = 13.6%

Of the 22 topics that comprise the interview, only three (or 13.6 per cent) were introduced by the patient: *breathing*, *heart*, and *smoking*. On the other hand, the doctor initiated and/or determined the other 19 (or 86.3 per cent). If one considers that in spontaneous discourse each participant is supposed to have an equal chance to present and develop his or her topic, it is evident that the doctor dominated this interview.

Moreover, a closer look at the doctor's speech (excerpts 1 and 2) reveals that he not only introduces 19 of the topics, but that interactionally he controls the conversation.

Excerpt 1

(02) - D - What's going on, Seu Francisco?
(03) - P - That's what happens,
(04) - P - The following, you see, doctor?
(05) - P - I'll tell something to you:
(06) - P - There's this ... lack of air, isn't it?
(07) - P - a VERY HARD lack of air,
(08) - P - It's so hard, you know? To take a good breath of air, you know?
(09) - P - So that if I make a lot of effort,
(10) - P - To take a breath of air without getting (fatigued), you know?
(11) - P - I can hardly sleep at night.
(12) - P - Awful hard breathing!
(13) - P - Sometimes it goes up ... it looks like I feel like

(14) - P - I get kind of dizzy like this, you know?
(15) - P - Then, also,
(16) - P - Then, this problem there.
(17) - D - How old are you, Francisco?
(18) - P - I'll be thirty-five.
(19) - D - Thirty-five ... How long have you been feeling like this?
(20) - P - Oh, this problem, it always comes, like ...
(21) - P - There's ... there's always some good times,
(22) - P - Now, in warm weather
(23) - P - I get more tired
(24) - P - I get like ... clogged like this,
(25) - P - The breathing blocked, you know?
(26) - P - It takes a lot of work,
(27) - P - To take a good breath of air, you know?

In excerpt 1, the patient gives an account of his breathing problem (03-16). He starts with a narrative opener, a routine formula in (03) and ends the story with a narrative coda, a conversational marker summarizing the whole episode in (16). At this point the doctor tries to change the topic, asking factual questions about the patient's *age* (17) and the *duration* of the problem (19). However, the patient uses these questions as an opportunity to talk about his breathing problem (21-27).

Excerpt 2

(33) - P - Heart problem, it isn't,
(34) - P - cause I had an electric taken, see?
(35) - P - It came out OK, you see?
(36) - P - BUT I DIDN'T HAVE THIS PROBLEM.
(37) - D - When was the electrocardiogram?
(38) - P - Electric? Oh, it's been some ... two ... or three months.
(39) - D - Right here?
(40) - P - Yeah ... I think with Doctor ... I think it's Dr Nereusa, isn't it?
(41) - D - Do you have a cough?
(42) - P - Oh, I have a cough, when I get a cold,
(43) - P - just that.
(44) - D - Umhum. And in your work?
(45) - D - How do you feel?
(46) - D - When you make some effort ...
(47) - P - Oh, ... in my work
(48) - P - When I ride my bicycle, like,
(49) - P - I feel like,
(50) - P - Just kind of tired only,
(51) - P - You know how it is like ...
(52) - P - (xxxxxxxxx) what a good breathing is like, isn't it?
(53) - P - Yeah. That's all.
(54) - D - I see.
(55) - D - But when you make an effort,
(56) - P - And ...
(57) - P - When I make an effort, I feel ...

(58) -	P -	I feel more tired, right?
(59) -	P -	But I don't know if it is a problem from smoking, too, isn't it?
(60 -	D -	Do you smoke a lot?
(61) -	P -	No. A pack of cigarettes every other day, only.
(62) -	D -	Uhm, YOUR LEGS,
(63) -	D-	Do they swell, or
(64) -	P -	No.

In excerpt 2 the patient introduces the topic of his *heart* (33), discards it as a possible source of the problem, as if he were self-diagnosing. But the doctor apparently decides to attend to this biomedical item of information (37), asking when the electrocardiogram was taken; then he shifts to some other items of interest to him: *place* (39), *cough* (41), *work* (44), *physical effort* (46). The patient replies briefly to each, still trying to emphasize his *breathing* problem. When the patient introduces the topic of smoking, in another attempt to self-diagnose (59), the doctor picks up on the topic asking the patient if he smokes a lot, looking for facts to specify the patient's account (60). The patient responds promptly; the doctor evaluates[4] his answer (61-62) and shifts the topic to legs (62-63).

In sum, though he may talk less, interactionally, the doctor has more influence in shaping the structure of the discourse. He opens and closes the conversation (see Table 11.1: 00 and 22); terminates the discussion on a topic, shifts to a new one as he wishes; or ignores the patient's remarks.

Participants' conversational strategies

The patient's language is highly evaluative[5] and involved as one can see from the number of intensifiers which abound in the text, e.g. 'hardly' (11); 'always' (20); pauses, hesitations, requests for confirmation and other discourse/conversational markers, e.g., 'you see' (04); 'you know' (08, 10, 14); 'isn't it' (06). His complaints are vague and diffuse (e.g. 13-16). The doctor, therefore, tries to medicalize these complaints into symptoms, by attending to the organic or clinical aspects of the patient's report. He attempts to collect factual details to specify the patient's account. In excerpt 3 he asks about his *age* (17) and the *duration* of the illness (19):

Excerpt 3

(17) -	D -	How old are you, Francisco?
(18) -	P -	I'll be thirty-five.
(19) -	D -	Thirty-five ... How long have you been feeling like this?

Excerpt 4 illustrates the doctor's attention to the *duration* of the medical problem and the patient's *previous history* (28-31):

Excerpt 4

(28) -	D -	Has this been going on for very long?
(29) -	P -	Oh, it's been ... some ... three, four months ... it's been like this, you know? This sort of problem, you know.
(30) -	D -	Before that, did you feel anything?
(31) -	P -	No.
(32) -	P -	Not before. And ...

In excerpt 5, facts about *time* and *place* are gathered:

Excerpt 5

(37) -	D -	When was the electrocardiogram?
(38) -	P -	Electric? Oh, it's been some ... two ... or three months.
(39) -	D -	Right here?
(40) -	P -	Yeah ... I think with Dr ... I think it's Dr Nereusa, isn't it?

Then, in excerpt 6, the doctor attends to other biomedical details such as the *position* in which the patient feels the problem and the *lack of air*:

Excerpt 6

(74) -	D -	Do you sleep with a thin pillow or with a big pillow?
(75) -	P -	Oh, normal pillow.
(76) -	D -	You don't feel any difficulty,
(77) -	P -	No
(78) -	D -	When you lie down,
(79) -	P -	(No), I don't feel.
(80) -	D -	Doesn't the lack of air get worse?
(81) -	P -	No the lack of ...
(82) -	P -	Air doesn't get worse.

Finally, near the end of the consultation (excerpt 7) the doctor runs a last check on some other organic aspects of the disease (96-99):

Excerpt 7

(96) -	D -	Your intestines function,
(97) -	P -	No, these things function all well
(98) -	D -	Urine?
(99) -	P -	No, all OK.

Topic recycling is a strategy the patient uses to deal with the doctor's control of the interview and to create as many opportunities as possible to talk about the topic of interest to him: his breathing problem. His attempts at self-diagnosis, e.g. heart and smoking (excerpt 2) are examples. In spite of the doctor's attempts to direct the discourse to biomedical items, such as *time* (excerpt 5), *pillow* and *position* (excerpt 6), the patient persists in taking every chance to recycle his *breathing* problem, his macro-proposal during the whole interview. Excerpt 8 is illustrative. In this final account of his breathing problem (85-93), he barely responds to the doctor's questions:

Excerpt 8

(84) -	D -	What do you FEEL?
(85) -	P -	I, when (I) get tired,
(86) -	P -	I get kind of
(87) -	P -	of having to
(88) -	P -	of having to take that good breath of air, you know?
(89) -	P -	Like this ... (sighs).
(90) -	P -	I have to struggle too hard, like,
(91) -	P -	To breathe.
(92) -	P -	it begins to hurt even ... my chest ... a little bit ...
(93) -	P -	to breathe.
(94) -	D -	Besides this, are there any other little problems?
(95) -	P -	/ no.
(96) -	D -	Your intestines function,
(97) -	P -	/ No, these things function all well.
(98) -	D -	Urine?
(99) -	P -	/ No, all OK.
(100)-	D -	(xxxxxxxxx) ... To the room next door. You may sit here. (Almost unintelligible).

Convergence and divergence of interest

In this paper, convergence and divergence refer to unilaterality or bilaterality in the introduction of proposals, that is, proposals that had a consensus and proposals which were of interest to only one of the participants.[6] In other words, convergence of interest or expectations means that the participants are on the same wavelength. Divergence, on the other hand, signals that the participants are out of synchrony with each other. That is, they are either talking out of turn or off the topic.

Convergence Table 11.3 illustrates convergence in doctor-patient conversation via consensus, i.e., bilateral proposals or topics which were personally interesting to both interactants.

Table 11.3
Convergence: Bilateral proposals

Topics	*Topic number*	*Percentage of talk*	*Total*	*Percentage*
Breathing	01, 05, 15, 16, 17, 18	47	100	47%
Work	10	11	100	11%
Effort	11	04	100	4%
Total		62	100	62%

The frequencies in Table 11.3 show that 62 per cent of the conversation was achieved when the doctor and the patient touched on a topic of mutual interest. This happened in the case of the convergent topics or bilateral proposals, i.e., those topics that reveal the patient's real problems. *Breathing*, the topic the patient wanted to discuss, appears to have been the most developed (see Table 11.1). In excerpt 1, the patient gives a rendition of his illness in the form of a narrative. In addition to the markers already pointed out earlier in this analysis, he uses a lot of concrete details to illustrate his breathing problem: *lack of air*, *physical effort*, *inhaling*, *difficulty to sleep*, *dizziness*. He explicitly says:

> Then this problem there (= That's the problem) (Excerpt 1:16)

In excerpt 2, he re-introduces the topic of breathing and adds further details in reply to the doctor's questions about his *age* and *when he feels the problem* (e.g., influence of warm weather on his breathing problems). *Work* and *physical effort*, two other topics introduced by the doctor, have the patient's approval and he talks extensively about them (44-58). In other words, in the case of bilateral proposals, even when the topic is initiated by the doctor, as is the case with topics 10 and 11 (*work* and *physical effort*), both participants develop the topic at length.

Divergence The divergent or unilateral topics, on the other hand, are shortlived and are quickly dropped and discarded altogether as illustrated in excerpt 9:

Excerpt 9

(62) -	D -	Uhm ... your legs,
(63) -	D -	Do they swell, or
(64) -	P -	no
(65) -	P -	No ...
(66) -	P -	Not the legs.
(67) -	P -	Leg problems I don't have at all, no.
(68) -	D -	What bothers you is only this breathing?
(69) -	P -	What bothers me is only this breathing.

The patient's negation (64) overlaps with the physician's question in (63). The patient, then, reinforces the negation and totally discards the possibility with the intensifier 'at all' (67). At this point, the doctor appears to have begun to concede to the patient's topic of interest (68-69). He asks if it is only the breathing that affects him and the patient repeats literally the physician's words so as to say 'yes, that's what I mean, that's the whole point, that's the matter'.

Other divergent topics introduced by the doctor are even more hurriedly discarded and not evaluated as in excerpt 10:

Excerpt 10

(94) - D - Besides this, are there any other little problems,
(95) - P - / no
(96) - D - Your intestines function,
(97) - P - / No, all these things function very well.
(98) - D - Urine?
(99) - P - / No, all OK.

Again, the sharp negation by the patient overlaps with the physician's question (94, 96 and 98). It appears that he can hardly wait till the doctor's question is over to counter it. Table 11.4 summarizes the percentage of talk taken up by these unilateral proposals:

Table 11.4
Divergence: Unilateral proposals

Topics	*Topic number*	*Percentage of talk*
all other topics	00, 02, 03, 04, 06, 07, 08, 09. 12, 13, 19, 20, 21	38%

Altogether, the divergent topics comprise only 38 per cent of the total amount of talk of the interview. These topics were originated mainly by the doctor through questions which intended to gather facts to specify the patient's account and/or biomedical information which would suggest symptoms that could serve as a basis for his diagnosis (transform into disease). Because they appear irrelevant to the patient who has a specific problem of his own, they were quickly discarded and dropped.

Yet another way to determine how meaning is negotiated in the medical discourse is to look at which interactant does the talking in the case of convergent and divergent topics.

Table 11.5
Dominance by number of utterances

	Who does the talking			
	Patient	*%*	*Doctor*	*%*
Convergent topics	40	85.11%	07	14.89%
Divergent Topics	33	62.27%	20	37.73%
Total	73	73%	27	27%

Table 11.5 illustrates that in this interview, as regards the convergent or consensus topics, the patient does 85.11 per cent of the talk and the doctor 14.89 per cent, his utterances consisting of prompting questions which give

the patient the floor and allow him to develop his account of his illness. In the case of the divergent topics, on the other hand, the doctor does most of the talking (62.27 per cent). This means that when the doctor agrees with the patient about what really seems to be the point of his story, the patient feels more stimulated to talk and to really contribute to the medical interview. In the other exchanges in which there is divergence, mostly topics introduced by the physician to get information, there is little response from the patient and little is revealed about the nature of the illness.

Discussion of the findings

This study has demonstrated the manner in which meaning is negotiated between physician and patient in a medical interview. The quantitative analysis of the patterns of topic management by the participants in the interview revealed that the doctor has hegemonic control of the conversation. Although he talks less in terms of the total time of the interview, it is the doctor who regulates the structures of participation, the content and the sequential organization or thematic progression of the topics in the conversation. While the patient talks more than the doctor in terms of the total time of the interview, he does so only in reply to the doctor's questions and imposed topics, which structure not only what he talks about but also when, how and in what order.

The qualitative analysis focused on the linguistic evidence of the conversational strategies used by the participants in the interview. Because the doctor is interested in obtaining enough good medical information for an accurate diagnosis and treatment, his conversational strategy is to attend to the organic, or biomedical items of information and to treat the patient's personal lifeworld problems as irrelevant to the interview. He relies mainly on specific questions in the search for symptoms to transform into his diagnosis. His topic management style[7] can be characterized as *talking about a topic*.

The patient's strategy, on the other hand, is to avoid talking about the topics that are introduced by the doctor. To do this he uses digressions, self-diagnosis, and topic association. In this way, not only does he avoid talking about the doctor's chosen topics, but he manages to recycle and to talk more about topics of interest to him personally and so to communicate what he deemed relevant to the consultation. Thus, although semi-illiterate, the patient reveals that he possesses the conversational skills he needs to give an account of his illness. His topic management style is *talking topically*, that is, talking centred on a topic. In the case of this analysis, the main topic was his *breathing* problem and others touched off by related words and/or ideas (e.g. *physical effort*, *smoking*, *work*, etc.).

As a consequence of this divergence in conversational strategies and topic management style, the topics introduced by the doctor are brief and remain unevaluated, quickly discarded by the patient. The bilateral, or convergent topics, on the other hand, are thoroughly developed and evaluated, thus affording the doctor with an opportunity to gather the information most relevant for diagnosis and treatment. Attending to the linguistic devices for involvement and evaluation the patient uses, he can learn not only what is of interest to him as a doctor but what is of concern to the patient.

To sum up, both the quantitative and the qualitative analyses point to a common conclusion: the importance of the quality of the communication between the doctor and the patient in the interview and a view of such a conversation as already being part of the healing process.

Training practitioners for change

From the very outset, this paper has pointed out the importance of viewing hospitals and doctors' offices or clinics as *contexts* for healing. This means considering the participants in doctor-patient communication as real people in interaction in the interest of a common pursuit: the restoration of the patient's health. To achieve this goal, the quality of the interaction that holds between the participants is of primary importance for it is a substantial part of the healing process. In fact, the correlation between the quality of the interaction and the degree of compliance with the prescription and treatment has been documented in many studies of doctor-patient communication.[8] This view is further emphasized in a recent article for the medical section of a major Brazilian daily paper[9] in which the writer (a physician) states:

> The difficulties in the relationship between doctors and patients generally undermine the successful outcomes of consultations and treatment for two reasons. First, the doctor's inability to approach the patient and second, the patient's resistance to accept what is proposed to him.

To solve this problem, the writer suggests that the "consideration given to the prescription should be equal to the concern with the patient's emotions", noting further:

> The good doctor should be concerned with the patient's story, not only with where his pains come from ... [that is] the problem is to find out what is important to the sick person and not only to the doctor.

It is suggested, therefore, that medical professionals develop a conscious knowledge of the characteristics and complexities of the discourse of healing. This would demand that doctors learn how to listen to understand rather than listen to question. In fact, their ability to question would be enhanced by their ability to listen for and identify contextual clues, such as evaluation and involvement, that point to their patients' real problems. Such an awareness would enable them to pinpoint their patients' medical problems more easily. However, as Shuy (1976) evidences, attitudes are very deeply rooted in daily practice and not very easy to change. The writer for the Brazilian paper mentioned above claims that doctors' resistance to change is due mainly to "... a mixture of prejudice and lack of knowledge about these changes." According to this same writer, doctors will have to face their prejudices and pride if they wish to improve their relationship with their patients. Mere knowledge of the problem will not guarantee change.

Such profound change, however, would call for a long-range integrated applied discourse analysis research project, involving linguistic researchers and medical practitioners in the collaborative research of doctors' workplace cultures and the nature of doctor-patient interaction. Findings from such research would serve as a basis for the training of other practitioners both in pre- and in-service training programmes.

In the film mentioned at the beginning of this paper, Dr Mackee suggests one approach to such training. Having undergone the process of becoming a patient, he had experienced a complete metamorphosis which changed his whole approach and attitude to medical practice and to life in general. He feels the need to have his students participate in such an experience as part of their medical formation. In one of the final scenes he enters the hall where his students wait for him and starts the following exchange:

> *Dr Mackee*: Every doctor becomes a patient sooner or later. And then it will hit you as it is hitting me. Doctors, you have spent a lot of time learning the Latin names for the diseases your patients might have. Now it's time to learn something simpler. All the patients have their own names. They feel frightened, embarrassed, feel sick. And most important, they wanna get better. Because of that they put their lives in your hands. I could try to explain what that means till I am blue in the face. But you know something. It wouldn't mean a thing. And sure as hell it never did to me. So for the next 72 hours you'll each be allocated a particular disease ...

Dr Mackee was giving his students a chance to become researchers of their own culture and to start transforming their own social practice, by changing themselves first.

Thus, it is suggested that, as researchers of their own workplace culture, doctors can begin by strangefying the familiar and familiarizing the strange in their own context. Then, with this critical attitude, arrived at by their insider and outsider perspective, they can become the main agents of transformation of their own social practice.

Notes

1 The film, *The Doctor,* was released by Touchstone Picture, 1991. It was produced by Randa Haines. Brazilian distributors are Abril Video.

2 Drew and Heritage (eds) (1992) bring together a collection of the latest advances in the study of interaction in institutional settings such as doctor-patient consultations, legal hearings, news interviews, visits by health visitors, psychiatric interviews and calls for emergency services. As illustrated in different articles in the collection, this mismatch between professionals' and their clients' views of the interaction seems to be a common feature not only of doctor-patient communication but of other genres of talk at work as well. Cautiousness seems to be a recurrent feature of professional discourse in institutionalized settings.

3 The participants are a male clinician and a working-class, middle-aged male patient. A detailed qualitative conversation microanalysis is conducted in the original paper but for this version I refer mainly to some quantitative aspects of the analysis.

4 This tripartite Initiation/Reply/Evaluation structure of the medical discourse is very similar to teacher-pupil interaction in the classroom (Sinclair and Coulthard, 1975). Like teachers in the classroom, the doctor also evaluates his patient's reply and shifts the topic to legs (62-63), that is, he starts another elicitation move to get some new medical information from the patient. Among other professionals, doctors, teachers and the police are questioners and, thus, a large part of their talk is constituted by questions. This is an important feature for the analysis of talk in those institutional settings.

5 The term 'evaluative' is used here in the Labov (1972) narrative analysis sense in which verbal and nonverbal devices such as adjectives and adverbs help reinforce the point of the story.

6 A further complicator of the medical discourse is the physician's technical expertise and vocabulary which may be an extra source of discrepancy and divergence in communication both at the conceptual and at the lexical level. Divergence at the conceptual level has to do with the categorization of objects and events by doctor and patient and the different beliefs and feelings associated with these categorizations. Divergence at the lexical level results from the different terminologies used by the speakers and it can yield various discrepancies. In Gonçalves (1981) these discrepancies are described in more depth in the analysis of the doctor's self-reported data.

7 For a complete description of patterns of topical development, see Gonçalves (1983) in which three topic management styles are illustrated.

8 In Drew and Heritage (eds) (1992, p. 236) Heath states, "It is, however, increasingly recognized by the profession itself that the relative absence of diagnostic and other forms of information provided by doctors to patients is consequential for compliance with treatment programs and undermines the possibility of encouraging prevention in medicine."

9 The paper is *Jornal do Brasil*, Sunday Issue, dated of 23 January 1994, Section Health & Medicine, Article: 'Such a Tender Relation'.

Appendix 1: Transcript of the interview

(Doctor calls patient's name):

(01) -	D -	Francisco de Paula! ... (tosse) ... (pausa, ruídos, pausa).
(01) -	*D -*	*Francisco de Paula! ... (coughs) ... (pause, noise, pause).*
(02) -	D -	O que está acontecendo, Seu Francisco?
(02) -	*D -*	*What's going on, Seu Francisco?*
(03) -	P -	Acontece
(03) -	*P -*	*That's what happens,*
(04) -	P -	O seguinte, sá dotô?
(04) -	*P -*	*the following, you see, doctor?*
(05) -	P -	Vou falar um assunto pro senhor
(05) -	*P -*	*I'll tell something to you:*
(06) -	P -	Faz assim ... uma falta de ar, né?
(06) -	*P -*	*There's this ... lack of air, isn't it?*
(07) -	P -	Falta BASTANTE de ar,
(07) -	*P -*	*a VERY HARD lack of air,*
(08) -	P -	Dá of que fazer, sá? Tomar uma respiração boa, sá?
(08) -	*P -*	*It's so hard, you know? To take a good breath of air, you know?*
(09) -	P -	De modo que se esforço bastante
(09) -	*P -*	*So that if I make a lot of effort,*
(10) -	P -	Pra tomar uma respiração boa sem ficar (fadigado)?
(10) -	*P -*	*To take a breath of air without getting (fatigued), you know?*
(11) -	P -	Quase não durmo de noite,
(11) -	*P -*	*I can hardly sleep at night.*
(12) -	P -	Uma ( ) tremenda!
(12) -	*P -*	*Awful hard breathing!*
(13) -	P -	Tem hora que sobe ... parece sentir assim
(13) -	*P -*	*sometimes it goes up ... it looks like I feel like*
(14) -	P -	Eu fico meio zonzo, sá?
(14) -	*P -*	*I get kind of dizzy like this, you know?*
(15) -	P -	Aí, também
(15) -	*P -*	*Then, also*
(16) -	P -	Aí, esse problema aí.
(16) -	*P -*	*Then, this problem there*
(17) -	D -	Quantos anos você tem, Francisco?
(17) -	*D -*	*How old are you, Francisco?*
(18) -	P -	Vou fazer 35 ...
(18) -	*P -*	*I'll be thirty-five*
(19) -	D -	Trinta e cinco..Há quanto tempo você está sentindo isso?
(19) -	*D -*	*Thirty five ... How long have you been feeling like this?*
(20) -	P -	Ah, esse problema, sempre dá ... assim ...
(20) -	*P -*	*Oh, this problem, it always comes, like ...*
(21) -	P -	passa ... sempre passa uns tempo bom ...
(21) -	*P -*	*there's ... there's always some good times,*
(22) -	P -	AGORA, sempre em tempo de calor,
(22) -	*P -*	*NOW, in warm weather,*
(23) -	P -	Eu fico mais fadigado.
(23) -	*P -*	*I get more tired*
(24) -	P -	fico assim ... preso assim,

(24) - P - I get like ... clogged like this,
(25) - P - a respiração presa, sá?
(25) - P - the breathing blocked, you know?
(26) - P - dá o que fazer,
(26) - P - It takes a lot of work,
(27) - P - pra tomar uma respiração boa assim, sá?
(27) - P - to take a good breath of air, you know?
(28) - D - E já faz muito tempo, isso?
(28) - D - Has this been going on for very long?
(29) - P - Ah, faz uns ... três, quatro meis ... que ... tá assim,sá? Problema assim, sá?
(29) - P - Oh, it's been ... some ... three, four months... it's been like this, you know? This sort of problem, you know.
(30) - D - Antes, você não sentia nada?
(30) - D - Before that, did you feel anything?
(31) - P - Não.
(31) - P - No.
(32) - P - Antes não. E ...
(32) - P - Not before. And ...
(33) - P - Problema de coração, não é,
(33) - P - Heart Problem, it isn't,
(34) - P - que eu tirei um elétrico, viu?
(34) - P - cause I had an electric taken, see?
(35) - P - deu tudo bom, sá?
(35) - P - It came out OK, you see?
(36) - P - MAS EU NÃO TINHA ESSE PROBLEMA.
(36) - P - BUT I DIDN'T HAVE THIS PROBLEM.
(37) - D - Quando foi o eletro?
(37) - D - When was the electrocardiogram?
(38) - P - Elétrico? ah, faz uns ... dois meis ... ou treis meis ...
(38) - P - Electric? Oh, it's been some ... two... or three months.
(39) - D - Aqui mesmo?
(39) - D - Right here?
(40) - P - É ... acho que com a dotora ... acho que é Nereusa, não é?
(40) - P - Yeah ... I think with Doctor... I think it's Dr Nereusa, isn't it?
(41) - D - Você tem tosse?
(41) - D - Do you have a cough?
(42) - P - Ah, tenho tosse, quando fico resfriado,
(42) - P - Oh, I have a cough, when I get a cold,
(43) - P - só assim.
(43) - P - just that.
(44) - D - Umhum. E no seu trabalho?
(44) - D - Umhum. And in your work?
(45) - D - Como é que você se sente?
(45) - D - How do you feel?
(46) - D - Quando você faz esforço ...
(46) - D - When you make some effort ...
(47) - P - Ah, ... no meu trabalho
(47) - P - Oh, ... in my work
(48) - P - Quando eu ando de bicicleta, assim
(48) - P - When I ride my bicycle, like,

(49) - P - Eu sinto assim,
(49) - P - I feel like,
(50) - P - Tipo cansado mesmo, só.
(50) - P - Just kind of tired only,
(51) - P - 'cê entende como é que é.
(51) - P - You know how it is like ...
(52) - P - (xxxxxxxxx) como é que é a respiração boa, né
(52) - P - (xxxxxxxxx) what a good breathing is like, isn't it?
(53) - P - É. Só isso.
(53) - P - Yeah. That's all.
(54) - D - Sei.
(54) - D - I see.
(55) - D - Mas quando você faz esforço,
(55) - D - But when you make an effort,
(56) - P - E ...
(56) - P - And ...
(57) - P - Quando eu faço esforço, eu sinto ...
(57) - P - When I make an effort, I feel ...
(58) - P - Eu sinto mais cansado, né?
(58) - P - I feel more tired, right?
(59) - P - Mas num sei se é problema de cigarro também, né?
(59) - P - But I don't know if it is a problem from smoking, too, isn't it?
(60) - D - Você fuma muito?
(60) - D - Do you smoke a lot?
(61) - P - Não. um maço de cigarros em dois dias, só.
(61) - P - No. A pack of cigarettes every other day, only.
(62) - D - Uhm. SUAS PERNAS,
(62) - D - Uhm, YOUR LEGS,
(63) - D - Costumam inchar, ou
(63) - D- Do they swell, or
(64) - P - Não.
(64) - P - No.
(65) - D - Não
(65) - D - No.
(66) - P - Perna, não
(66) - P - No, not the legs
(67) - P - Problema de perna não sinto nada não.
(67) - P - Leg problems I don't have at all, no.
(68) - D - O que atrapalha é só essa falta ...
(68) - D - What bothers you is just this lack ...
(69) - P - O que atrapalha é só essa falta.
(69) - P - What bothers is just this lack.
(70) - D - E isso piora a noite?
(70) - D - And does it get worse at night?
(71) - P - Ah, sempre, e ... algum,
(71) - P - Oh, always, ... there're some
(72) - P - Alguma noite assim que eu
(72) - P - Some nights, like I,
(73) - P - fico meio fadigado, sá?
(73) - P - I get kind of tired, you know
(74) - D - Você dorme com travesseiro baixo, ou com travesseiro alto?

(74) - D - Do you sleep with a thin pillow or with a big pillow?
(75) - P - Ah, travesseiro normal.
(75) - P - Oh, normal pillow.
(76) - D - Não sente dificuldade,
(76) - D - You dont't feel any difficulty,
(77) - P - Não.
(77) - P - No.
(78) - D - quando deita
(78) - D - when you lie down,
(79) - P - Não sinto.
(79) - P - (No) I don't feel.
(80) - D - A falta de ar não piora?
(80) - D - Doesn't the lack of air get worse?
(81) - P - Não, a falta de ...
(81) - P - No the lack of ...
(82) - P - ar não piora.
(82) - P - Air doesn't get worse.
(83) - P - é ... alguma vez só, sá?
(83) - P - It's ... only sometimes, you see?
(84) - D - O que que SENTE?
(84) - D - What do you FEEL?
(85) - P - Eu, quando fico fadigado,
(85) - P - I, when (I) get tired,
(86) - P - Fico meio
(86) - P - I get kind of
(87) - P - De tanto ficar
(87) - P - of having to
(88) - P - de ter de tomar aquela respiração boa, sá?
(88) - P - of having to take that good breath of air, you know?
(89) - P - isso assim ...(suspiro)
(89) - P - Like this ... (sighs).
(90) - P - Começo esforcar demais, assim,
(90) - P - I have to struggle too hard, like,
(91) - P - pra respirar.
(91) - P - To breathe.
(92) - P - começa a doer até ... o peito ... um pouquinho,
(92) - P - it begins to hurt even ... my chest ... a little bit ...
(93) - P - pra respirar.
(93) - P - to breathe.
(94) - D - Fora isso, tem mais algum probleminha ...
(94) - D - Besides this, are there any other little problems?
(95) - P - Não.
(95) - P - No.
(96) - D - O intestino funciona ...
(96) - D - Your intestines function,
(97) - P - Não, essas coisa funciona tudo bem.
(97) - P - No, these things function all well.
(98) - D - A urina?
(98) - D - Urine?
(99) - P - Não, tudo em orde.
(99) - P - No, all OK.

(100) - D - (xxxxxxxxx) ... para a sala ao lado ... pode sentar-se aqui. (Quase inaudível).

(100) - D - (xxxxxxxxx*) ... to the room next door. You may sit here. (Almost unintelligible).*

12 Perceptions of Language in L1 and L2 Teacher-Pupil Interaction: The Construction of Readers' Social Identities

LUIZ PAULO DA MOITA LOPES

Introduction

The central role of language in education can never be emphasized enough since language is the means through which the different components of the school curriculum are imparted to learners. That is, access to explicit and implicit curriculum content is made possible through teacher and pupil interaction. Therefore, the way teachers and learners conceptualize the nature of language seems to be crucial in determining beliefs about how knowledge and meaning are generated in society, i.e., in defining who has access to discourse and, therefore, to power. As Foucault (1984, p. 110) says, "discourse is not simply that which translates struggles or systems of domination, but [it] is the thing for which and by which there is struggle, discourse is the power which is to be seized." Because of the centrality of written language in the world of schools and because children go to school to be given the tools which will provide access to written language as a means of further access to different bodies of knowledge, the teaching of reading is paramount in defining these beliefs. That is, language teachers play a crucial role in developing learners' views of the function of language in society.

This paper, therefore, reports on a study which investigates[1] how teachers and learners operating in L1 and L2 reading classes in the public sector of the school system of the city of Rio de Janeiro perceive the nature of language. Conclusions are derived from an ethnographic analysis of the interaction between teachers and learners. The analysis was undertaken from a theoretical perspective which places meaning, comprehension, learning and knowledge as being socially constructed by participants in discourse. First, theoretical issues in connection with the relationship between discourse and society will be introduced. Then, the research methodology and context of the investigation will be described and the data analysed. Finally, some conclusions regarding the relationship between the teaching of reading and the formation of learners' beliefs concerning the role of language in society and their social identities as language users will be outlined.

Discourse and society

Models of language put forward in what is called mainstream linguistics have been extremely influential in determining teachers' and learners' views of language, thus accounting for particular methods used in the teaching/learning of languages, that, in turn, shape learners' views on the role of language in society. Despite the fact that linguists themselves have been rather sceptical about the relevance of their theoretical claims as regards the work of teachers in language classrooms (see, e.g., Chomsky, 1971, p. 153), there has been a long tradition of applying theoretical principles directly to language teaching contexts (cf. the application of Linguistics versus Applied Linguistics traditions in Widdowson, 1979, p. 243). These models of language were constructed on the basis of a standardized view of language, thus excluding from their scope the actual realization of language in society: the socio-historical facts which condition whatever we do when we use language. In the interests of concentrating on what is said to be the core in a description of language (syntax, morphology, phonology and semantics), mainstream linguists have idealized language by putting aside, among other factors, its function in society. They have omitted what, as I will try to show below, is essential to understanding the very nature of language: its use in society, i.e., discourse.

According to the traditional view referred to above, meaning is logocentric, that is, inherent in language. Such a view is based on the illusion that meaning pre-exists language itself (Derrida, 1973, p.17) and is, consequently, anterior to its use by humans. From this it follows that meaning is found in the printed text and is not affected by the intersubjectivity of language users. Theories of reading comprehension based on this view assume that reading comprehension is limited to decoding the linguistic system (see Gough, 1976; Gibson and Levin, 1975) and that learning to read solely implies the acquisition of this system.

A model of language of this nature does not seem to be useful in language education since it does not take into consideration language use, i.e., how participants get involved and involve others in discourse in particular socio-historical circumstances. Teachers and learners need a model of language which takes into consideration the use of language in society, what I shall refer to here as a discourse model of language. That is, language teachers and learners need to operate from a model which accounts for meaning as being socially constructed: there is no meaning outside the use language is put to by language users. Therefore, besides accounting for what is systemic in language, a discourse model of language which is useful in educational terms has to account for interaction and context (see Fairclough, 1989, p. 238), thus addressing issues which have a direct bearing on how participants construct meaning through social interaction.

This view of discourse as being socially constructed is similar to a growing tradition prevalent in our times, which treats learning and the construction of knowledge as forms of social co-participation (see Lave and Wenger, 1991; Wertsch, ed., 1985; Edwards and Mercer, 1987). This emerging tradition places great emphasis on interactional contexts as the crucial element in a theory of meaning, comprehension and learning: there is "a growing literature in cognitive studies, discourse analysis and sociolinguistics, which treats verbal meaning as the product of speakers' interpretive activities, and not merely as the 'content' of linguistic forms" (Hanks, 1991, p. 15). These different areas of investigation, therefore, have placed the interaction between social participants as the initial point of analysis.

In the discourse model of language argued for here, participants involved in the social construction of meaning through interaction make use of their schematic knowledge (see Rumelhart, 1977). In addition to involving knowledge of particular content areas and rhetorical routines (as in Widdowson, 1983), schematic knowledge is represented here as encompassing values, political ideologies and beliefs. Such a view of meaning, therefore, centres on the idea that, because meaning is socially constructed, discourse "shapes and is shaped by society" (Fairclough, 1992b, p. 8). Thus, the construction of meaning reflects the political and economic interests of more powerfully positioned social participants involved in particular discursive practices (see Foucault, 1984): the notion of power struggles is intrinsic here. These struggles, from the perspective of neo-Marxist social theory (see Anderson, 1989, p. 251) followed in this paper, go beyond social class struggle. They involve any kind of social relations constructed on the basis of social inequalities, including men versus women, heterosexuals versus gays, whites versus blacks, users of hegemonic languages/dialects versus users of minority languages/dialects, professionals versus clients (for example, teachers and pupils, doctors and patients), etc.

Freire (1969) and Fairclough (1992b), among others, have drawn attention to the need for what Freire refers to as *Conscientization* and Fairclough as *Critical language awareness* in education so that one can fight the types of oppressive discursive practices mentioned above and change society by taking control of one's own processes in unequal social relations. The essential point here is that society is conceptualized as a process - rather than a given - upon which one can act. This consciousness will lead to emancipatory discourse, which Janks and Ivanic (1992, p. 306) describe as "discourse which does not disempower others, and discourse which resists disempowerment."

In this view, reading comprehension becomes a social act, for meaning is not in the written text but is made possible because readers interact with writers through the written text within a particular socio-historical moment to socially construct meaning. These socio-historical conditions together with the interpretive community to which readers belong (Fish, 1980, p. 331) circumscribe readers' possible readings of a text. In other words, there is no meaning outside the subjectivity (or better, intersubjectivity) of language users (i.e., readers and writers).

In light of the views of language presented here, the relevance of investigating teachers' and learners' perceptions of language in L1 and L2 reading classes should be evident. It is their own position as subjects or objects in society which is at issue: their social identity as language users. According to the decoding view of reading, learner-readers are not expected to participate in the construction of meaning, which is said to be inherent in a text. Rather they are seen as occupying an object position in the sense that they are affected by the meaning produced by others who have access to discourse. On the other hand, when reading comprehension is viewed as the social construction of meaning, learner-readers occupy a subject position in the sense that they are portrayed as actively engaged in the production of meaning, i.e., they become engaged and engage others in discourse within particular socio-historical circumstances.

Which of these views of language are adopted by a teacher in helping students learn how to deal with written discourse is crucial because learners' social identities as readers are basically constructed in reading classes. This is due to the relative lack of familiarity that most learners have with written language when they go to school. If learner-readers perceive meaning as inherent in written language, and if this view is reinforced by the teacher, learning to read at school may contribute to learners' construing their social identities as objects of social processes. Thus, language education may reinforce the position of speechlessness and powerlessness which particular social groups have in society. This is a vital issue when teaching children who are socially oppressed, as is the case of the learners participating in this research.

Research methodology and context

The research reported on in this paper subscribes to the above view of interaction in learning and comprehension. It investigates the interaction between discourse participants in L1 and L2 classrooms in order to discover their perceptions of language. The research methodology further draws upon the interpretativist tradition of investigation in the social sciences. This tradition argues that research is an intersubjective activity and that the only way to have access to knowledge about the social world is through the reconstruction of the kinds of meanings discourse participants use to interpret and re-interpret the world around them: "unlike physical phenomena, social actors give meaning to themselves, to others and to the social environments in which they live" (Hughes, 1990, p. 96). To investigate the social world, one needs to reconstruct it through recovering participants' views of what is going on in the contexts in which they are acting. This is done here in the framework of ethnographic research.

The investigation reported in this paper involves data derived from two research projects (the English as a Foreign Language [EFL] and the Portuguese as a Mother Tongue [PMT] Projects), which centred on the evaluation of two different sets of materials for the teaching of reading in EFL and in PMT in public sector schools in Rio de Janeiro. These two sets of materials were designed on the basis of the same theoretical principles: an ethnomethodological view of discourse (see Widdowson, 1983; Psathas, ed., 1979), a socio-interactional view of reading (see Rumelhart, 1977; Widdowson, 1984) and a cognitivist view of learning. These projects represent attempts to collaborate with a central area of educational concern in Brazilian secondary schools in the public sector: the improvement of reading performance.

Brazilian schools in the public sector are mainly attended by children who come from a socially deprived background (see Salm and Fogaça, 1992, p. 123). These schools have been unable to raise levels of reading performance. One of the reasons for such a problem has to do with the almost total absence of social function for the use of written discourse in the students' social world and their consequent inability to represent such a function (see Moita Lopes, 1993; Terzi, 1992).

The EFL Project extended over a period of three years (two classes of 45 minutes each a week for twenty-seven months) in Escola Francisco Cabrita and the PMT Project over a period of one year (two classes of 45 minutes each a week for a period of nine months) in Escola Eurico Gaspar Dutra. Each project investigated two groups of pupils in each school. The EFL Project followed the same groups for three years, starting to work with them when they were fifth graders (about eleven years old), and the PMT Project concentrated on two fifth grade groups - group 501 (about eleven years old) and group 504 (about fifteen years old). The EFL groups had two different teachers and the PMT groups had the same teacher. The four groups had about thirty-five pupils each. The groups were chosen because their teachers[2] volunteered to participate in the projects.

The classes were tape-recorded and observed with field-notes being taken by four research assistants and by the project coordinator. At the end of the school year, semi-structured interviews were conducted with the teachers and three pupils of each group chosen on the basis of the teachers' informal evaluation of their motivation for reading classes in EFL and PMT, i.e., high, middle and low level of motivation. The data presented in this paper come mostly from the transcription of the tape-recorded classes, although data derived from interviews are also used. The class sequences included in the discussion of data below were selected because they typically indicate teachers' and pupils' perception of language.

Analysis and discussion of data

By centring on teachers' and pupils' interaction, the focus of this analysis is geared towards the content of what is being said, by whom and to whom, in line with Edwards and Mercer (1987, p. 10). Following a hermeneutic tactics of analysis, I tried to recover the meanings constructed by discourse participants by interpreting what one participant said in view of what another had said. My interpretation of what was going on in the interaction between teachers and learners was retrospectively checked with the teachers and is also supported by data derived from interviews with learners, as shown below.

The analysis of the interaction between teacher and pupils in both L1 and L2 classrooms indicates that a logocentric view of meaning underlies teaching and learning.[3] The data from the PMT reading classroom will be first considered.

PMT reading classes

In excerpt 1 (Unit 4: 4 June 1992), a view of reading as decodification is identified. The teacher not only refers to what the text is about before learner-readers actually get involved with the reading, but also requires that they underline the words which present some difficulty. This may convey to learner-readers the ideas that (1) meaning pre-exists reading; and (2) if they know the meaning of the words in the text they can understand it: meaning is equal to the sum of the different words in the text. It is, therefore, seen as being inherent in language, i.e., textually marked.

Excerpt 1[4]

T: So, let's see the text that says that the preoccupation with the environment begins at home. Then, let's first read the text silently. I would like you to underline the words which offer some difficulty to you while you read the text. Underline the words which prevent you from understanding the sentence. OK? ...

T: Now, let's see the difficulties with vocabulary. Did anyone underline any word in the first paragraph?

P1: Devastation.

T: Just a minute. Devastation. Could anyone explain the meaning of devastation to P1?

P2: It is as if it were a forest where there were lots of trees and the trees were destroyed.

In excerpts 2 and 3 (Unit 4: 4 June 1992) and in excerpt 4 below (Unit 11: 26 October 1992), the teacher requires the learner-reader to reply to her comprehension questions on the basis of the words in the text, i.e., the same logocentric view of meaning is detected.

Excerpt 2

T: According to the text, i.e., according to the words in the text, what would make this subject a fashionable subject?

P1: Everybody's responsibility.

T: Is this written in the text? ...

T: And how do you become aware of this fact in the text, i.e., that they did not respect this environmental issue?

P1: They had a lollipop and littered the street with the wrapper.

T: Aha! Quite right!

Excerpt 3

T: What?

P6: Environment pollution.

T: OK. Environment pollution. But did you understand that environment pollution in the text is equal to dirty beaches, noise and forest devastation? That is what matters.

Excerpt 4

P1: The answer is in the text?

T: Yes, an answer that is based on what is written in the text. ...

T: P2, have you found the answer there, have you found the passage in the text where you find this answer? ...

P2: Here, I found this here: "as a way of reacting against politicians' awareness".

T: What? 'Awareness'?

P2: 'Unawareness'.

In excerpt 5 below (Unit 4: 4 June 1992), a pupil is reading a section of the text aloud and changes the order of two words. Although that syntactic alteration is grammatical in Portuguese and does not affect the semantic level, the teacher, in a subservient attitude to the text corrects the learner-reader's change. Textual marks are conceived as the essential determinants of meaning.

Excerpt 5

T: Environment. That is right. P7, would you go on reading?

P7: 'This all, however, ...'

T: No! 'All this, however, ...'

P7: Right! 'All this, however, is treated as if somebody else caused environmental problems and not ourselves.'

In excerpts 6 and 7 below (Unit 8: 17 August 1992), the teacher invalidates the learner-readers' attempts to collaborate with the construction of meaning by insisting that meaning is in the text. In excerpt 6, P8 tries to give his own reading of a particular passage, but the teacher corrects his reading by saying that it does not correspond to what is in the text. The teacher says that P8 has modified the idea presented in the text. In excerpt 7, the teacher evaluates the learner-readers' interpretations as wrong because they did not look for meaning in the text. In other words, the same view that meaning is found in language is transparent here.

Excerpt 6

T: Just a minute, what did you say?

P8: There is nothing one can do.

T: Listen, P8. That is not what is in the text. She is not going to act this way. She identifies this attitude in her son. You tried to change the sentence as it is found in the text. The problem is that you also modified the idea. And that is not possible.

Excerpt 7

P3: Teacher.

T: OK, now let's pay attention to your interpretations, i.e., ... wrong interpretations. You need to pay attention to the text.

EFL reading classes

The focus of the analysis now moves to the interaction between teachers and pupils in EFL reading classes. The logocentric view of meaning found in PMT classes is also prevalent in the EFL classes. In learning to read English, learner-readers are also prompted to find the meaning of the text embedded in language. They are not encouraged to participate in the social construction of meaning. In excerpts 8 (Unit 3: 23 May 1988), 9 (Unit 5: 27 June 1988), 10 (Unit 8: 19 August 1988) and 11 (Unit 21: 28 August 1990) below, the teacher requires that learner-readers look for meaning in language, by focusing on the text, on individual words, and by paying attention to language as form.

Excerpt 8[5]

T: These words were at the beginning of the sentence and they are the subject. Do you know what the subject is?

P5: No.

Excerpt 9

T: What happened in the third paragraph?

P1: The life-guard saved him.

P2: The life-guard took him out of the sea. ...

T: What does 'break-time' mean?

P3: 'Break-time' [in Portuguese].

T: What is the text about?

P5: About what happens when kids are playing.

T: Does the text say that?

Excerpt 10

T: What does 'nurse' mean?

P5: 'Nurse' [in Portuguese].

T: What does 'their' mean?

P5: 'Their' [in Portuguese].

T: And [what is the meaning of the word] 'because'? [The teacher has one of her hands on one of her ears].

P5: 'Ear' [in Portuguese]. [The pupils actually thought that the teacher was indicating the meaning of the word 'because' to them by pointing to her ear.]

Excerpt 11

T: What is the text about?

P5: Too many people in the cities.

T: [T reads the first sentence of the text aloud] What does 'better' mean?

P5: 'Better' [in Portuguese].

T: What grade is that?

P5: Comparative.

T: The comparative form of what word?

In excerpt 12 (Unit 15: 29 May 1989) below, the teacher tests reading comprehension by asking learner-readers to summarize the text and evaluates their reading comprehension on the basis of the details from the text included in their summary. Comprehension is, therefore, perceived as the inclusion of text content in the summary.

Excerpt 12

T: P5, would you summarize the text?

P5: Italo dropped coffee.

T: Not enough. P6, would you like to take a chance? Let's listen to *P6*.

[P6 summarizes the text].

T: You didn't include all the details, but you summarized all the ideas.

In excerpt 13 (Unit 19: 4 August 1989) below, the teacher asks learners to read a composite text (i.e., a text specially constructed for teaching reading comprehension in a foreign language, containing English and Portuguese words) and equates reading as the ability to decode the meaning of individual words.

Excerpt 13

T: Let's read to find out the message of the text. ...

T: Have you figured out what the Portuguese words mean? You'll need to do that first in order to figure out the meaning of the English words. Then you should understand what the text means.

P5: Yes.

T: Did you understand what is written? And the message? What is the text about?

In excerpt 14 (Unit 21: 28 August 1990) below, the teacher asks learner-readers to construct sentences about the text and does not accept a pupil's sentence because it is about a consequence (i.e., slums) of the issue dealt with in the text (i.e., overpopulation) and not in the text itself. That is, the teacher operates with a view of meaning as being found in the text: the learner-readers' contribution to meaning construction is not accepted.

Excerpt 14

P9: There are slums in big cities.

T: Does the text talk about this? Does the text talk about slums?

P7: Who said that?

T: Slums are a consequence of overpopulation. That is in our experiences and not in the text.

Data derived from interviews conducted with both EFL and PMT learners at the end of the school year about their attitudes to written language also support my claim that both teachers and pupils in the Brazilian context conceive of meaning as being inherent in language. Pupils have indicated that (1) reading comprehension involves finding out meaning in text ("To understand a text, all you need to know is the meaning of the words" - fifth grade PMT pupil, 11 December 1992); and (2) written language contains the truth ("The written text tells the truth" - seventh grade EFL pupil, 28 November 1990; " I think I trust the text" - seventh grade EFL pupil, 28 November 1990). This perception of written language as truth revealing may be in fact seen as a corollary of the view of meaning as intrinsic to language typical of the reading classes investigated here. This perception may be said to be damaging to the learner-readers' construction of their social identities as readers since, by representing written language as truth revealing, they are clearly excluding themselves from the participation of meaning construction in reading comprehension.

Conclusion

The analysis of L1 and L2 teachers' and pupils' perceptions of the nature of language undertaken here demonstrates that teachers and learners in the Brazilian secondary schools of the public sector may be operating in classrooms with a logocentric view of meaning. They do not seem to perceive language as a social phenomenon, through which people construct and deconstruct meaning interactionally according to their own socio-political projects. That is, they seem to operate from a perception of language as form rather than of language as discourse. Because this perception sees meaning as inherent in language, i.e., anterior to language use in society, it naturalizes the existing power struggles in society which construct the meanings by which we live. These perceptions are, in fact, congruent with EFL and PMT classroom research findings (see Almeida

Filho et al., 1991), which indicate a tendency to teach form rather than use in Brazilian language classrooms in general, i.e., with teaching language as the formal manifestation of the language system. The findings reported in this paper, therefore, seem to indicate that language teachers in Brazil are not being educated from the perspective of what I have called here a discourse model of language. As pointed out above, this model seems to be more adequate from an educational perspective because it takes into account language use in society, i.e., how discourse participants construct meaning socially and, by so doing, construct society and are constituted by it.

Instead, the model of language in use in schools may be helping (1) to construct a view of written language as even more socially distant since it focuses on language as form, thus nurturing a logocentric view of language and making the acquisition of reading even more problematic; and (2) to consolidate the alienation of learner-readers since in the last analysis they are being taught to ignore their rights and responsibilities as citizens. The data suggest that in Brazilian schools the social identity of the learner-reader that is being constructed is that of language user as object. This may inhibit pupils from learning to operate in society as agents, who, by becoming aware of the discursive practices in which they are involved, are capable of emancipatory discourse and, therefore, of taking on the responsibilities of citizenship. This issue becomes particularly relevant if we take into account the fact that the data used in this research are derived from reading classrooms in schools attended by socially oppressed learners for whom written discourse seems to have relatively no social justification and for whom the great battle to be fought in school is the learning of reading. In other words, language education may be excluding learners from the hegemonic discursive practice implicit in written language use. This, therefore, may be making the seizure of power through discourse even more difficult for these pupils.

In a society where social inequalities are so flagrant, the issues raised here need to be addressed by those involved in language education. There seems to be a need for the design of language teacher education programmes and language teaching syllabi, informed by the discourse model of language argued for here. Finally, from a yet broader perspective, this paper draws attention to the need to continue the investigation of language use in schools as well as in other Brazilian institutions so that discourse participants involved in unequal social relations in these contexts, being made critically aware of the nature of language, can move forward to assume a subject position in society.

Notes

1 The research reported on here is derived from two different projects sponsored by Brazilian Research Council (CNPq) (CNPq 300194-86/2) and FUJB grants. I am grateful to Alice Freire (UFRJ), Branca Ribeiro (UFRJ) and Rodrigo Fernandes (UFRJ) for their suggestions on a first version of this paper.

2 The teachers participating in this research are extremely dedicated professionals, who, despite the poor salaries they make, are bravely fighting the everyday battle of education in the public sector. The critical points to be raised below as regards their views of the nature of language do not imply criticism of their professional skills but rather of an educational system, which has not invested in ongoing professional development that would keep teachers theoretically informed about new developments in language education, and, therefore, able to look critically at their own practices.

3 It should be made clear that this analysis does not imply that the language system is unimportant or that there is no need to attend to the language system or to its formal manifestation as found in the text when we read or when we teach reading comprehension since after all there is no comprehension without recourse to the language system as manifested in the text. What the interpretation of the data implies, however, is that the text should be seen as a resource for the construction of meaning, which has no meaning of itself. As argued above, meaning is viewed in this paper as being socio-interactionally constructed by discourse participants. Therefore, from this perspective, the formal manifestation of the language system in the text should not be treated in reading classes as if meaning resided in it.

4 Since classes were taught in Portuguese, I have translated the transcriptions of the excerpts of the classes presented here for the purpose of this paper. I will be using the initials *T* for teacher and *P* for pupil.

5 Although these are excerpts of EFL classes, they were conducted in Portuguese because they are reading classes, i.e., the syllabus aims at the teaching of reading comprehension. I have translated the transcriptions for the purpose of this paper.

13 Critical Language Education

ANITA L. WENDEN

Introduction

In his plenary address to the 9th AILA Congress (1990), Halliday challenged applied linguists to use their expertise to shed light on the social and ecological problems of our time. Pointing out that it is language which constructs the ideologies that sustain the social institutions and practices causing these problems, he urged them to show, for example, "how the grammar produces the ideology of growth and growthism"; to replace "war discourse with peace discourse ...". Other linguists, who share Halliday's view on the social utility of linguistic research, further argue that language is a factor, like political, economic, and cultural factors, which needs to be investigated in the search for insight into critical social problems (e.g. Urban, 1988; Wertsch, 1987; Connor-Linton et al., 1987; Mehan and Wills, 1988). These same concerns underlie the work of the applied (critical) linguists who have contributed to *Language and Peace*. Their research illustrates the role played by language in social life, especially those aspects of social practice that inhibit the achievement of a comprehensive peace, i.e. a peace marked by an absence of social discrimination be it based on ethnicity, race, gender, or class, and the absence of physical and psychological violence as the means of dealing with human conflict.[1] The research shows how language works through discourse to communicate and reproduce ideologies that support the use of war as a legitimate option for resolving national conflicts as well as inegalitarian and discriminatory social institutions and practices.

These insights on language use support and illustrate earlier conclusions presented in the Seville Statement on Violence (1986). Prepared by social, behavioural, and natural scientists from twelve nations and five continents, who met under the auspices of the Spanish National Commission for UNESCO, the document debunks the myths that contribute to the belief that violence is innate in humans. One of their conclusions points to the role played by social institutions and learned skills, *including language*, in socializing citizens into the use of violence:

> It is scientifically incorrect to say that war is caused by instinct or any single motivation. Here our social scientists took the leading role and showed how modern war is not a matter of emotion so much as the institutional use of obedience, suggestibility, idealism and social skills, such as language ... traits of violence are exaggerated in the training of soldiers and in the preparation of support for war in the general populations. (UNESCO, 1986)

If, as has just been noted, language socializes into violence, it can also contribute to socializing for peace. This points to another dimension of the social utility of research studies inspired by critical linguistics, such as those presented in the preceding chapters. That is, insights from the research and the framework of concepts that guide it can be used as a basis for enhancing both peace education and language education.[2] All language users need to be made aware of the subtle role language plays in developing and consolidating ideologies. They need to realize that as participants in social discourse, they may unconsciously contribute to the reproduction of these ideologies and, in some cases, the maintenance of social practices of which they disapprove (see Fowler and Kress, 1979).

This last chapter will, therefore, present a content schema to guide curriculum development in critical language education. The schema will consist of discourse structures that are the focus of analysis in critical linguistics (or critical discourse analysis). First, a rationale for making critical language education a core objective in curricula for peace education and language education will be offered. Then, the discourse structures that make up the schema will be described. Following each description a set of questions that can be used to guide the discussion and critique of a particular discourse in terms of that discourse structure will be outlined.[3]

Social need

Together with its responsibility to nurture personal development, society has always assigned to its educational institutions the task of preparing students to understand and even remedy its problems (see, e.g., Smith, 1950; Taba, 1962). Today, however, the educational mission is qualitatively different, for it is necessary to prepare students to participate as citizens and professionals in a globally interdependent world. Learners of all ages must be provided with the knowledge, skills, and attitudes they will need to play an active role in the development and processes of what Elise Boulding (1988) has referred to as the emerging global civic culture.

Civic culture, as defined by Boulding, refers to the interactions that create and maintain the common public interest which, in turn, provides the context within which we can pursue our private lives with our families and friends. It includes physical space we share in common with others and social space. Social space refers to the activities whereby we provide for our basic needs and, generally, enhance our mutual well-being as a society. To date, our experience of civic culture has been local and national. Interdependence among nations is creating a global civic culture. The United Nations, transnational corporations, nongovernmental organizations, professional organizations, and grassroots movements are all instances of this emerging global civic culture. They represent attempts on the part of international and transnational groups to forge a framework based on a common global interest within which to pursue their common purposes. Problems of international complexity which cross national frontiers to touch upon the lives of ordinary citizens are further evidence of global interdependence. The reports in the previous chapters have pointed to some of these - the ongoing presence of social discrimination based on class (e.g. Haidar and Rodríguez, Moita Lopes), race (e.g. Clyne), ethnicity (e.g. Blommaert and Verschueren, Lowenberg) and the emergence of regional and ethnic wars despite the termination of the Cold War (e.g. Vaughan, Musolff). These are problems that do not respect political divisions, nor are they inhibited by distance. They can only be resolved on a global scale demanding global cooperation for a solution.

Educational response

Comprehensive peace education is a long term educational strategy that intends to respond to the challenges of interdependence. It provides a framework for the planning of educational activities that will prepare present and future citizens to participate in the development of the emerging global civic culture and to deal with the social and ecological problems that beset it. The curriculum of the University for Peace[4] (Reardon, 1988) outlines three substantive areas of study that constitute comprehensive peace education, i.e. quality of life, planetary civic order, global problematique. Central to each of these three areas is the need for critical language education (CLE).

The rubric *quality of life* deals with social, economic and cultural topics. Notable among them is culture and languages. According to Reardon (1988) who served on the University of Peace Council (1983-86):

> Quality of life in a planetary society requires sophisticated and sensitive understanding of other cultures and the ability to communicate across cultures ... Knowledge of the earth's cultures and the ways of life of its many peoples is perhaps the first and fundamental form of peace knowledge. Human languages are the medium for encoding and transmitting knowledge. (Reardon, 1988, p. 43).

Under the rubric *global problematique,* research and study will be dedicated to the elimination of poverty and to an equitable global development that can provide adequately for the needs of the world's people while sustaining the basic life support system of the planet. The curriculum "recasts the human role as that of functioning as an integral part, rather than as master of the ecology of planet earth" (Reardon, 1988, p. 43). Finally, the rubric *planetary civic order* will deal with the political, administrative and organizational aspects of the international order. Education for participation in a just and peaceful planetary social order will require "knowledge and understanding of comparative and conflicting values ...". It will seek to address the causes of conflict, including 'the mindset' that produces it. Such education will remain sensitive to the fact that conflicts are going to be viewed differently "... depending upon the ideological, political and geographic and cultural frameworks they bring to the viewing of the problems" (Reardon, 1988, p. 44).

CLE has a key role to play in promoting the research and study included in each of these substantive areas. It can contribute to the learnings included under 'quality of life' by helping learners gain insight into culture specific mindsets[5] underlying and encoded in language. In this way it can enable them to discover and appreciate the distinct social values and attitudes particular to ethnic/culture groups. Equitable development and respect for earth systems will require serious value and attitudinal changes. To be achieved, a severe critique of the ideologies that have contributed to social inequity and the destruction of earth systems will be necessary. CLE could provide the first step in this process by helping develop an awareness of how these ideologies are firmly naturalized in our discourse practices. Finally the resolution of the problems facing the international order will require an understanding of the varied ideological, political, cultural frameworks people bring to the negotiation of solutions to problems. Again, CLE can facilitate the development of this understanding.

A content schema for critical language education

Table 13.1 presents a content schema that is intended to serve as a guide to peace educators and language educators who wish to make critical language education a part of their curriculum.

Table 13.1
Content schema for critical language education

The content
Explicit propositions
(1) Recurring keywords
(2) Related themes

The framework
Text schemas
(1) Kinds
(2) Significance of schema structure

Scope of identification
(1) Global
(2) National
(3) Local/regional

The presentation
Modes of legitimation
(1) Argumentation
(2) Characterizations
(3) Explicitness
(4) Specificity
(5) Rhetorical devices

Lexicalization*
(1) Lexical choices
(2) Lexical transfer
(3) Pronominals

* The subcategories listed under lexicalization are intended to be illustrative of the many ways word choice can support propositions and ideologies.

Derived primarily (though not exclusively) from the discourse structures that guided the research presented in the previous chapters of this volume, the schema outlines a set of categories that can guide the critical comprehension of discourse in printed texts (e.g. a newspaper editorial, a chapter in a scholarly book, a governmental document, a conference report) or oral media (e.g. a public debate, a TV news report or panel discussion, a political speech, trade union negotiations). The categories represent aspects of discourse that readers/listeners (R/L's) need to become aware of in order to understand how language works to communicate and reproduce the ideologies that underlie communications about controversial issues.[6] Based upon group value systems and shaping social attitudes, these ideologies are key to understanding why certain beliefs and social institutions, which condone and sustain the practice of physical, psychological, structural and ecological violence in our societies, are tolerated, supported and, in some cases, defended.[7]

R/L's need to understand what these various discourse structures are and how they work, especially in discourse about global issues, such as war, ecological deterioration, social discrimination and inequality. For all of these topics refer to conditions that are obstacles to a comprehensive peace. Of course, it is not intended that lay persons become critical discourse analysts, but they do need to learn to go beyond the decoding of surface linguistic structures to a critical analysis of how language is used to construe meaning and so, to communicate and reproduce particular ideologies in written and oral discourse.

Language and discourse

R/Ls should first be made aware of the following basic notions about language and the function of discourse:

(1) Language actively shapes and gives meaning to human experience

That is, language is not "a neutral medium for the description of reality" (Hook, 1984, p. 259). It is not to be looked through, like a windowpane, to see the real world (Mehan and Wills, 1988). Rather the choice of certain ways of talking constitutes different versions of the world and influences actual practice and the way in which people think about particular objects, events, situations. In other words, it is language that gives meaning to the categories and concepts we select to represent a particular view of human experience (Halliday, 1990).

(2) Social groups have differing views of the same event

The construction of meaning depends upon the biographical, historical, socio-cultural and political perspectives of various groups. That is, it is individuals and the groups of which they are a member that assign meaning to or determine how to interpret a particular object, event, or situation. Thus, meanings will vary and there may be a competition among groups to determine whose representation is to be accepted as the correct or appropriate version, with each view striving to have their view dominate.[8]

(3) Discourse is the basic unit through which meaning is represented and interpreted [9]

Meaning is neither represented nor interpreted word by word or sentence by sentence or even paragraph by paragraph. It is the discourse that must first be examined and analysed, i.e. that coherent whole constituted of these smaller linguistic units and unified by a semantic topic or event.

(4) Discourse is not limited to one article, report or speech event

Discourse can consist of the several texts or speech events that focus on a particular topic or event. That is, it is not necessarily limited to one text or oral presentation. For example, to clarify and contrast views on the 1982 war between Lebanon and Israel, editorials from four different newspapers written over the period of a summer were examined (Vaughan, Chapter 4); to understand how the balance metaphor shaped views on European security, leading articles from the British weekly *The Economist*, which appeared over a period of about ten years, were read (Schäffner, Chapter 5).

A global view of discourse

The R/L, then, needs to understand that discourse must be viewed globally to determine what content it carries and how this content is organized and presented or framed.

Propositions, keywords and themes

In order to comprehend and critically evaluate discourse on global issues, it is necessary to identify or abstract from the information the main or overarching propositions that are made about the topic under discussion. These will represent the writer/speaker's view on the topic or event that is the focus of the discourse. In a well written piece of exposition, these propositions may be easily found in a writer's thesis statement and/or the subpoints used to develop it. However, in other types of writing, especially media reports and opinion pieces, these propositions are not always so clearly evident. The R/L will need to learn to look for recurring keywords and themes that constitute the propositions.[10]

Vaughan (Chapter 4), for example, found that editorials in four newspapers, each representing the view of one of the key actors in the 1982 war between Lebanon and Israel, agreed on the following propositions regarding war, peace, and the role of nations, i.e. that:

(1) War is justified, if not required, under certain circumstances.

(2) Property destruction, displacement of people, injuries and deaths are justified in large numbers if key political goals are achieved.

(3) The massacring of defenceless civilians is wrong.

Schäffner's analysis (Chapter 5) abstracted two main propositions that dominated thinking during the early 1980s, at the height of the Cold War, from articles in *The Economist,* i.e. that (1) Russia had achieved military superiority, and (2) The West had to restore the balance (to keep the peace). In their analysis of articles from mainstream daily newspapers in about twelve European countries over a three-month period, Blommaert and Verschueren (Chapter 9) identified what they refer to as the doctrine of homogeneity underlying nationalist movements, i.e. the view that ethnicity - similarity in descent, history, culture, religion and language - is the basis for identifying a 'nation' or 'people'.

Table 13.2 lists questions that can help the R/L identify themes and propositions.

Table 13.2
Themes and propositions

(1) What keywords does the writer/speaker use to discuss the topic of the discourse? Which of these are repeated most often?

(2) What key themes does the writer/speaker present about the topic of the discourse? Which of these themes recur?

(3) What propositions (i.e. basic views on the event, problem, ...) are made with the keywords? implied by the recurring themes?

(4) Consider the keywords, propositions and themes. Can you infer what the writer believes about the issue that is the focus of the discourse?

Text schemas

Text schemas or schematic structures refer to ways in which the information in a communication can be organized. They are a type of plan or blueprint that writers or speakers must follow.

These 'plans' may be determined by the rhetorical schema writers select. Do they wish to focus on causes? consequences? problem/solutions? Do they prefer to highlight similarities or differences? The selection of a rhetorical schema reflects how writers wish to construe a topic/problem. For example, the articles that advocated the need to balance the nuclear arsenal of both the former USSR and the

West were written according to a problem/solution text schema (Schäffner, Chapter 5). Text schemas are also determined by the kind of genre used to communicate. Is it an editorial? a narrative? a TV debate? a negotiation? a government document? The various genres analysed in previous chapters, for example, include editorials (Vaughan, Chapter 4), TV news reports (Musolff, Chapter 6), radio talkback shows (Clyne, Chapter 7), trade union negotiations (Haidar and Rodríguez, Chapter 8), newspaper articles (Blommaert and Verschueren, Chapter 9; Lowenberg, Chapter 10), doctor-patient discourse (Gonçalves, Chapter 11), teacher-student discourse (Moita Lopes, Chapter 12).

Each genre of communication has its own purpose and inbuilt script, which determines its basic structure. An editorial, for example, highlights an event or set of events that readers expect to be of importance and deserving of their attention. The event or set of events is organized within the context of a framework (selected by the writer) that establishes its logical consistency and that is also expected to make sense, i.e. be familiar, to the readers (Vaughan, Chapter 4).

Furthermore, each component of the script has a particular function. Van Dijk (1987a) describes the function of the component parts of narratives told about foreigners (usually to communicate ethnic prejudice). The stories begin with a description of the *setting*, which may include both time and place. The *orientation* refers to a usually trivial daily situation and is followed by the *complication*, usually an account of the social deviancy of the 'foreigner', and the *resolution*, which contrasts such behaviour with the rational and calm response of the non-foreigner. A concluding *evaluation* may be made either by the story-teller or by one of the characters in the story. Thus, while a text schema is basically neutral, as exemplified by 'foreigner stories', it may be used to highlight information that represents an outgroup negatively and, therefore, to communicate the ideology that underlies the writer's attitude towards that group, in this case, racism. Those parts of a script which have more prominence than others, such as the headlines in a news report, can also be used for the same purpose.

Table 13.3 (page 220) lists questions the R/L can use to analyse how the text schema is used to present information in a particular discourse.

Scope of identification

Scope of identification, a factor defined in the research on the nuclear debate (e.g. Wertsch, 1987), should also be taken into account to understand how a writer frames the content of a communication. That is, how broadly does the speaker/writer define the *scope* of the problem, event, ...? Is it a local matter? national? regional? global? In discussing the problem, with whom does the writer identify? with a particular group? a country? the whole world?

Table 13.3
Text schema

---

(1) *What kind of rhetorical plan does the writer/speaker use to organize the information? e.g. cause and effect, problem and solution, ...?*

(2) *Could the same topic be presented using a different plan? Would the writer need more or different information to do so? How might you react to a different plan?*

(3) *What kind of discourse genre is used to present this issue (i.e. editorial, TV debate, ...)?*

(4) *How can this discourse be analysed (i.e. broken up into different parts)? What is the function of each part?*

(5) *Which part do you pay most attention to? Why? What kind of information has the speaker/writer put into this part/section?*

(6) *Consider your answers to the above questions. What do they suggest about the ideology implicit in the discourse?*

As noted in several of the preceding chapters, a narrow scope of identification, which sets up an *us* versus *them* dichotomy, can manifest and maintain inegalitarian ideologies (e.g. van Dijk, Chapter 2; Clyne, Chapter 7; Haidar and Rodríguez, Chapter 8) as well as pro-war ideologies when the 'them' is explicitly portrayed as 'the enemy' (e.g. Vaughan, Chapter 4; Musolff, Chapter 6).

Table 13.4 lists questions that the R/L can use to analyse a discourse for scope of identification.

Table 13.4
Scope of identification

---

(1) *What group(s) does the writer/speaker refer to in this communication?*

(2) *Does the writer identify with any one of the groups referred to?*

(3) *Is the problem/topic presented as a matter of concern for one group of people within a country? a world region? the whole world/global community?*

(4) *Is the problem/topic presented in such a way that it sets up conflict, opposition, competition between groups?*

(5) *Consider the scope of the problem. What clues does it provide, if any, regarding the beliefs underlying this communication?*

A micro perspective

At the micro or local level the reader/listener must be able to understand (1) how basic propositions are legitimated and justified and (2) what aspects of the language system are utilized to communicate these proposals and convey the ideology that underlies them.

Modes of legitimation

Argumentation According to Wertsch (1987) it is important to examine the forms of reasoning by which arguments used to legitimate a particular proposition or theme are presented. For example, during the Cold War, in the debate over the development and use of nuclear weapons, defence intellectuals and government officials couched their arguments in terms of formal logic. They used a decontextualized mode of reasoning that disallows concrete particulars regarding the human impact of nuclear war in favour of abstract generalizations and statistics (Cohn, 1988). In contrast, members of the peace movement, such as MEND (Mothers Embracing Nuclear Disarmament)[11] used a contextualized mode of reasoning (see Mehan and Wills, 1988). Such a mode of reasoning emphasized the human aspects of war in concrete detail, making emotional and moral appeals. Differences in argumentation of first, second and third world country participants in the Law of the Seas conference have also been documented.[12] Countries were distinguished by either an inductive or deductive approach to reasoning and by arguments that were pragmatic and legalistic or emotional and imagistic (Walker, 1990).

When the modes of argumentation among participants in a discourse differ or when discourse participants select a mode of argumentation that other participants do not consider appropriate to the topic and/or context, the result is what Wertsch (1987) referred to as 'fragmented discourse', which often leads to a loss of credibility between or among discourse participants and a breakdown in communication.

Characterization Ideology can also be indirectly supported by the way in which various actions, events and/or persons are characterized. Van Dijk refers to 'biased' reasons and causes which attribute blame to one group as opposed to another. The same kind of one-sided approach to characterizing was identified in Haidar and Rodríguez's (Chapter 8) analysis of how workers involved in a trade union-management dispute characterized themselves and their opponents; how members of the subordinated urban group characterized the causes of Mexico's economic problems. On the other hand, as demonstrated by Vaughan's (Chapter 4) analysis of editorials from American, Palestinian, Lebanese and Israeli newspapers during the 1982 war with Lebanon, the four groups represented by these newspapers, who differed on almost every issue relating to the war and its causes, did agree on one particular set of characterizations, i.e. that

(1) Lebanon was foundering as a country,
(2) Israel was reacting too violently,
(3) the Palestinian problem needed to be solved, and
(4) the United States was the nation with the most power and, by inference, likely to have the greatest influence on the crisis.

Explicitness In examining the kind of information presented in a discourse, it is also important to consider what has been left unsaid and why. What other information might have been included and why was it not? In some cases, as noted by van Dijk (Chapter 2), such choices are made to enhance a positive self-representation of one's own group and negative representation of the other group. Haidar and Rodríguez (Chapter 8) refer to rules of exclusion, which determine what one may or may not talk about in a particular discourse. In their research, for example, trade union leaders were not allowed to talk about matters which might lead to worker dissidence. Rather they were expected to discuss worker-employer relations in a positive way. In their discourse with university administrators, students were not supposed to discuss politics (though they did) but were forced to talk about topics imposed by the university administration. Such rules, as Haidar and Rodríguez have noted, serve an ideology that maintains social inequality.

Specificity Related to but distinct from explicitness of information in a discourse is the degree of specificity (or generality) of the information. As noted above, the war rhetoric of government officials and defence intellectuals de-emphasizes specific details about the human impact. Similarly, during the Gulf War, the Allies were constrained by the 'Rescue Scenario', through which they chose to represent their engagement, to avoid concrete details about the human impact of their weaponry on civilians. On the other hand, they were anxious to highlight as specifically as possible the barbarous and 'ruffianlike' behaviour of the Iraqi soldiers (Musolff, Chapter 6).

Rhetorical devices Rhetorical devices are specific ways of using language so as to enhance the effectiveness of the processes of argumentation and characterization described above. Van Dijk (Chapter 2) refers to some of these, such as hyperbole, understatements, irony and metaphor, as having a close relationship to social beliefs. Three are described, here, for illustrative purposes: metaphors, cultural analogies, and euphemisms.

(1) Metaphors

As noted in Part II (cf. Chilton and Lakoff, Schäffner, Musolff) metaphors are our primary means of conceptualizing the world. The power of the metaphor derives from its ability to assimilate new experiences to familiar patterns of perception; to project one knowledge domain onto another so as to allow the newer or abstract domain of experience to be understood in terms of the former and more concrete. As aptly illustrated by each of the above mentioned authors, metaphors have served as a basis and justification for policy making. The 'state-as-person' guided American foreign policy during and after the Cold War (Chilton and Lakoff, Chapter 3). The 'balance metaphor' essentially shaped discussions regarding nuclear policy and national security during that same period (Schäffner, Chapter 5), and the 'Rescue Scenario', the metaphorical frame used to represent American involvement in the Gulf War, served both to justify their participation and to determine which events would signal the beginning and the ending of the war (Musolff, Chapter 6).

(2) Cultural analogies

Cultural analogies are metaphors that draw upon well known domestic images to give war a human face. They personalize the acts of war in terms of cultural experiences so as to win sympathy and understanding for something that is both difficult to understand and traumatic to contemplate. Examples from Moss's (1985) analysis of presidential addresses include the comparison of international negotiations with industrial relations and the upgrading of missile systems with making new car models.

(3) Euphemisms

A euphemism is an alternative choice of word used to disguise something unpleasant or undesirable. Clyne (Chapter 7) refers to euphemisms used to describe (disguise) the work of racists ('care of Jews in a concentration camp'). Technostrategic language (see Cohn, 1988; Ross, 1984)[13] is replete with euphemisms and abstract terms, such as statistics and acronyms, all of which serve to depersonalize the consequences of war, i.e. to disguise its human impact (e.g. 'collateral damage'; 'urban targets'; 'countervalue attacks'; 'servicing targets') and to give it the appearance of scientific credibility (e.g. 'the attack consists of <u>6559 MT</u>, of which <u>5951 MT</u> are groundbursts on ... targets', from Ross, 1984).

Table 13.5 lists questions that the R/L can use to identify and evaluate the ways in which a writer/speaker legitimates his/her views (or propositions) in a particular discourse.

Table 13.5
Questions to identify modes of legitimation

(1) *What arguments does the writer/speaker put forth to support his/her propositions?*

(2) *What mode of reasoning is used? Is it intuitive or deductive? Does it appeal to the emotions or to reason? What effect does the writer's mode of reasoning have on you? Why?*

(3) *What kinds of arguments are used? Are they based on fact? moral principles? legalistic? Do you agree with the arguments? Why?*

(4) *How do these arguments and other information represent or characterize the groups, events, topics discussed in the communication? Is the characterization positive or negative? one-sided? stereotypical?*

(5) *How has the writer/speaker's characterization influenced your view of these groups? events? topics?*

(6) *What information is presented in detail and which ideas/facts remain general and vague? How does this influence the characterization of the groups, event and/or topic under discussion?*

(7) *What other information might the writer/speaker have presented about the groups, events, and/or topic under discussion? Why might that information not have been included?*

(8) *List the rhetorical devices (e.g. metaphors, euphemisms, ...) used in the discourse. What ideas do the figures in these rhetorical devices represent? What attitudes do they evoke? Can these ideas and attitudes be correctly applied to the propositions in the discourse? Why? Why not?*

(9) *Consider the various dimensions of discourse referred to in (1)-(8). What do they reveal about the ideology underlying this discourse?*

Lexicalization

What words do writer/speakers use to argue, characterize, legitimate their propositions? From among the wide range available to them, which ones do they choose and what do these word choices reveal about the underlying ideology?

(1) Lexical choices

Clyne (Chapter 7) describes and illustrates the following categories of words that overtly sustain a racist ideology, i.e. words which

(1) nurture separateness among groups (e.g. 'black' versus 'white');
(2) represent people in terms of group affiliation and, thus, deprive them of their individuality (e.g. 'Asians' - to include Chinese, Turks, Indians, ...);
(3) are selected from the strong end of the lexical field (i.e. dysphemisms) for victims of racism ('Asylum seekers out.');
(4) label a group in negative terms (e.g. 'power hungry Jews', 'uncivilized black Africans').

(2) Lexical transfer

Lexical choice, in the case of multilingual speakers, can also entail lexical transfer with words from a first language being transferred into the second language. As Lowenberg (Chapter 10) indicates such shifts can contribute to the development and maintenance of a nationalist ideology based on group homogeneity (cf. Blommaert and Verschueren, Chapter 9). Lowenberg describes how the replacement of certain English words with words from Malay have, on the one hand, excluded from certain opportunities those who are not Malay or Malay speaking or, on the other hand, defined them in Malay terms and so neutralized their ethnic identity.

(3) Pronominals

Haidar and Rodríguez (Chapter 8) show how the choice of pronouns represents and sustains collectivist and individualist ideologies. Speakers from their 'subordinated urban group', for example, made scant use of 'yo' ['I'] and frequent use of 'uno' ['one'] whereby the subject speaks in the name of the collectivity (rather than her/himself) and 'nosotros' ['we'] which shows adherence to the social group. In contrast, speakers from the 'dominant urban group' made frequent use of 'yo' ['I'] thus manifesting individuality and freedom in contrast to the collectivist view of self underlying the subordinated group speakers. The use of the respectful version of 'you', i.e. 'usted', by the subordinated group speakers and the familiar version, i.e. 'tú' by the dominant group speakers is another example of how power distance is revealed and maintained through language use. Pronominals have also been used to support a pro-war ideology as when they are used to draw in a reader to identify with a writer's or speaker's perspective and evoke a positive affective response to the basic proposition of a text (Urban, 1988) or to coalesce speaker, audience and theme so that the immediate impression is that of unity (Moss, 1985).

Table 13.6 lists questions that the R/L can use to analyse and discuss word choice.

Table 13.6
Word choice

(1) *Make a list of the words and phrases used to describe:*
– the various groups referred to in the communication
– the topic that is the main focus of the article

(2) *How do these words influence the way you think about the groups? the topic?*

(3) *Separate the words into groups according to those that separate, deny individuality, have negative meanings and other differences that may characterize lexical choice in a particular discourse.*

(4) *Make a list of the pronouns. To whom do they refer? Are they used to create a sense of unity between the reader/listener and the writer/speaker? between/among the groups discussed? Or are they used to separate?*

(5) *Consider the words listed in (1) and the use of pronouns. What do they reveal about the ideology that underlies this discourse?*

Conclusion

Most educational institutions will include citizenship courses in their curricula. Social studies courses in primary and secondary schools are also intended to contribute to the development of a civically literate citizen. Twenty years ago, when the oil boycott made the notion of global interdependence palpable to citizens of the Western world, the term 'new civic literacy' appeared in the writings of some adult educators (e.g. Morehouse, 1975) in recognition of the fact that a literate citizen needed to acquire an understanding of the complexities of global interdependence. Under the rubric 'just and peaceful planetary order' discussed above, the United Nations curriculum for peace has expanded even further the skills and knowledge needed by a civically literate citizen in our day, making global civic education an integral part of peace education. This paper has argued that critical language education be included as a part of global citizenship education. It especially challenges applied linguists and foreign and second language educators to lead the way in translating insights from the research into educational tasks and materials.

Notes

1 The term comprehensive peace was introduced by Betty Reardon, an American peace educator, who is one of the leading theorists and practitioners in the field internationally. See Chapter 1 for a brief description of the evolution of the field of peace education that led to this term and Reardon (1988) for an extended discussion.

2 See earlier chapters by Vaughan, Schäffner, Clyne, Haidar and Rodríguez, Gonçalves, Moita Lopes for similar views on the educational implications of these research findings.

3 The questions are intended to be selected, specified and adapted to the particular text/oral communication being analysed and discussed and to the linguistic and background knowledge of the students.

4 The University for Peace was established by the United Nations in 1980; it is based in Costa Rica. During the first planning phase, the University council and staff conducted a study of the content and practice of peace education around the world. From a long and varied list of topics a general conceptual framework was distilled to serve as a possible framework for curriculum development (Reardon, 1988).

5 The term 'mindset' is based on Fisher (1988).

6 The set of discourse structures included in the schema is not intended to be comprehensive. See van Dijk (this volume), for others.

7 While the chapter focuses on the use of CLE to understand how ideologies are communicated, with some adaptation, the same could be used to understand cultural mindsets as well.

8 See Holquist (1983) for a discussion of the politics of representation.

9 The term 'discourse' as it is intended in this chapter, does not refer to the process of discourse in general but to any one instance of a discourse type, e.g. a particular editorial or a series of editorials, one or several TV newscasts, etc.

10 See Vaughan and Schäffner (this volume) for illustrations of procedures for identifying keywords and themes.

11 MEND is an American anti-nuclear group that was particularly active in the United States in the 1980s.

12 The Law of the Sea conference actually refers to the Third United Nations Conference on the Law of the Sea (UNCLOS III) convened in Caracas, Venezuela in 1974.

13 As defined by Cohn (1988) technostrategic language refers to the specialized language used by defence intellectuals to talk about the development of weaponry and strategy for making nuclear war.

Bibliography

Abrams, Irwin (1986), 'Nobel Peace Prizes' in Laszlo, Erwin and Yoo, Jong Youl (eds), *World Encylopedia for Peace*, Pergamon Press, Oxford, pp. 52-6.

Acheson, D. (1987), *Present at the Creation*, Norton, New York.

Adams, K.L. and Brink, D.T. (eds) (1990), *Perspectives on Official English: The Campaign for English as the Official Language of the USA*, Mouton de Gruyter, Berlin.

Alisjahbana, S.T. (1976), *Language Planning and Modernization: The Case of Indonesian and Malaysian*, Mouton, The Hague.

Allan, K. and Burridge, K. (1991), *Euphemisms and Dysphemisms*, Oxford University Press, New York.

Almeida Filho, Jose Carlos; Baghin, Debora; Consolo, Douglas; Santos, Joao C.; Alvarenga, Mangali and Viana, Nelson (1991), 'A Representação do Processo de Aprender no Livro Didático Nacional de Língua Estrangeira Moderna no 1o. grau', *Trabalhoe de Linguistica Aplicada*, vol. 17, January/June, pp. 67-97.

Anderson, B. (1983), *Imagined Communities: Reflections on the Origin and Spread of Nationalism*, Verso, London.

Anderson, Gary L. (1989), 'Critical Ethnography in Education: Origins, Current Status, and New Directions', *Review of Educational Research*, vol. 59, no. 3, pp. 249-70.

Asmah, H. O. (1979), *Language Planning for Unity and Efficiency*, Penerbit Universiti Malaya, Kuala Lumpur.

Asmah, Haji Omar (1982), 'Language Spread and Recession in Malaysia and the Malay Archipelago' in Cooper, Robert L. (ed.), *Language Spread: Studies in Diffusion and Social Change*, Indiana University Press, Bloomington, IN, pp. 198-213.

Asmah, Haji Omar (1985), 'Patterns of Language Communication in Malaysia', *Southeast Asian Journal of Social Science*, vol. 13, no. 1, pp. 229-50.

Aspelagh, Robert (1986), 'Peace Education' in Laszlo, Erwin and Yoo, Jong Youl (eds), *World Encylopedia for Peace*, Pergamon Press, Oxford, pp. 182-90.

Augustin, John (1982), 'Regional Standards of English in Peninsular Malaysia' in Pride, John B. (ed.), *New Englishes*, Newbury House, Rowley, MA, pp. 248-58.

Austin, J.L. (1962), *How to do Things with Words*, Oxford University Press, London.

Barker, M. (1981), *The New Racism*, Junction Press, London.

Barth, F. (ed.) (1982), *Ethnic Groups and Boundaries: The Social Organization of Culture Differences*, Universitetsforlaget, Oslo.

Baudrillard, Jean (1991), 'The Reality Gulf', *The Guardian*, 11 January 1991.

Bedarida, Catherine (1988), 'University Leaders Seek to Expand Study of Peace', *The Chronicle of Higher Education*, 28 September 1988.

Billig, M. (1991), *Ideology and Opinions. Studies in Rhetorical Psychology*, Sage, Newbury Park, CA.

Billig, M., et al. (1988), *Ideological Dilemmas*, Sage, London.

Blommaert, Jan and Verschueren, Jef (1991), 'The Pragmatics of Minority Politics in Belgium', *Language in Society*, vol. 20, no. 4, pp. 503-31.

Blommaert, Jan and Verschueren, Jef (1992), *Het Belgische Migrantendebat. De Pragmatiek van de Abnormalisering* [The Belgian Migrant Debate. The Pragmatics of Abnormalization], International Pragmatics Association, Antwerp.

Blommaert, Jan and Verschueren, Jef (1993a), 'European Concepts of Nation-building', Paper presented at the conference on *Ethnicity, Identity and Nationalism in South Africa: Comparative Perspectives*, Grahamstown, South Africa, 20-24 April 1993.

Blommaert, Jan and Verschueren, Jef (1993b), 'The Rhetoric of Tolerance, or, What Police Officers are Taught about Migrants', *Journal of Intercultural Studies*, vol. 14, no. 1, pp. 49-63.

Boden, D. and Zimmerman, D. H. (eds) (1991), *Talk and Social Structure. Studies in Ethnomethodology and Conversation Analysis*, Polity Press, Cambridge.

Bok, S. (1990), *A Strategy for Peace: Human Values and the Threat of War*, Random House, New York.

Booth, Ken and Wheeler, Nicholas (1992), 'Contending Philosophies about Security in Europe' in McInnes, Colin (ed.), *Security and Strategy in the New Europe*, Routledge, London and New York, pp. 3-36.

Boulding, E. (1988), *Building a Global Civic Culture: Education for an Interdependent World*, Teachers College Press, New York.

Boutros-Ghali, Boutros (1992), *An Agenda for Peace: Preventive Diplomacy, Peacemaking and Peace-Keeping*, Report of the Secretary-General pursuant to the Statement adopted by the Summit Meeting of the Security Council on 31 January 1992, United Nations, New York.

Brock-Utne, B. (1989), *Feminist Perspectives on Peace and Peace Education*, Pergamon Press, New York.

Brown, G. and Yule, G. (1983), *Discourse Analysis*, Cambridge University Press, Cambridge.

Brown, P. and Levinson, S.C. (1987), *Politeness: Some Universals in Language Use*, Cambridge University Press, Cambridge.

Bruck, Peter and Roach, Colleen (1993), 'Dealing with Reality: The News Media and the Promotion of Peace' in Roach, Colleen (ed.), *Communication and Culture in War and Peace*, Sage, Newbury Park, CA, pp. 71-96.

Bunge, F.M. (1985), *Malaysia: A Country Study*, Foreign Area Studies, The American University, Washington, DC.

Burkhardt, A., Hebel, F. and Hoberg, R. (eds) (1989), *Sprache zwischen Militär und Frieden: Aufrüstung der Begriffe?*, Narr, Tübingen.

Buzan, B. (1991), *People, States and Fear: An Agenda for Security Studies in the Post-Cold War Era* [second edition], Harvester Wheatsheaf, London.

Camilleri, J.A. and Falk, J. (1992), *The End of Sovereignty? The Politics of a Shrinking and Fragmenting World*, Edward Elgar, Aldershot.

Carbonell, J.G. and Minton, S. (1983), 'Metaphor and Common-Sense Reasoning', (manuscript), Pittsburgh.

Carstens, Sharon A. (1986), 'Introduction' in Carstens, Sharon A. (ed.), *Cultural Identity in Northern Peninsular Malaysia*, Ohio University Center for International Studies, Athens, OH, pp. 1-11.

Chernus, Ira (1993), 'Order and Disorder in the Definition of Peace', *Peace and Change* , vol. 18, no. 2, pp. 99-125.

Chilton, Paul (1985), 'Words, Discourse and Metaphors: The Meanings of *deter*, *deterrent* and *deterrence*' in Chilton, Paul (ed.), *Language and the Nuclear Arms Debate: Nukespeak Today*, Pinter, London, pp. 103-27.

Chilton, Paul (1986), 'Metaphor, Euphemism and the Militarization of Language', Paper presented at the Biannual meeting of the International Peace Research Association, Sussex, England, quoted in Mehan, Hugh and Skelley, James M. (eds), *Discourse of the Nuclear Arms Debate*, (= *Multilingua*, vol. 7, no. 1/2).

Chilton, Paul (1989), 'Safe as Houses?', *Peace Review* , vol. 1, no. 2, pp. 12-17.

Chilton, Paul (1991a), 'Métaphore et Légitimation de la Guerre du Golfe', *Alternatives non-violentes*, no. 79, juin, pp. 54-60.

Chilton, Paul (1991b): 'Getting the Message Through. Metaphor and the Legitimation of War', (manuscript), University of Warwick.

Chilton, Paul (1994), '"La plaie qu'il convient de fermer" Les métaphores du Discours Raciste', *Journal of Pragmatics*, vol. 21, no. 6, pp. 583-620.

Chilton, Paul (ed.) (1985), *Language and the Nuclear Arms Debate: Nukespeak Today*, Pinter, London.

Chilton, Paul and Ilyin, Mikhail (1993), 'Metaphor in Political Discourse: the Case of the "Common European House"', *Discourse and Society*, vol. 4 no. 1, pp. 7-31.

Chitoran, Dimitru and Symonides, Janusz (1992), 'UNESCO Approaches to International Education in Universities', *Peace, Environment and Education*, vol. 3, no. 4, pp. 3-12.

Chomsky, Noam (1971), 'Language Teaching' in Allen, J.P.B. and van Buren, Paul (eds), *Chomsky: Selected Readings*, Oxford University Press, London, pp. 149-59.

Chomsky, Noam (1991a), 'A stand on low moral ground', *The Guardian,* 10 January 1991.

Chomsky, Noam (1991b), 'The weak shall inherit nothing', *The Guardian,* 25 March 1991.

Chomsky, N. (1992), *Deterring Democracy*, Vintage, London.

Clutterbuck, R. (1985), *Conflict and Violence in Singapore and Malaysia, 1945-1983*, Westview Press, Boulder, CO.

Clyne, Michael (1986), 'Language and Racism' in Markus, Andrew and Rasmussen, Radha (eds), *Prejudice in the Public Arena: Racism*, Monash University, Centre for Migrant and Multicultural Studies, pp. 35-44.

Cohn, Carol (1988), 'Sex and Death and the Rational World of Defense Intellectuals' in Gioseffi, Daniela (ed.), *Women on War*, Simon and Schuster/Touchstone, New York, pp. 84-99.

Connor-Linton, Jeff; Taylor, Carolyn; Landlofi Liliana and Seki, Minako (1987), 'Soviet and American Expression of Personal Involvement: Some Implications for Cross-cultural and Cross-gender Communication', *Multilingua*, vol. 6, no. 3, pp. 257-86.

Cooper, Sandi (1986), 'Peace Movements of the Nineteenth Century' in Laszlo, Erwin and Yoo, Jong Youl (eds), *World Encylopedia for Peace*, Pergamon Press, Oxford, pp. 230-34.

Coulter, J. (1989), *Mind in Action*, Polity Press, Cambridge.

Davey, William G. (1990), 'The Legislation of Bahasa Malaysia as the Official Language of Malaysia' in Adams, Karen L. and Brink, Daniel T. (eds), *Perspectives on Official English: The Campaign for English as the Official Language of the USA*, Mouton de Gruyter, Berlin, pp. 95-103.

Davis, Howard H. and Walton, Paul A. (1983), 'Sources of Variation in News Vocabulary: A Comparative Analysis', *International Journal of the Sociology of Language*, no. 40, pp. 59-75.

de Beaugrande, R. and Dressler, W. (1981), *Introduction to Text Linguistics*, Longman, London.

De Ipola, E. (1982), *Ideología y Discurso Populista*, Folios Ediciones, México.

Delbridge, A., et al (eds) (1981), *The Macquarie Dictionary*, Macquarie Library, St. Leonards.

Derrida, J. (1973), *Gramatologia*, Perspectiva, S. Paulo.

Di Pietro, R. (ed.) (1982), *Linguistics and the Professions*, Ablex, Norwood, NJ.

Dieckmann, W. (1981), *Politische Sprache. Politische Kommunikation,* Carl Winter Universitätsverlag, Heidelberg.

Dittmar, Norbert and von Stutterheim, Christiane (1985), 'On the Discourse of Immigrant Workers' in van Dijk, Teun A. (ed.), *Handbook of Discourse Analysis, vol. 4, Discourse Analysis in Society*, Academic Press, London, pp. 125-52.

Diuk, N. and Karatnycky, A. (1990), *The Hidden Nations: The People Challenge the Soviet Union*, William Morrow and Company, New York.

Drew, P. and Heritage, J. (eds) (1992), *Talk at Work. Interaction in Institutional Settings*, Cambridge University Press, Cambridge.

Ducrot, Oswald (1979), 'Les Lois de Discours', *Langue Française*, no. 42, pp. 21-33.

Ducrot, Oswald (1980), 'Je trouve que' in Ducrot, Oswald et al., *Les Mots du Discours*, Minuit, Paris, pp. 57-92.

Ducrot, O. et al., (1981), *L'Argumentation*, Lyon Presses Universitaires de Lyon, Lyon.

Eagleton, T. (1991), *Ideology. An Introduction*, Verso, London.

Edelman, M.J. (1977), *Political Language: Words that Succeed and Policies that Fail*, Academic Press, New York.

Edelman, M.J. (1985), *The Symbolic Uses of Politics*, University of Illinois Press, Urbana, IL.

Edwards, D. and Mercer, N. (1987), *Common Knowledge*, Routledge, London.

Ehlich, K. (ed.) (1989), *Sprache im Faschismus*, Suhrkamp, Frankfurt.

Essed, P. (1991), *Understanding Everyday Racism. An Interdisciplinary Theory*, Sage, Newbury Park, CA.

Essed, Philomena (1993), 'Things They Say Straight to your Face: Socio-political Implications of the Usage of Racist Slurs', Paper presented at the International Conference *Others in Discourse*, Toronto, 6-8 May 1993.

Europa Year Book (1987), Europa Publications Limited, London.

Fairclough, N. (1989), *Language and Power*, Longman, London.

Fairclough, N. (1992a), *Discourse and Social Change*, Polity Press, Cambridge.

Fairclough, Norman (1992b), 'Introduction' in Fairclough, Norman (ed.), *Critical Language Awareness*, Longman, London, pp. 1-29.

Fairclough, Norman (1993), 'Critical Discourse Analysis and the Marketization of Public Discourse: The Universities' in van Dijk, Teun A. (ed.), *Critical Discourse Analysis*, special issue of *Discourse & Society*, vol. 4, no. 2, pp. 133-68.

Ferguson, Charles A. (1992), 'Forward to the First Edition' in Kachru, Braj B. (ed.) *The Other Tongue: English Across Cultures* [second edition], University of Illinois Press, Urbana, IL, pp. vii-xi.

Fish, S. (1980), *Is There a Text in this Class? The Authority of Interpretive Communities*, Harvard University Press, Cambridge, Mass.

Fisher, G. (1988), *Mindsets: Role of Culture and Perception in International Relations*, Intercultural Press, Yarmouth, ME.

Fisher, S. and Todd, A.D. (eds) (1986), *Discourse and Institutional Authority: Medicine, Education, and Law*, Ablex, Norwood, NJ.

Fiske, S.T. and Taylor, S.E. (1991), *Social Cognition* [second edition], McGraw-Hill, New York.

Fleischer, Wolfgang (1977), 'Zur Rolle der Sprache bei der Bewußtseinsbildung', (= *Linguistische Studien*, LS/ZISW/A, 41), Zentralinstitut für Sprachwissenschaft, Berlin, pp. 1-31.

Foucault, M. (1972), *La Arqueología del Saber*, Siglo XXI, México.

Foucault, M. (1980), *El Orden del Discurso*, Tusquets Editores, Barcelona.

Foucault, Michel (1984), 'The Order of Discourse' in Shapiro, Michael (ed.), *Language and Politics*, Blackwell, London, pp. 108-38.

Fowler, R. (1991), *Language in the News. Discourse and Ideology in the Press*, Routledge, London.

Fowler, R., Hodge, B., Kress, G., and Trew, T. (1979), *Language and Control*, Routledge and Kegan Paul, London.

Fowler, Roger and Kress, Gunther (1979), 'Critical Linguistics' in Fowler, Roger; Hodge, Bob; Kress, Gunther and Trew, Tony, *Language and Control*, Routledge and Kegan Paul, London, pp. 185-213.

Freire, P. (1969), *Educação como Prática de Liberdade*, Paz e Terra, Rio de Janeiro.

Galtung, Johann (1964), 'Editorial', *Journal of Peace Research*, vol. 1, no. 1, pp. 1-4.

Galtung, Johann (1969), 'Violence, Peace, and Peace Research', *Journal of Peace Research*, vol. 6, no. 3, pp. 167-92.

Garfinkel, H. (1967), *Studies in Ethnomethodology*, Prentice Hall, Englewood Cliffs, NJ.

Geis, M.L. (1987a), *The Language of Politics*, Springer, New York.

Geis, Michael (1987b), 'Language and Media' in Kaplan, Robert B. (ed.), *Annual Review of Applied Linguistics*, vol. 7, pp. 64-73.

Ghadessy, M. (ed.) (1988), *Registers of Written English. Situational Factors and Linguistic Features*, Pinter, London.

Gibson, E. and Levin, H. (1975), *The Psychology of Reading*, The MIT Press, Cambridge, Mass.

Giles, H. and Coupland, N. (1991), *Language: Context and Consequences*, Open University Press, Milton Keynes.

Glasgow University Media Group (1982), *Really Bad News*, Writers and Readers, London.

Goffman, E. (1967), *The Presentation of Self in Everyday Life*, Penguin, Harmondsworth.

Goffman, E. (1974), *Frame Analysis*, Harper and Row, New York.

Goldstein, E. (1992), *War and Peace Treaties 1816-1991*, Routledge, London/New York.

Gonçalves, J.C. (1981), *Personalization and Objectification of the Interview in the Doctor-Patient Negotiation of Illness*, Georgetown University, Graduate School of Languages and Linguistics, Washington, DC.

Gonçalves, J.C. (1983), *A Study of Topic Management in the Acquisition of Portuguese as a Second Language in Classroom Interaction and Natural Conversations* (unpublished PhD dissertation), School of Languages and Linguistics, Georgetown University, Washington, DC.

Gough, Philip B. (1976), 'One Second of Reading' in Singer, Harry and Ruddel, Robert B. (eds), *Theoretical Models and Processes of Reading*, International Reading Association, Newark, Del., pp. 331-58.

Greenberg, Jeff; Kirkland, S.L. and Pyszczynski, Tom (1987), 'Some Theoretical Notions and Preliminary Research Concerning Derogatory Labels' in

Smitherman-Donaldson, Geneva and van Dijk, Teun A. (eds), *Discourse and Communication*, Wayne State University, Detroit, MI, pp. 74-92.

Gruber, H. and Wodak, R. (1992), *Ein Fall für den Staatsanwalt*, (= *Wiener Linguistische Gazette 11*), Department of Linguistics, University of Vienna.

Haidar, J. (1980), *Discurso Sindical y Procesos de Fetichización*, INAH, México.

Haidar, Julieta (1988), 'El Debate CEU-Rectoría: Estrategias Discursivas' (to be published).

Haidar, Julieta (1992), 'Las Materialidades Discursivas: un Problema Interdisciplinario', *Revista Alfa*, no. 36, pp. 139-47.

Halliday, M.A.K. (1985), *An Introduction to Functional Grammar*, Edward Arnold, London.

Halliday, Michael A.K. (1988), 'The Language of Physical Science' in Ghadessy, Mohsen (ed.), *Registers of Written English. Situational Factors and Linguistic Features*, Pinter, London, pp. 162-78.

Halliday, Michael (1990), 'New Ways of Meaning: A Challenge to Applied Linguistics', Plenary address presented at the Ninth World Congress of Applied Linguistics, Thessaloniki, Greece, *Journal of Applied Linguistics*, Thessaloniki, no. 6, pp. 7-36.

Halliday, Michael. A.K. (1993), 'The Act of Meaning' in Alatis, James E. (ed.), *Language, Communication, and Social Meaning*, Georgetown University Press, Washington, DC, pp. 7-21.

Hamilton, David L. and Trolier, Tina K. (1986), 'Stereotypes and Stereotyping: An Overview of the Cognitive Approach' in Dovidio, John and Gaertner, Samuel L. (eds), *Prejudice, Discrimination and Racism: Theory and Research*, Academic Press, New York, pp. 127-63.

Hanks, William F. (1991), 'Foreword' in Lave, Jean and Wenger, Etienne (eds), *Situated Learning*, Cambridge University Press, Cambridge, pp. 13-24.

Hassan, Abdullah (1975), 'The Standardization and Promotion of Bahasa Malaysia', Paper given at Regional English Language Centre Conference, January, Bangkok, Thailand.

Heath, Christian (1992), 'The Delivery and Reception of Diagnosis in the General-Practice Consultation' in Drew, Paul and Heritage, John (eds), *Talk at Work: Interaction in Institutional Settings*, Cambridge University Press, Cambridge, pp. 235-67.

Hebert, Hugh (1991), 'Propaganda War', *The Guardian*, 4 February 1991.

Heinemann, W. and Viehweger, D. (1991), *Textlinguistik. Eine Einführung*, Niemeyer, Tübingen.

Hirschman, Charles (1985), 'The Society and its Environment' in Bunge, Frederica M. (ed.), *Malaysia: A Country Study*, Foreign Area Studies, The American University, Washington, DC, pp. 67-127.

Hobsbawm, E.J. (1990), *Nations and Nationalism since 1780: Programme, Myth, Reality*, Cambridge University Press, Cambridge.

Holquist, Michael (1983), 'The Politics of Representation', *Quarterly Newsletter of the Laboratory of Comparative Human Cognition*, vol. 5, no. 1, pp. 2-9.

Hook, Glenn (1984), 'The Nuclearization of Language: Nuclear Allergy as Political Metaphor', *Journal of Peace Research*, vol. 21, no. 3, pp. 259-75.

Hua, W.Y. (1983), *Class and Communalism in Malaysia*, Marram Books, London.

Hughes, J. (1990), *The Philosophy of Social Research*, University of Chicago Press, Chicago.

Hurtado, A. and Arce, C.H. (1987), 'Mexicans, Chicanos, Mexican Americans, or Pochos ...? Que somos? The Impact of Language and Nativity on Ethnic Labelling', *Aztlan*, vol. 17, pp. 103-29

Hutchison, Frank (1992), 'Making Peace with People and Planet: Some Important Lessons from the Gandhian Tradition in Educating for the 2lst Century', *Peace, Environment, and Education*, vol. 3, no. 3, pp. 3-14.

Ishida, Takeshi (1969), 'Beyond the Traditional Concepts of Peace in Different Cultures', *Journal of Peace Research*, vol. 6, no. 2, pp. 133-45.

Jäger, Siegfried (1985), 'Der Begriff des Friedens und sein politischer Gebrauch' in Lison, Rüdiger (ed.), *Wissenschaftler zu Frieden und Abrüstung*, Duisburg, pp. 115-32.

Janks, Hilary and Ivanic, Roz (1992), 'Critical Language Awareness and Emancipatory Discourse' in Fairclough, Norman (ed.), *Critical Language Awareness*, Longman, London, pp. 305-31.

Jarvis, Simon (1992), 'The Annihilation of Truth by Power', Review of Norris, C. (1992), *Uncritical Theory. Postmodernism, Intellectuals and the Gulf War*, Lawrence & Wishart, London, *The Times Higher Education Supplement*, 17 April 1992, p. 28.

Johnson-Laird, P.N. (1983), *Mental Models*, Cambridge University Press, Cambridge.

Kachru, Braj B. (1985), 'The Bilingual's Creativity', *Annual Review of Applied Linguistics*, vol. 6, pp. 20-33.

Kachru, B.B. (1986) *The Alchemy of English*, Pergamon Press, Oxford [Reprinted, 1990, University of Illinois Press, Urbana, IL].

Kachru, Braj B. (1992), 'Meaning in Deviation: Toward Understanding Non-native English Texts' in Kachru, Braj B. (ed.), *The Other Tongue: English Across Cultures* [second edition], University of Illinois Press, Urbana, IL, pp. 301-26.

Kahane, H. (1971), *Logic and Contemporary Rhetoric*, Wadsworth, Belmont, CA.

Kellner, D. (1992), *The Persian Gulf TV War*, Westview Press, Boulder/San Francisco/Oxford.

Kennan, George F. (1946), 'Telegram', *Foreign Relations of the United States*, vol. 6, pp. 696-709.

Kövecses, Z. (1986), *Metaphors of Anger, Pride, and Love. A Lexical Approach to the Structure of Concepts*, John Benjamins, Amsterdam.

Kövecses, Z. (1989), *Minimal and Full Definitions of Meaning*, L.A.U.D. Series A, no. 252, Duisburg.

Kramarae, C. (1981), *Women and Men Speaking: Frameworks for Analysis*, Newbury House, Rowley, MA.

Kress, G. and Hodge, B. (1979), *Language as Ideology*, Routledge and Kegan Paul, London.

Kress, G. and Hodge, B. (1993), *Language as Ideology* [second edition], Routledge and Kegan Paul, London.

Krumeich, Gerd (1989), 'Einkreisung. Zur Entstehung und Bedeutung eines politischen Schlagwortes', *Sprache und Literatur in Wissenschaft und Unterricht,* no. 63, pp. 99-104.

Kuhn, E.D. (1992), *Gender and Authority. Classroom Diplomacy at German and American Universities*, Narr, Tübingen.

Labov, W. (1972), *Language in the Inner City*, University of Pennsylvania Press, Philadelphia.

Lakoff, G. (1986), *Cognitive Semantics*, (Berkeley Cognitive Science Report, no. 36), Berkeley.

Lakoff, G. (1987), *Women, Fire and Dangerous Things: What Categories Reveal about the Mind,* University of Chicago Press, Chicago.

Lakoff, G. (1989), *The Invariance Hypothesis: Do Metaphors Preserve Cognitive Topology?*, L.A.U.D. Series A, no. 266, Duisburg.

Lakoff, George (1990), 'Metaphor and War: The Metaphor System Used to Justify War in the Gulf', Paper distributed publicly over the internet by electronic mail, December, 1990.

Lakoff, George (1992): 'Metaphor and War. The Metaphor System Used to Justify War in the Gulf', in Pütz, Martin (ed.), *Thirty Years of Linguistic Evolution. Studies in the Honour of René Dirven,* J.Benjamins, Philadelphia/Amsterdam, pp. 463-81.

Lakoff, G. and Johnson, M. (1980), *Metaphors We Live By*, University of Chicago Press, Chicago.

Lakoff, R.T. (1990), *Talking Power. The Politics of Language*, Basic Books, New York.

Larrain, J. (1979), *The Concept of Ideology*, Hutchinson, London.

Laszlo, Erwin and Yoo, Jong Youl (eds) (1986), *World Encyclopedia of Peace,* Pergamon Books, Oxford (with Linus Pauling as honorary editor-in-chief).

Lave, J. and Wenger, E. (1991), *Situated Learning*, Cambridge University Press, Cambridge.

Le Page, Robert B. (1962), 'Multilingualism in Malaya' in *Symposium on Multilingualism,* [Proceedings of the second meeting of the Inter-African Committee on Linguistics, 16-21 July 1962, Brazzaville], Committee for Technical Cooperation in Africa, London.

Le Page, Robert B. (1984), 'Retrospect and Prognosis in Malaysia and Singapore', *International Journal of the Sociology of Language*, no. 45, pp. 113-26.

Lee, D. (1992), *Competing Discourses: Perspective and Ideology in Language,* Longman, London.

Levertov, Denise (1988), 'Making Peace' in Gioseffi, Daniela (ed.), *Women on War,* Simon and Schuster/Touchstone, New York, pp. 326-27.

Link, Jürgen (1991), 'Der irre Saddam setzt seinen Krummdolch an meine Gurgel', *Frankfurter Rundschau,* 16 January 1991.

Llamzon, Teodoro A. (1978), 'English and the National Languages in Malaysia, Singapore, and the Philippines: A Sociolinguistic Comparison', *Cross Currents*, vol. 5, no. 1, pp. 87-104.

Lowenberg, Peter H. (1988), 'Malay in Indonesia, Malaysia, and Singapore: Three Faces of a National Language' in Coulmas, Florian (ed.), *With Forked Tongues: What are National Languages Good for?*, Karoma Publishers, Ann Arbor, MI, pp. 146-79.

Maingueneau, D. (1976), *Introducción a los Métodos de Análisis del Discurso*, Hachette, Buenos Aires.

Mandelbaum, M. (1988), *The Fate of Nations: The Search for National Security in the Nineteenth and Twentieth Centuries*, Cambridge University Press, Cambridge.

Markus, Andrew (1986), 'Land Rights, Immigration and Multiculturalism' in Markus, Andrew and Rasmussen, Radha (eds), *Prejudice in the Public Arena: Racism*, Monash University, Centre for Migrant and Multicultural Studies, pp. 21-34.

McConahay, M.J. (1993), 'Rigoberta Menchú', *The Progressive*, no. 1, pp. 28-31.

McInnes, C. (ed.) (1992), *Security and Strategy in the New Europe*, Routledge, London.

McQuail, Denis (1972), 'Introduction' in McQuail, Denis (ed.), *Sociology of Mass Communications*, Penguin, Harmondsworth, pp. 9-16.

Means, G.P. (1991), *Malaysian Politics: The Second Generation*, Oxford University Press, Singapore.

Media Development (1991), *Reporting the Gulf War*, Special issue, October 1991.

Meeuwis, Michael (1993), 'Nationalist Ideology in News Reporting on the Yugoslav Crisis: A Pragmatic Analysis', *Journal of Pragmatics*, vol. 20, no. 3, pp. 217-37.

Mehan, Hugh and Skelley, James M. (1988), 'Reykjavik: The Breach and Repair of the Pure War Script' in Mehan, Hugh and Skelley, James M. (eds), *Discourse of the Nuclear Arms Debate*, (= *Multilingua*, vol. 7, no. 1/2), pp. 35-66.

Mehan, Hugh and Wills, John (1988), 'MEND: A Nurturing Voice in the Nuclear Arms Debate', *Social Problems*, vol. 35, no. 4, pp. 363-83.

Metzler, Helmut and Römer, Christine (1990), 'Möglichkeiten und Grenzen der Sprachanalyse des politischen Begriffs *Frieden*', *Pro pace mundi*, no. 7, Friedrich-Schiller-Universität, Jena, pp. 7-21.

Miller, N. and Allen, R. (eds) (1991), *And now for the BBC...: Proceedings of the 22nd University of Manchester Broadcasting Symposion*, J.Libbey, London.

Moita Lopes, Luiz Paulo (1993), 'Representação Social e Encaminhamento Pedagógico da Leitura na Escola Pública Brasileira', *Revista Letra*, vol. 4, November, pp. 137-47.

Montgomery, M. (1986), *An Introduction to Language and Society*, Methuen, London.

Morehouse, Ward (1975), *A New Civic Literacy: American Education and Global Interdependence*, Aspen Institute for Humanistic Studies, Aspen Colorado.

Morgenthau, H.J. (1973), *Politics among Nations: The Struggle for Power and Peace* [fifth edition], Alfred A. Knopf, New York.

Moss, Peter (1985), 'Rhetoric of Defence in the United States: Language, Myth, and Ideology' in Chilton, Paul (ed.), *Language and the Nuclear Arms Debate: Nukespeak Today*, Pinter, London, pp. 45-63.

Musolff, Andreas (1994), 'Der Golfkrieg von 1991 als Medien-Ereignis', in Reiher, Ruth (ed.), *Sprache im Konflikt*, de Gruyter, Berlin, pp. 1-13.

Norris, C. (1992), *Uncritical Theory. Postmodernism, Intellectuals and the Gulf War*, Lawrence & Wishart, London.

Noss, R. B. (ed.) (1984), *An Overview of Language Issues in South-East Asia 1950-1980*, Oxford University Press, Singapore.

Opp de Hipt, M. (1987), *Denkbilder in der Politik. Der Staat in der Sprache von CDU und SPD*, Westdeutscher Verlag, Opladen.

Osgood, R. and Tucker, R. (1967), *Force, Order, and Justice*, The Johns Hopkins University Press, Baltimore.

Paine, Robert (1981), 'When Saying is Doing' in Paine, Robert (ed.), *Politically Speaking*, Institute for the Study of Human Issues, Philadelphia, pp. 9-23.

Parkin, David (1984), 'Political Language', *Annual Review of Anthropology*, vol. 13, pp. 345-65.

Parmer, J. Norman (1959), 'Malaya and Singapore' in Kahin, George (ed.), *Governments and Politics of Southeast Asia*, Cornell University Press, Ithaca, NY, pp. 239-312.

Pasierbsky, F. (1983), *Krieg und Frieden in der Sprache*, Fischer, Frankfurt/M.

Pêcheux, M. (1969), *Hacia el Análisis Automático del Discurso*, Gredos, Madrid.

Pettigrew, Thomas F. (1979), 'The Ultimate Attribution Error: Extending Allport's Cognitive Analysis of Prejudice', *Personality and Social Psychology Bulletin*, vol. 5, pp. 461-76

Platt, J. and Weber, H. (1980), *English in Singapore and Malaysia*, Oxford University Press, Kuala Lumpur.

Platt, J., Weber, H. and Lian Ho, M. (1983), *Singapore and Malaysia*, John Benjamins, Amsterdam and Philadelphia [*Varieties of English around the World*, vol. 4].

Polanyi, Livia (1979), 'So What's the Point?', *Semiotica*, vol. 25, no. 3/4, pp. 207-41.

Pradhan, Ram Chandra (1986), 'Peace Education and Human Rights' in Laszlo, Erwin and Yoo, Jong Youl (eds), *World Encylopedia for Peace*, Pergamon Press, Oxford, pp. 190-4.

Psathas, G. (ed.) (1979), *Everyday Language: Studies in Ethnomethodology*, Irvington Publishers, Inc., New York.

Reardon, B. (1988), *Comprehensive Peace Education: Educating for Global Responsibility*, Teachers College Press, New York.

Reboul, O. (1980), *Lenguaje e Ideología*, Fondo de Cultura Económica, México.

Renkema, J. (1981), *De Taal van 'Den Haag'*, [The language of 'The Hague'], Staatsuitgeverij, Den Haag.

Resnick, L.B., Levine, J.M. and Teasley, S.D. (eds) (1991), *Perspectives on Socially Shared Cognition*, American Psychological Association, Washington, DC.

Richards, Jack C. (1979), 'Rhetorical and Communicative Styles in the New Varieties of English', *Language Learning*, vol. 29, no. 1, pp. 1-25.

Robin, R. (1973), *Histoire et linguistique*, Librairie Armand Colin, Paris.

Robin, Régine (1976), *Discours Politique et Conjoncture. L'Analyse du Discours*, Centre Educatif et Culturel, Montreal.

Rodríguez, L. (1993), 'Deixis y Modalización: Funcionamiento Ideológico en el Discurso de dos Grupos Sociales de Monterrey', (to be published).

Rodríguez, Lidia (in print), 'La Función Expresiva y la Apelativa: Mecanismos de la Subjetividad en el Discurso', *La Imaginación y la Inteligencia en el Lenguaje. Homenaje a Roman Jakobson*, ENAH, México.

Rosch, Eleanor (1977), 'Human Categorization' in Warren, Neil (ed.), *Studies in Cross-Cultural Psychology*, vol. 1, Academic Press, New York, pp. 1-49.

Rosenberg, S.W. (1988), *Reason, Ideology, and Politics*, Princeton University Press, Princeton, NJ.

Ross, John Haj (1984), 'Speaking the Unspeakable:The Language of Civil Defence' in Leaning, Jennifer and Keyes, Langley (eds), *Research in the Counterfeit Ark: Crisis Relocation for Nuclear War*, Ballinger, Cambridge, pp. 48-54.

Rumelhart, David E. (1977), 'Toward an Interactive Model of Reading' in Dornic, Stanislav (ed.), *Attention and Performance VI*, Lawrence Erlbaum Associates, Hillsdale, NJ, pp. 573-603.

Ryan, W. (1976), *Blaming the Victim* [revised edition], Vintage Books, New York.

Said, E. (1981), *Covering Islam: How the Media and the Experts Determine How We See the Rest of the World*, Pantheon Press, New York.

Salm, Claudio and Fogaça, Azuete (1992), 'Modernização Industrial e a Questão dos Recursos Humanos', *Economia e Sociedade*, vol. 1, no. 1, pp. 111-33.

Samora, J., Saunders, L. and Larson, R.F. (1961), 'Medical Vocabulary Knowledge Among Hospital Patients', *Journal of Health and Social Behavior*, vol. 2, pp. 83-92.

Sandig, B. (1986), *Stilistik der deutschen Sprache*, de Gruyter, Berlin.

Schäffner, Christina (1986), 'Themawörter zum NATO-Doppelbeschluß in bürgerlichen Zeitungen: *The Economist* und *The Guardian*' in Schäffner, Christina and Neubert, Albrecht (eds), *Politischer Wortschatz in textueller Sicht*, (= *Linguistische Studien*, LS/ZISW/A, 146), Zentralinstitut für Sprachwissenschaft, Berlin, pp. 55-71.

Schäffner, Christina (1990), 'A New Way of Looking at Meanings of Political Words' in Bahner, Werner; Schildt, Jochen and Viehweger, Dieter (eds), *Proceedings of the Fourteenth International Congress of Linguists. Berlin/GDR, August 10 - August 15, 1987*, vol. II, Akademie-Verlag, Berlin, pp. 1241-4.

Schäffner, Christina (1993), 'Die europäische Architektur - Metaphern der Einigung Europas in der deutschen, britischen und amerikanischen Presse' in Grewenig, Adi (ed.), *Inszenierte Information. Politik und strategische Kommunikation in den Medien*, Westdeutscher Verlag, Opladen, pp. 13-30.

Schäffner, Christina (1994), 'Die multipolare Welt - eine konzeptuelle Herausforderung', in Reiher, Ruth (ed.), *Sprache im Konflikt*, de Gruyter, Berlin, pp. 97-105.

Schäffner, Christina (in print), 'The Concept of Europe - a Network of Metaphors', Paper presented at the Conference *Europe on the Move*, Jyväskylä, March 1994.

Schäffner, Christina and Neubert, Albrecht (eds) (1986), *Politischer Wortschatz in textueller Sicht*, (= *Linguistische Studien*, LS/ZISW/A, 146), Zentralinstitut für Sprachwissenschaft, Berlin.

Schäffner, Christina and Porsch, Peter (1993), 'Meeting the Challenge on the Path to Democracy: Discursive Strategies in Government Declarations in Germany and the Former GDR, *Discourse & Society*, vol. 4, no. 1, pp. 33-56.

Schäffner, Christina and Trommer, Sylvia (1990), 'Das Konzept des *gemeinsamen europäischen Hauses* im Russischen und Englischen' in Schäffner, Christina (ed.), *Gibt es eine prototypische Wortschatzbeschreibung? Eine Problemdiskussion* (= *Linguistische Studien*, LS/ZISW/A, 202), Zentralinstitut für Sprachwissenschaft, Berlin, pp. 80-91.

Schäffner, Christina; Shreve, Gregory M. and Wiesemann, Uwe (1987), 'A Procedural Analysis of Argumentative Political Texts. Case Studies from *The Economist*', *Zeitschrift für Anglistik und Amerikanistik*, vol. 35, no.2, pp. 105-17.

Schmidt, Wilhelm (1969), 'Zur Ideologiegebundenheit der politischen Lexik', *Zeitschrift für Phonetik, Sprachwissenschaft und Kommunikationsforschung*, vol. 23, no. 3, pp. 255-71.

Schultz, Muriel (1975), 'The Semantic Derogation of Woman' in Thorne, Barrie and Henley, Nancy (eds), *Language and Sex: Difference and Dominance*, Newbury House, Rowley, MA, pp. 64-75.

Schuman, H., Steeh, C, and Bobo, L. (1985), *Racial Attitudes in America. Trends and Interpretations*, Harvard University Press, Cambridge, Mass.

Schwilk, H. (1992), *Was man uns verschwieg. Der Golfkrieg in der Zensur*, Ullstein, Frankfurt a.M./Berlin.

Searle, J.R. (1969), *Speech Acts*, Cambridge University Press, London.

Shinn, Rinn-Sup (1985), 'Government and Politics' in Bunge, Frederica M. (ed.), *Malaysia: A Country Study*, Foreign Area Studies, The American University, Washington, DC, pp. 185-231.

Shuy, Roger W. (1976), 'The Medical Interview: Problems in Communication', *Primary Care*, vol. 3, no. 3, pp. 365-86.

Sinclair, John (1985), 'Lexicographic evidence' in Ilson, Robert (ed.), *Dictionaries, Lexicography, and Language Learning*, Pergamon Press, Oxford, pp. 81-92.

Sinclair, J. and Coulthard, M. (1975), *Towards an Analysis of Discourse*, Oxford University Press, Oxford.

Smith, O. (1950), *Fundamentals of Curriculum Development*, World Book Company, New York.

Stanford, Barbara (ed.) (1976), *Peacemaking: A Guide to Conflict Resolution*, Bantam Books, New York.

Taba, H. (1962), *Curriculum Development: Theory and Practice*, Harcourt, Brace & World Inc., New York.

Taylor, Philipp M. (1992), *War and the Media. Propaganda and Persuasion in the Gulf War*, Manchester University Press, Manchester.

Tedeschi, J.T (ed.) (1981), *Impression Management. Theory and Social Psychological Research*, Academic Press, New York.

Terzi, Silvia B. (1992), *Ruptura e Retomada na Comunicação: o Processo de Construção de Leitura por Crianças de Periferia*, (unpublished PhD Thesis), UNICAMP.

Thomas, R. Murray (1983), 'Malaysia: Cooperation versus Competition - or National Unity versus Favored Access to Education' in Thomas, R. Murray (ed.), *Politics and Education: Case Studies from Eleven Nations*, Pergamon Press, Oxford, pp. 149-68.

Thompson, J.B. (1984), *Studies in the Theory of Ideology*, University of California Press Berkeley, CA.

Thompson, J. B. (1990), *Ideology and Modern Culture: Critical Social Theory in the Era of Mass Communication*, Stanford University Press, Stanford.

Thornborrow, Joanna (1993), 'Metaphors of Security: A Comparison of Representations in Defence Discourse in Post-Cold-War France and Britain', *Discourse & Society*, vol. 4, no. 1, pp. 99-119.

Tongue, R.K. (1979), *The English of Singapore and Malaysia* [second, revised edition], Eastern Universities Press, Singapore.

Trew, Tony (1979), 'Linguistic Variation and Ideological Difference' in Fowler, Roger, Hodge, Bob, Kress, Gunther and Trew, Tony (eds), *Language and Control*, Routledge and Kegan Paul, London, pp. 117-56.

Trömel-Plötz, Senta (1981), 'Languages of oppression', *Journal of Pragmatics*, vol. 6, no. 5, pp. 67-80.

Trömel-Plötz, S. (ed.) (1984), *Gewalt durch Sprache. Die Vergewaltigung von Frauen in Gesprächen*, Fischer, Frankfurt.

Tuchman, G. (1978), *Making News*, Free Press, New York.

Tucker, Erin (1986), 'Old Racism, New Racism' in Markus, Andrew and Rasmussen, Radha (eds), *Prejudice in the Public Arena: Racism*, Monash University, Centre for Migrant and Multicultural Studies, pp. 16-20.

UNESCO (1986), *The Seville Statement on Violence.*

Urban, Gregg (1988), 'Pronominal Pragmatics of Nuclear War Discourse', *Multilingua*, vol. 7, no. 1/2, pp. 67-93.

van Dijk, T.A. (1980a), *Macrostructures. An Interdisciplinary Study of Global Structures in Discourse, Interaction and Cognition*, Erlbaum, Hillsdale, NJ.

van Dijk, T.A. (1980b), *Texto y Contexto*, Cátedra, Madrid.

van Dijk, T.A. (1982), *When Majorities Talk about Minorities*, University of Amsterdam, Amsterdam.

van Dijk, Teun A. (1985), 'Levels and Dimensions of Discourse Analysis' in van Dijk, Teun A. (ed.), *Handbook of Discourse Analysis*, vol. 2, Academic Press, New York, pp. 1-12.

van Dijk, T.A. (1987a), *Communicating Racism: Ethnic Prejudice in Thought and Talk*, Sage Publications, Inc., California.

van Dijk, Teun A. (1987b), 'Episodic Models in Discourse Processing. 1983' in Horowitz, Rosalind and Samuels, S. Jay (eds), *Comprehending Oral and Written Language*, Academic Press, New York, pp. 161-96.

van Dijk, T. A. (1988a), *News Analysis. Case Studies of International and National News in the Press*, Erlbaum, Hillsdale, NJ.

van Dijk, T.A. (1988b), *News as Discourse*, Erlbaum, Hillsdale, NJ.

van Dijk, Teun A. (1988c), 'The Tamil Panic in the Press' in van Dijk, Teun A., *News Analysis. Case studies of International and National News in the Press*, Erlbaum, Hillsdale, NJ, pp. 215-54.

van Dijk, Teun A. (1990), 'Social Cognition and Discourse' in Giles, Howard and Robinson, R. Peter (eds), *Handbook of Social Psychology and Language*, Wiley, Chichester, pp. 163-83.

van Dijk, T.A. (1991a), *Racism and the Press*, Routledge, London.

van Dijk, Teun A. (1991b), 'Discourse and the Denial of Racism', *Discourse & Society*, vol. 3, no. 1, pp. 87-118.

van Dijk, Teun A. (1992), 'Racism and Argumentation' in van Eemeren, Frans H., et al. (eds), *Argumentation Illuminated* Foris, Dordrecht, pp. 242-59.

van Dijk, T. A. (1993a), *Elite Discourse and Racism*, Sage, Newbury Park, CA.

van Dijk, Teun A. (1993b), 'Principles of Critical Discourse Analysis' in van Dijk, Teun A. (ed.), *Critical Discourse Analysis*, special issue of *Discourse & Society*, vol. 4, no. 2, pp. 249-83.

van Dijk, Teun A. (1993c), 'Editor's Foreword to Critical Discourse Analysis' in van Dijk, Teun A. (ed.), *Critical Discourse Analysis*, special issue of *Discourse & Society*, vol. 4, no. 2, pp. 131-2.

van Dijk, Teun A. (1993d), 'The Meaning of 'Ideology'', Paper presented at the Tenth World Congress of Applied Linguistics, August 1993, Amsterdam.

van Dijk, Teun A. (in print), 'Discourse, Power and Access' in Coulthard, Malcolm and Caldas-Coulthard, Carmen R. (eds), *Critical Discourse Analysis*, Routledge, London.

van Dijk, T.A. and Kintsch, W. (1983), *Strategies of Discourse Comprehension*, Academic Press, New York.

van Eemeren, F.H. and Grootendorst, R. (1992), *Argumentation, Communication and Fallacies*, Erlbaum, Hillsdale, NJ.

Vellinga, M. (1988a), *Desigualdad, Poder y Cambio Social en Monterrey*, Siglo XXI, México.

Vellinga, Menno (1988b), 'La Dinámica del Desarrollo Capitalista Periférico' in Cerutti, Mario (ed.), *Monterrey, Siete Estudios Contemporáneos*, Facultad de Filosofía y Letras de la Universidad Autónoma de Nuevo León, Monterrey, pp. 21-53.

Verschueren, Jef (forthcoming), *The Pragmatic Return to Meaning: Notes on the Dynamics of Communication, Conceptual Accessibility and Communicative Transparency*.

Volmert, Johannes (1993), "'While the World Prayed for Peace, Saddam Prepared for War." Bushs Fernsehrede zur Eröffnung des Bombenkrieges gegen den Irak' [appendix: Address to the Nation by President George Bush on 16 January 1991] in Grewenig, Adi (ed.), *Inszenierte Kommunikation*, Westdeutscher Verlag, Opladen, pp. 198-230.

Vreeland, N., et al. (1977), *Area Handbook for Malaysia* [third edition], The American University, Washington, DC.

Walker, Gregg B. (1990), 'Cultural Orientations of Argument in International Disputes' in Korzenny, Felipe and Ting Toomey, Stella (eds), *Communicating for Peace*, Sage Publications, Inc., California, pp. 96-117.

Walker, R.B.J. (1993), *Inside/Outside: International Relations as Political Theory*, Cambridge University Press, Cambridge.

Waltz, K. (1979), *Theory of International Relations*, Addison-Wesley, Reading, Mass.

Watson, J. Keith P. (1984), 'Cultural Pluralism, Nation-building and Educational Policies in Peninsular Malaysia' in Kennedy, Chris (ed.), *Language Planning and Language Education*, George Allen and Unwin, London, pp. 132-50.

Wertsch, James V. (1987), 'Modes of Discourse in the Nuclear Arms Debate', *Current Research on Peace and Violence*, Tampere Peace Research Institute, Tampere, Finland.

Wertsch, J.V. (ed.) (1985), *Culture, Communication and Cognition: Vygotskian Perspectives*, Cambridge University Press, Cambridge.

West, C. (1984), *Routine Complications. Troubles with Talk between Doctors and Patients*, Indiana University Press, Bloomington, IN.

Wickman, Stephen B. (1983), 'The Economy' in Bunge, Frederica M. (ed.), *Indonesia: A Country Study*, Foreign Area Studies, The American University, Washington, DC, pp. 119-74.

Widdowson, H.G. (1979), *Explorations in Applied Linguistics*, Oxford University Press, Oxford.

Widdowson, H.G. (1983), *Learning Purpose and Language Use*, Oxford University Press, Oxford.

Widdowson, Henry G. (1984), 'Reading and Communication' in Alderson, J. Charles and Urquhart, A.H. (eds), *Reading in a Foreign Language*, Longman, London, pp. 213-26.

Wild, Stefan (1991), 'Karriere einer Metapher', *Frankfurter Rundschau*, 12 March 1991.

Windisch, U. (1990), *Speech and Reasoning in Everyday Life*, Cambridge University Press, Cambridge.

Wodak, Ruth (1987), ''And where is the Lebanon?' A Socio-psycholinguistic Investigation of Comprehension and Intelligibility of News', *Text*, vol. 7, no. 4, pp. 377-410.

Wodak, Ruth (1991), 'Turning the Tables: Antisemitic Discourse in post-war Austria', *Discourse & Society*, vol. 2, no. 1, pp. 65-83.

Wodak, Ruth and Matouschek, Bernd (1993), ''We are Dealing with People whose Origins one can Clearly Tell just by Looking': Critical Discourse Analysis and the Study of Neo-racism in Contemporary Austria', in van Dijk, Teun A. (ed.), *Critical Discourse Analysis*, special issue of *Discourse & Society*, vol. 4, no. 2, pp. 225-48.

Wodak, R. and Menz, F. (eds) (1990), *Sprache in der Politik, Politik in der Sprache. Analysen zum öffentlichen Sprachgebrauch*, Drava, Klagenfurt.

Wodak, R., Menz, F. and Lalouschek, J. (1989), *Sprachbarrieren. Die Verständigungskrise der Gesellschaft*, Atelier, Wien.

Wong, Irene F.H. (1983), 'Simplification Features in the Structure of Colloquial Malaysian English' in Noss, Richard B. (ed.), *Varieties of English in Southeast Asia*, SEAMEO Regional Language Centre, Singapore [Anthology Series 11], pp. 125-49.

Woolard, K.A. (1989), *Double Talk: Bilingualism and the Politics of Ethnicity in Catalonia*, Stanford University Press, Stanford.

Wright, Q. (1942), *A Study of War*, University of Chicago Press, Chicago.

Index